The Venetian
School of Painting
BY
EVELYN MARCH
PHILLIPPS

PREFACE

Many visits to Venice have brought home the fact that there exists, in English at least, no work which deals as a whole with the Venetian School and its masters. Biographical catalogues there are in plenty, but these, though useful for reference, say little to readers who are not already acquainted with the painters whose career and works are briefly recorded. "Lives" of individual masters abound, but however excellent and essential these may be to an advanced study of the school, the volumes containing them make too large a library to be easily carried about, and a great deal of reading and assimilation is required to set each painter in his place in the long story. Crowe and Cavalcaselle's *History of Painting in North Italy* still remains our sheet anchor; but it is lengthy, over full of detail of minor painters, and lacks the interesting criticism which of late years has collected round each master. There seems room for a portable volume, making an attempt to consider the Venetian painters, in relation to one another, and to help the visitor not only to trace the evolution of the school from its dawn, through its full splendour and to its declining rays, but to realise what the Venetian School was, and what was the philosophy of life which it represented.

Such a book does not pretend to vie with, much less to supersede, the masterly treatises on the subject which have from time to time appeared, or to take the place of exhaustive histories, such as that of Professor Leonello Venturi on the Italian primitives. It should but serve to pave the way to deeper and more detailed reading. It does not aspire to give a complete and comprehensive list of the painters; some of the minor ones may not even be mentioned. The mere inclusion of names, dates, and facts would add unduly to the size of the book, and, when without real bearing on the course of Venetian art, would have little significance. What the book does aim at is to enable those who care for art, but may not have mastered its history, to rear a framework on which to found their own observations and appreciations; to supply that coherent knowledge which is beneficial even to a passing acquaintance with beautiful things, and to place the unscientific observer in a position to take greater advantage of opportunities, and to achieve a wide and interesting outlook on that cycle of artistic apprehension which the Venetian School comprises, and which marks it as the outcome and the symbol of a great historic age.

The works cited have been principally those with which the ordinary traveller is likely to come into contact in the chief European galleries, and, above all, in Venice itself. The lists do not propose to be exhaustive, but merely indicate the principal works of the artists. Those in private galleries, unless easy of access or of first-rate importance, are usually eliminated. It has not been thought necessary to use profuse illustrations, as the book is intended primarily for use when visiting the original works.

PART I

CHAPTER I
VENICE AND HER ART

Venetian painting in its prime differs altogether in character from that of every other part of Italy. The Venetian is the most marked and recognisable of all the schools; its singularity is such that a novice in art can easily, in a miscellaneous collection, sort out the works belonging to it, and added to this unique character is the position it occupies in the domain of art. Venice alone of Italian States can boast an epoch of art comparable in originality and splendour to that of her great Florentine rival; an epoch which is to be classed among the great art manifestations of the world, which has exerted, and continues to exert, incalculable power over painting, and which is the inspiration as well as the despair of those who try to master its secret.

The other schools of Italy, with all their superficial varieties of treatment and feeling, depended for their very life upon the extent to which they were able to imbibe the Florentine influence. Siena rejected that strength and perished; Venice bided her time and suddenly struck out on independent lines, achieving a magnificent victory.

Art in Florence made a strictly logical progress. As civilisation awoke in the old Latin race, it went back in every domain of learning to the rich subsoil which still underlay the ruin and the alien structures left by the long barbaric dominion, for the Italian in his darkest hour had never been a barbarian; and as the mind was once more roused to conscious life, Florence entered readily upon that great intellectual movement which she was destined to lead. Her cast of thought was, from the first, realistic and scientific. Its whole endeavour was to know the truth, to weigh evidences, to elaborate experiments, to see things as they really were; and when she reached the point at which art was ready to speak, we find that the governing motive of her language was this same predilection for reality, and it was with this meaning that her typical artists found a voice. No artist ever sought for truth, both physical and spiritual, more resolutely than Giotto, and none ever spoke more distinctly the mind of his age and country; and as one generation follows another, art in Tuscany becomes more and more closely allied to the intellectual movement. The scientific predilection for *form*, for the representation of things as they really are, characterises not Florentine painting alone, but the whole of Florentine art. It is an art of contributions and discoveries, marked, it is needless to say, at every step by dominating personalities, positively as well as relatively great, but with each member consciously absorbed in "going one better" than his predecessors, in solving problems and in mastering methods. Florentine art is the outcome of Florentine life and thought. It is part of the definite clear-cut view of thought and reason, of that exactitude of apprehension towards which the whole Florentine mind was bent, and the lesser tributaries, as they flowed towards her, formed themselves on her pattern and worked upon the same lines, so that they have a certain general resemblance, and their excellence is in proportion to the thoroughness with which they have learned their lesson.

The difference which separates Venetian from the rest of Italian painting is a fundamental one. Venice attains to an equally distinguished place, but the way in which she does it and the character of her contribution are both so absolutely distinct that her art seems to be the outcome of another race, with alien temperament and standards. Venice had, indeed, a history and a life of her own. Her entire isolation, from her foundation, gave her an independent government and customs peculiar to herself, but at the same time her people, even in their earliest and most precarious struggles, were no barbarians who had slowly to acquire the arts of civilised life. Among the refugees were persons of high birth and great traditions, and they brought with them to the first crazy settlement on the lagoons some political training and some idea of how to reconstruct their shattered social fabric. The Venetian Republic rose rapidly to a position of influence in Europe. Small and circumscribed as its area was, every feature and sentiment was concentrated and intensified. But one element above all permeates it and sets it apart from other European States. The Oriental element in Venice must never be lost sight of if we wish to understand her philosophy of art.

There are some grounds, seriously accepted by the most recent historians, for believing that the first Venetian colonists were the descendants of emigrants who in prehistoric times had established themselves in Asia and who had returned from thence to Northern Italy. "These colonists," says Hazlitt, "were called Tyrrhenians, and from their settlements round the mouth of the Po the Venetian stock was ultimately derived." If the tradition has any truth, we think with a deeper interest of that instinct for commerce which seems to have been in the very blood of the early Venetians. Did it, indeed, come down to them from the merchants of Tyre and Carthage? From that wonderful trading race which stretched out its arms all over Europe and penetrated even to our own island? From the first, Venice cut herself adrift, as far as possible, from Western ties, but she turned to Eastern people and to intercourse with the East with a natural affinity which savours of racial instinct. All her greatness was derived from her Asiatic trade, and her bazaars, heaped with Eastern riches, must have assumed a deeply Oriental aspect. Her customs long retained many details peculiar to the East. The people observed a custom for choosing and dowering brides, which was of Asia. The national treatment of women was akin to that of an Oriental State; Venetian women lived in a retirement which recalled the life of the harem, only appearing on great occasions to display their brocades and jewels. Girls were closely veiled when they passed through the streets. The attachment of men to women had no intellectual bias, scarcely any sentiment, but "went straight to the mark: the enjoyment of physical beauty." The position of women in Venice was a great contrast to that attained by the Florentine lady of the Renaissance, who was highly educated, deeply versed in men and in affairs, the fine flower of culture, and the queen of a brilliant society. The love for colour and gorgeous pageantry was of Semitic intensity and seemed insatiable, and the gratification of the senses was a deliberate State policy. But passionate as was the spirit of patriotism, enthusiastic the love and loyalty of the people, the civic spirit was absent. The masses were contented to live under a despotic rule and to be little despots in their own houses. In the twelfth century the people saw power pass into the hands of the aristocracy, and as long as the despotism was a benevolent one, the event aroused no opposition. Like Orientals, the Venetians had wild outbursts, and like them they quieted down and nothing came of them. As Mr. Hazlitt remarks, "their occasional resistance to tyranny, though marked by deeds of horrid and dark cruelty, left no deep or enduring traces behind it. It established no principle. It taught no lesson." Venice was a Republic only in name. The whole aspect of her government is Eastern. Its system of espionage, its secret tribunals, its swift and silent blows,—these are all Oriental traits, and the East entering into her whole life from without found a natural home awaiting it. We should be mistaken, however, in thinking that the Venetians in their great days were enervated and lapped in the sensuality which we are apt to associate with Eastern ideals. Sensuality did in the end drain the life out of her. "It is the disease which attacks sensuousness, but it is not the same thing." The Venetians were by nature men with a deep capacity for feeling, and it is this deep feeling which has so large a share in Venetian art.

The painters of Venice were of the people and had no wide intellectual outlook at its most splendid moment, such as was possessed by those men who in Florence were drawn into the company of the Medici and their court of scholars, and who all their lives were in the midst of a society of large aims and a free public spirit, in which men took their share of the responsibilities and honours of a citizen's life. The merchant-patrons of Venice are quite uninterested in the solving of problems. They pay a price, and they want a good show of colour and gilding for their money. Presently they buy from outside, and a half-hearted imitation of foreigners is the best ambition of Venetian artists. Art, it has been said, does not declare itself with true spontaneity till it feels behind it the weight and unanimity of the whole body of the people. That true outburst was long in coming, but its seeds were fructifying deep in a congenial soil. They were fostered by the warmth and colour of Oriental intercourse, and at last the racial instinct speaks with no uncertain accent in the great domain of art, and speaks in a new and unexpected way; as splendid as, yet utterly unlike, the grand intellectual declaration of Florence.

Let us bear in mind, then, that Venice in all her history, in all her character, is Eastern rather than Western. Hers is the kingdom of feeling rather than that of thought, of emotion as opposed to intellect. Her whole story tells of a profoundly emotional and sensuous apprehension of the nature of things; and till the time comes when her artists are inspired to express that, their creations may be interesting enough, but they fail to reveal the true workings of her mind. When they do, they find a new medium and use it in a new way. Venetian colour, when it comes into its kingdom, speaks for a whole people, sensuous and of deep feeling, able for the first time to utter itself in art.

We have to divide the history of the Venetian School into three parts. The first extends from the primitives to the end of Giovanni Bellini's life. He forms a link between the first and second periods. The second begins with Giorgione and ends with Tintoretto and Bassano, and is the Venetian School proper. Thirdly, we have the eighteenth-century revival, in which Tiepolo is the most conspicuous figure, and which is in an equal degree the expression of the life of its time.

CHAPTER II
PRIMITIVE ART IN VENICE

The school of Byzantium, so widespread in its influence, was particularly strong in Venice, where mosaics adorned the cathedral of Torcello from the ninth century and St. Mark's became a splendid storehouse of Byzantine art. The earliest mosaic on the façade of St. Mark's was executed about the year 1250, those in the Baptistery date during the reign of Andrea Dandolo, who was Doge from 1342 to 1354. Yet though the life of Giotto lies between these two dates, and his frescoes at Padua were within a few hours' journey, there is no sign that the great revolution in painting, which was making itself felt in every principal centre of Italy, had touched the richest and most peaceful of all her States.

Yet local art in Venice was no outcome of Byzantinism. It rose as that of the mosaicists fell, but its rise differs from that of Florence and Siena in being for long almost imperceptible. Artists were looked upon merely as artisans in all the cities of Italy, but in Venice before any other city they had been placed among the craftsmen. The statute of the Guild of Siena was not formulated till 1355; that of Venice is the earliest of which we have any record, and bears the date of 1272. There is scarcely a word to indicate that pictures in the modern sense of the term existed. Painters were employed on the adornment of arms and of household furniture. Leather helmets and shields were painted, and such banners as we see in Paolo Uccello's battlepieces. Painted chests and *cassoni* were already in demand, dishes and plates for the table and the surface of the table itself were treated in a similar way. Special regulations dealt with all these, and it is only at the end of the list that anconæ are mentioned. The ancona was a gilded framework, having a compartment containing a picture of the Madonna and Child, and others with single figures of the saints, and these were the only pictures proper produced at this date. The demand for anconæ was, however, large, and they were very early placed, not only in the churches, but in the houses of patricians and burghers. Constant disputes arose between the painters and the gilders. Pictures were habitually painted upon a gold ground, but the painters were forbidden to gild the backgrounds themselves. "Gilding is the business of the gilder, painting that of the painter," says a contemporary record. "Now the gilder contends that if a frame has to be gilt and then touched with colour, he is entitled to perform both operations, but the painter disputes this right, and maintains that the gilder should return it to him when the addition of painting is desired." It was, however, finally decided by law that each should exercise both professions, when one or the other played a subordinate part in the finished work. Though the art of mosaic was falling into decay as painting began to emerge, yet the commercial manufactory of Byzantine Madonnas, which had been established as early as 600, went on, on the Rialto, without any variation of the traditional forms.

Florence very early discarded the temptation to cling to material splendour, but as we pass into the Hall of the Primitives in the Venetian Academy, we see at once that Venetian art, in its earlier stages, has more to do with the gilder than the painter. The Holy Personages are merely accessories to the gorgeous framework, the embossed ornaments, the real jewels, which were in favour with the rich and magnificent patrons. There is no sign of any feeling for painting as painting, no craving after the study of form as the outcome of intellectual activity, no zest of discovery, such as made the painter's life in Florence an excitement in which the public shared. What little Venice imbibes of these things is from outside influence, after due lapse of time. A prosperous, luxurious city of merchants and statesmen, she was too much bound up in the transactions and sensations of actual life to develop any abstract and thoughtful ideals.

Perhaps the first painting we can discover which shows any sign of independent effort is the series which Paolo da Venezia painted on the back of the Pala d' Oro, over the high altar of St. Mark, when it was restored in the fourteenth century. This reveals an artist with some pictorial aptitude and one alive to the subjects that surround him. It tells the story of St. Mark's corpse transported to Venice. The first panel contains a group of cardinals of varying types and expressions; in another the disciple listening to St. Mark's teaching, and crouching with his elbows on his knees, has a true, natural touch. The dramatic feeling here and there is considerable. The scene of the guards watching the imprisoned Saint through the window and seeing the shadow of two heads, as the Saviour visits him, imparts a distinct emotion; and there is force as well as feeling for decorative composition in the panel in which the Saint's body lies at the feet of the sailors, while his vision appears shining upon the sails.

Except for the exaggerated insistence on the gilded elaborations of the early ancona, there is not much to differentiate the early art of Venice from that of other centres; but we notice that it persevered longer in the material and mechanical art of the craftsman. Tuscan taste made little impression, and many years elapsed before work akin to that of Giotto attracted attention and was admired and imitated. A man like Antonio Veneziano met with

4

the fate of the innovator in Venice. He had too much of the simplicity of the Tuscan and was compelled to carry his work to Pisa, where his naïf and humorous narratives still delight us in the Campo Santo. It was in 1384 that he was employed to finish the frescoes of the life of S. Ranieri, which had been left uncompleted at Andrea da Firenze's death, and the fondness for architecture and surroundings in the Florentine taste, which secured him a welcome, may, as Vasari says, be derived from Agnolo Gaddi, who had already visited Padua and Venice.

In the last years of the fourteenth century tributary streams begin to feed the feeble main current. In 1365 Guariento, a Paduan, was employed by the State to paint a huge fresco of Paradise in the Hall of the Gran Consiglio of the Ducal Palace. This, which lay hid for centuries under the painting by Tintoretto, was uncovered in 1909 and found to be in fairly good preservation. It can now be seen in a side room. It tells us that Guariento had to some extent been influenced by Giotto. The thrones have long Gothic pendatives, the faces have more the Giottesque than the Byzantine cast and show that the old traditions were crumbling.

When painting in Venice first begins to live a life of its own, Jacobello del Fiore stands out as the most conspicuous of the indigenous Venetians. His father had been president of the Painters' Guild. Jacopo himself was president from 1415 to 1436. He was a rich and popular member of the State and a man of high character. His works, to judge by the specimens left, hardly attained the dignity of art, though in the banner of "Justice," in the Academy, the space is filled in a monumental fashion and the figure of St. Gabriel with the lily has something grand and graceful. We trace the same treatment of flying banners and draperies and rippling hair in the fantastic but picturesque S. Grisogono in the left transept of San Trovaso. Jacobello's will, executed in 1439 in favour of his wife Lucia and his son, Ercole, with provision for a possible posthumous son, shows him to have been a man of considerable possessions. He owned a slave and had other servants, a house, money, and books. Among his fellow-workers who are represented in Venice are Niccolo Semitocolo, Niccolo di Pietro, and Lorenzo Veneziano. The important altarpiece by the last, in the Academy, has evidently been reconstructed; two Eternal Fathers hover over the Annunciation, and the Saints have been restored to the framework in such wise that the backs of many of them are turned on the momentous central event. In the "Marriage of St. Catherine," in the same gallery, Lorenzo gets more natural. The Child, in a light green dress with gold buttons, has a lively expression, and looks round at His Mother as if playing a game. The chapel of San Tarasio in San Zaccaria contains an ancona of which the central panel was only inserted in 1839, and is identical with Lorenzo's other work. One of the finest and most elaborate of all the anconæ is in San Giovanni in Bragora, and is also the work of Lorenzo. In this, as well as in that of San Tarasio, the Mother offers the Child the apple, signifying the fruit of the Tree of Jesse and symbolical of the Incarnation. This incident, which is found thus early in art, was evidently felt to raise the group of the Mother and Child from a representation of a merely earthly relationship to a spiritual scene of the deepest meaning and the highest dignity.

Niccolo di Pietro has several early works of the last decade of the fourteenth century, from which we gather that he began as a Byzantine, but that he imitated Guariento and was tentatively drawn to the Giottesque movement, but not, we may remember, before Giotto had been dead for some sixty years. Niccolo di Pietro has been confounded with Niccolo Semitocolo, but it is now realised that they were two distinct masters. The most important work of Michele Giambono which has come down to us is the signed ancona with five saints, now in the Venetian Academy. It is unusual to find a saint in the central panel instead of the Madonna. The saint is on a larger scale than his companions, and has hitherto passed as the Redeemer, but Professor Venturi has identified him as St. James the Great. He has the gold scallop-shell and pilgrim's staff. It is clear from his size and position that the ancona has been painted for an altar specially dedicated to this Apostle.

The saints on the right are S. Michael and S. Louis of Toulouse. Between S. John the Evangelist and S. James is a monastic figure which has evidently changed places with S. John at some moment of restoration. If the two figures are transposed, their attitudes become intelligible. S. John is inculcating a message inscribed in his open book, while the monk is displaying his humble answer on his own page. The use in it of the term *servus*suggests that he is a Servite, though the want of the nimbus precludes the idea that he is one of the founders. It is probable that he is S. Filipo Benizzi, who, though considered as a saint from the time of his death, was not canonised for several centuries.

The Mond Collection includes a glowing picture by Giambono; a seated figure clad in rich vestments and holding an orb, probably representing a "Throne," one of the angelic orders of the celestial Hierarchy.[1]

Works are still in existence which may be ascribed to one or other of these masters, or of which no attribution can be made, but we know nothing positive of any other artists of the time which preceded the influence of Gentile da Fabriano. Nothing leads us to suppose that the Venetian School in its origin had any pretension to be a school of colour, or that it could claim anything like real excellence at a time when the Republic first became alive to the movement which was going on in other parts of Italy, and decided to call in foreign talent.

PRINCIPAL WORKS

Paolo da Venezia.

	Venice.	St. Mark's: The Pala d' Oro.
	Vicenza.	Death of the Virgin.

Lorenzo da Venezia.

	Venice.	Academy: Altarpiece.
		Correr Museum: Saviour giving Keys to St. Peter.
		S. Giovanni in Bragora: Ancona.
	Berlin.	Two Saints.

Nicoletto Semitocolo.

	Venice.	Academy: Altarpiece.
	Padua.	Biblioteca Archivescovo: Altarpiece.

Stefano da Venezia.

	Venice.	Academy: Coronation of Virgin, with false signature of Semitocolo.

Jacobello del Fiore.

	Venice.	Academy: Justice.
		S. Trovaso: S. Grisogono.

Niccolo di Pietro.

	Venice.	S. Maria dei Miracoli: Altarpiece.

Michele Giambono.

	Venice.	Academy: St. James the Great and other Saints.
	London.	Mond Collection: A "Throne."

CHAPTER III
INFLUENCES OF UMBRIA AND VERONA

Gentile da Fabriano, the Umbrian master, when he reached Venice in the early years of the fifteenth century, was already a man of note. He had received his art education in Florence, and he brought with him fresh and delicate devices for the enrichment of painting with gold, which, derived as it was from the Sienese assimilation of Byzantine methods, was very superior in fancy and refinement to anything that Venice had to show. He was a man of a gentle, mystic temperament, but he was accustomed to courts, and a finished master whose technique and artistic value was far beyond anything that the local painters were capable of. He spent some years in Venice, adorning the great hall with episodes from the legend of Barbarossa; one of these, which is specially cited, was of the battle between the Emperor and the Venetians. Gentile was working till about 1414, and the walls, finished by Pisanello, were covered by 1416. After this Gentile remained some time in Bergamo and Brescia, and settled in Florence about 1422. The year after reaching Florence, he painted the famous "Adoration of the Magi," now in the Florentine Academy. Even after leaving Venice his fame survived; pictures went from his workshop in the Popolo S. Trinità, and he sent back two portraits after he had returned to his native Fabriano.

We have no positive record of Gentile and Vittore Pisano, commonly called Pisanello, having met in Venice, but there is every evidence in their work that they did so, and that one overlapped the other in the paintings for the Ducal Palace.

The School of Verona already had an honourable record, and its Guild dates from 1303. The following are its rules, the document of which is still preserved, while that of Venice has been lost:

RULES OF THE VERONESE GUILD (*abridged*)

1. No one to become a member who had not practised art for twelve years.
2. Twelve artists to be elected members.
3. The reception of a new member depends on his being a senior.
4. The members are obliged in the winter season to take upon themselves the instruction of all the pupils in turn.
5. A member is liable to be expelled for theft.
6. Each member is bound to extend to another fraternal assistance in necessity.
7. To maintain general agreement in any controversies.
8. To extend hospitality to strange artists.
9. To offer to one another reciprocal comfort.
10. To follow the funerals of members with torches.
11. The President is to exercise reference authority.
12. The member who has the longest membership to be President.

There were also by-laws, which provided that no master should accept a pupil for less than three years, and this acceptance had to be definitely registered by the public notary, a son, brother, grandson, or nephew being the only exceptions. No master might receive an apprentice who should have left another master before his time was out, unless with that master's free consent. There were penalties for enticing away a pupil, and others to be enforced against pupils who broke the agreement. Severe restrictions existed with regard to the sale of pictures, no one but a member of the Guild being allowed to sell them. No one might bring a work from any foreign place for purposes of sale. It might not even be brought to the town without the special permission of the *Gastaldiones*, or trustees of the Guild, and those trustees were permitted to search for and destroy forged pictures. Every painter, therefore, had to subordinate his interests and inclinations to the local school. It helps us to understand why the individual character of the different masters is so perceptible, and one of the primary causes of this must have been the careful training of the pupils in the master's workshop.

The fresco left by Altichiero, Pisanello's first master, in the Church of S. Anastasia in Verona, shows how worthily a Veronese painter was at this early time following in the footsteps of Giotto. Three knights of the Cavalli family are presented by their patron saints to the Madonna. The composition has a large simplicity, a breadth of feeling which is carried into each gesture. The knights with their raised helmets, in the pattern of horses' heads, are full of reality, the Madonna is sweet and dignified, and the saints are grand and stately. The picture has a delightful suavity and ease, and the colouring has evidently been lovely. The setting is in good proportion and more satisfactory than that of the Giottesques. From the series of frescoes in S. Antonio, Verona, we gather that while Venice was still limited to stiff anconæ, the Veronese masters were managing crowds of figures and rendering distances successfully. Altichiero puts in homely touches from everyday life with a freedom which shows he has not yet mastered the principles of selection or the dignified fitness which guided the great masters; as, for instance, in the case of the old woman, among the spectators of the Crucifixion, who shows her grief by blowing her nose. He lets himself be drawn off by all manner of trivial detail and of gay costume; but again in such frescoes as S. Lucia, or the "Beheading of St. George," in the Paduan chapel of the Santo, he proves how well he understands the force of solid, simply-draped figures, direct in gesture and expression, while the decorative use he makes of lances against the background was long afterwards perhaps imitated, but hardly surpassed, by Tintoretto.

Pisanello, who followed quickly upon Altichiero and his assistant, Avanzi, exhibits the same chivalresque and courtly inclinations which commended Gentile da Fabriano to the splendour-loving Venetians. Verona, under the peaceful but gallant government of the Scaligeri, had long been the home of all knightly lore, and the artists had been employed to decorate chapels for the families of the great nobles. Among these, Pisanello had attained a high place. Though very few of his paintings remain, they all show these influences, and his subtly modelled medals establish him as a master of the most finished type. A much destroyed fresco in S. Anastasia, Verona, portrays the history of St. George and the Dragon. In the St. George we probably see the portrait of the great personage in whose honour the fresco was painted. He is mounting his horse, which, seen from behind, reminds us of the fore-shortened chargers of Paolo Uccello. The rescued princess, also a portrait, wears a magnificent dress and an elaborate headgear in the fashion of the day. Other horses, fiery and spirited, are grouped around, and in the band of cavaliers, beyond St. George, every head is individualised; one is beautiful, another brutal, and so on through the seven. A greyhound and spaniel in the foreground are superbly painted, the background is excellent, and a realistic touch is given by the corpses which dangle unheeded from the trees outside the castle-gate. A ruined, but fortunately not restored, "Annunciation" in S. Fermo, has a simple, slender figure of the Virgin sitting by her white bed, and the angel, with great sweeping, rushing wings and bowed, child-like head with fair hair, is a most sweet and keen figure, thrilling and convincing, in contrast to all the dead, over-worked frescoes round the church. All these paintings are too small to be the least effective at the height at which they are placed, and can only be seen with a good glass. Pisanello's art is not well adapted to wide, frescoed walls, and he seems to have enjoyed painting miniature panels, such as the two we possess. In these he is full of originality, and shows his love for the knightly life, the life of courts, in the armed *cap-à-pied* figure of St. George, whose point-device armour is crowned by a wide Tuscan hat and feather. The artist's knowledge and love of animals and wild nature comes out in them, and his interest in beauty and chivalry as opposed to the outworn conventionalities of ecclesiastic demands.

We shall be able to trace the influence of both the Umbrian and the Veronese painter on men like Antonio di Murano and Jacopo Bellini, and it is important to note the likeness of the two to one another. In Gentile's "Adoration" we have on the one hand the Holy Family and the gay pageant of the kings, of which we could find the prototype in many an Umbrian panel. On the other we see those contrasting elements which were struggling in Pisanello; the delight in flowers and animals, in gaily apparelled figures, in dogs and horses. The two have no lasting effect, but though they created no actual school, they gave a stimulus to Venetian art, and started it on a new tack, enabling it to open its channels to fresh ideas. During the time they were in Venice, Jacobello del Fiore shows some signs of adapting the new fashion to his early style, and the horse of S. Grisogono is very like that of Gentile in the "Adoration," or like Pisano's horses. Michele Giambono is actually found in collaboration, in the chapel of the Madonna da Mascoli in St. Mark's, with such a virile painter as the Florentine, Andrea del Castagno, who is evidently responsible for God the Father and two of the Apostles; but Castagno must have been thoroughly antipathetic to the Venetians, and though he may have taught them the way to draw, he has not left any traces of a following.

Facio, writing in 1455, speaks of Gentile's work in the Ducal Palace as already decaying, while Pisanello's was painted out by Alvise Vivarini and Bellini.

PRINCIPAL WORKS

Gentile da Fabriano.

	Florence.	Academy: Adoration of the Magi.
	Milan.	Brera: Altarpiece.

Altichiero.

	Padua.	Capella S. Felice, S. Antonio: Frescoes.
		Capella S. Giorgio, S. Anastasia: The Cavalli Family.

Pisanello.

	Padua.	S. Anastasia: St. George and the Dragon.
	Verona.	S. Fermo: Annunciation.
	London.	S. George and S. Jerome; S. Eustace and the Stag.

CHAPTER IV
THE SCHOOL OF MURANO

The important little town of Murano, a satellite of Venice, lies upon an island, some ten minutes' row from the mother State, distinct from which it preserved separate interests and regulations. Its glass manufacture was safeguarded by the most stringent decrees, which forbade members of the Guild to leave the islet under pain of death. Its mosaics, stone work, and architecture speak of an early artistic existence, and we recognise the justice of the claim of Muranese painters to be the first to strike out into a more emancipated type than that of the primitives. The painter Giovanni of Murano, called Giovanni Alemanus or d' Alemagna, names between which Venetian jealousy for a time drew an imaginary distinction, had certainly received his early education in Germany, and betrays it by his heavier ornamentation and more Gothic style; but he was a fellow-worker with Antonio of Murano, the founder of the great Vivarini family, and the Academy contains several large altarpieces in which they collaborated. "Christ and the Virgin in Glory" was painted for a church in Venice in 1440, and has an inscription with both names on a banderol across the foreground. The Eternal Father, with His hands on the shoulders of the Mother and Son, makes a group of which we find the origin in Gentile da Fabriano's altarpiece in the Brera, and it is probable that one if not both masters had been studying with the Umbrian and absorbing the principles he had brought to Venice. It is easy to trace the influence of Giovanni d' Alemagna, though not always easy to pick out which part of a picture belongs to him and which to Antonio working under his influence. In S. Pantaleone is a "Coronation of the Virgin," with Gothic ornaments such as are not found in purely Italian art at this period, but the example in which both masters can be most closely followed is the great picture in the Academy, the "Madonna enthroned," where she sits under a baldaquin surrounded by saints. Here the Gothic surroundings become very florid, and have a gingerbread-cake effect, which Italian taste would hardly have tolerated. Many features are characteristic of the German; the huge crown worn by the Mother, the floriated ornament of the quadrangle, the almost baroque appearance of the throne. Through it all, heavily repainted as it is, shines the dawn of the tender expression which came into Venetian art with Gentile.

Antonio da Murano. ADORATION OF THE MAGI. *Berlin.*
(*Photo, Hanfstängl.*)

9

Giovanni d' Alemagna and Antonio da Murano were no doubt widely employed, and when the former died Antonio founded and carried on a real school in Venice. In 1446 he was living in the parish of S. Maria Formosa with his wife, who was the daughter of a fruit merchant, and the wills of both are still preserved in the parish archives. Gentile da Fabriano had set the example for gorgeous processions with gay dresses and strange animals; winding paths in the background and foreshortened limbs prove that attention had been drawn to Paolo Uccello's studies in perspective, while many figures and horses recall Pisanello. A striking proof of the sojourn of Gentile and Pisanello in Venice is found in an "Adoration of Magi," now ascribed to Antonio da Murano, in which the central group, the oldest king kissing the Child's foot, is very like that in Gentile's "Adoration," but the foreshortened horses and the attendants argue the painter's knowledge of Pisanello's work. A comparison of the architecture in the background with that in the "St. George" in S. Anastasia shows the same derivation, and the dainty cavalier, who holds a flag and is in attendance on the youngest king, is reminiscent of St. George and St. Eustace in Pisanello's paintings in the National Gallery, so that in this one picture the influences of the two artists are combined.

Antonio took his younger brother, Bartolommeo, into partnership, and the title of da Murano was presently dropped for the more modern designation of Vivarini. Both brothers are fine and delicate in work, but from the outset of their collaboration the younger man is more advanced and more full of the spirit of the innovator. In his altarpiece in the first hall of the Academy the Nativity has already a new realism; Joseph leans his head upon his hand, crushing up his cheek. The saints are particularly vivid in expression, especially the old hermit holding the bell, whose face is brimming with ardent feeling.

PRINCIPAL WORKS

Giovanni d' Alemanus and Antonio da Murano.
Venice.   Christ and the Virgin in Glory; Virgin
enthroned, with Saints.

Antonio da Murano.
Berlin.   Adoration of Magi.

CHAPTER V
THE PADUAN INFLUENCE

And now into this dawning school, employed chiefly in the service of the Church, with its tentative and languid essays to understand Florentine composition, resulting in what is scarcely more than a mindless imitation, and with its rather more intelligent perception of the Humanist qualities of Pisanello's work, there enters a new factor; or rather a new agency makes a slightly more successful attempt than Gentile and Castagno had done to help the Venetians to realise the supreme importance of the human figure, its power in relation to other objects to determine space, its modelling and the significance of its attitude in conveying movement. Giotto had been able to present all these qualities in the human form, but he had done so by the light of genius, and had never formulated any sufficient rules for his followers' guidance. In Ghiberti's school, at the beginning of the fifteenth century, the fascination of the antique in art was making itself felt, but Donatello had escaped from the artificial trammels it threatened to exercise, and had carried the Florentine school with him in his profound researches into the human form itself. Donatello had been working in Padua for ten years before Pisanello's death, and in an indirect way the Venetians were experiencing some after-results of the systematising and formulating of the new pictorial elements. Though the intellectual life had met with little encouragement among the positive, practical inhabitants of Venice, in Padua, which had been subject to her since 1405, speculative thought and ideal studies were in full swing. There was no re-birth in Venice, whose tradition was unbroken and where "men were too genuinely pagan to care about the echo of a paganism in the remote past." St. Mark was the deity of Venice, and "the other twelve Apostles" were only obscurely connected with her religious life, which was strong and orthodox, but untroubled by metaphysical enthusiasms and inconvenient heresies. Padua, on the other hand, was absorbed in questions of learning and religion. A university had been established here for two centuries. The abstract study of the antique was carried on with fervour, and the memory of Livy threw a lustre over the city which had never quite died out. It seemed perfectly right and respectable to the Venetians that the *savants*, lying safely removed from the busy stream of commercial life, should cultivate inquiries into theology and the classics, which would only have been a hindrance to their own practical business; but such, as it was well known, were of absorbing interest in the circles which gathered round the Medici in Florence. The school of art, which was now arising in Padua, was fed from such sources as these. The love of the antique was becoming a fashion and a guiding principle, and influenced the art of painting more formally than it could succeed in doing among the independent and original Florentines.

Francesco Squarcione, though, as Vasari says, he may not have been the best of painters, has left work (now at Berlin) which is accepted as genuine and which shows that he was more than the mere organiser he is sometimes called. He had travelled in Greece, and was apparently a dealer, supplying the demand for classic fragments, which was becoming widespread. When he founded his school in Padua he evidently was its leading spirit and a powerful artistic influence. His pupils, even the greatest, were long in breaking away from his convention, and few of them threw it off entirely, even in after life. That convention was carried with undeviating thoroughness into every detail. Draperies are arranged in statuesque folds, designed to display every turn of the form beneath; the figures are moulded with all the precision and limitations of statuary. The very landscape becomes sculpturesque, and rocks of a volcanic character are constructed with the regularity of masonry. The colour and technique are equally uncompromising, and the surface becomes a beautiful enamel, unyielding, definite in its lines, lacquer-like in its firmness of finish, while the Gothic forms, which had hitherto been so prevalent, were replaced by more or less pedantic adaptations from Roman bas-reliefs. This system of design was practised most determinedly in Padua itself, but it soon spread to Venice. Squarcione himself was employed there after 1440, and though Antonio da Murano clung to the old archaic style he saw the Paduan manner invading his kingdom, and his own brother became strongly Squarcionesque.

The two brothers of Murano come most closely together in an altarpiece in the gallery of Bologna, where the framework is more simple than Alemanus's German taste would have permitted, and the Madonna and Child have some natural ease, and the delicacy of feeling of primitive art. Bartolommeo, when he breaks away and sets out to paint by himself, is crude and strong, but full of vital force. In his altarpiece of 1464, in the Academy, he gives his saints reality by taking them off their pedestals and making them stand upon the ground, and though they are still isolated from one another in the partitions of an ancona, their sparkling eyes, individual features, and curly beards give them a look of life. The draperies, thin and clinging, with little rucked folds, which display the forms, and the drawing of the bony structure, exaggerated in the arms and legs, are Squarcionesque. The rocks and stones, too, show the Paduan convention. In several of his other altarpieces, Bartolommeo introduces rich ornaments and swags of fruit, such as Donatello had first brought to Padua, or which Paduan artists delighted to copy from classic columns. Antonio's manner to the end is the local Venetian manner, infused as it was with the soft and charming influence of Gentile da Fabriano and Pisanello, but Bartolommeo adopts the new and more ambitious style. Though not a very good painter, and inclined to be puffy and shapeless in his flesh forms, he was the head of a crowd of artists, and works of his school, signed *Opus factum*, went all over Italy, and are found as far south as Bari. Works of his pupils are numerous; the "St. Mark enthroned" in the Frari is as good if not better than the master's own work, and the triptych in the Correr Museum is a free imitation.

Round this early school gathered such painters as Antonio da Negroponte and Quirizio da Murano, who were both working in 1450. Negroponte has left an enthroned Madonna in S. Francesco della Vigna, which is one of the most beautiful examples of colour and of the fanciful charm of the Renaissance that the early art of Venice has to show. The Mother and Child are placed in a marble shrine, adorned with antique reliefs, rich wreaths of fruit swag above her head, a little Gothic loggia is full of flowers and fruit, and birds are perched on cornucopias. On either side, four badly drawn little angels, with ugly faces and awkwardly foreshortened forms, foreshadow the beautiful, music-making angels which became such a feature of North Italian art. The Divine Mother, adoring the Child lying across her knees, has an exquisite, pensive face, conceived with all the delicacy and simplicity of early art. It seems quite possible, as Professor Leonello Venturi suggests, that we have here the early master of Crivelli, in whom we find the love of fruit garlands, of chains of beads and rich brocades carried to its farthest limits, who takes keen pleasure in introducing the ugly but lively little angels, and who gives the same pensive and almost mincing expression to his Madonnas.

PRINCIPAL WORKS

Antonio da Murano and Bartolommeo Vivarini.

Bologna.	Altarpiece.

Bartolommeo Vivarini.

Venice.	Academy: Altarpiece, 1464; Two Saints.
	Frari: Madonna and four Saints.
	S. Giovanni in Bragora: Madonna and two Saints.
	S. Maria Formosa: Triptych.
London.	Madonna and Saints.
Vienna.	S. Ambrose and Saints.

Antonio da Negroponte.

Venice.	S. Francesco della Vigna: Altarpiece.

CHAPTER VI
JACOPO BELLINI

While Venice was assimilating the spirit of the school of Squarcione, which in the next few years was to be rendered famous by Mantegna, another influence was asserting itself, which was sufficient to counteract the hard formalism of Paduan methods.

When Gentile da Fabriano left Venice, he carried with him, and presently established with him in Florence, a young man, Jacopo Bellini, who had already been working with him and Pisanello, and who was an ardent disciple of the new naturalistic and humanist movement. Both Gentile and his apprentice were subjected to annoyance from the time they arrived in Florence, where the strict regulations which governed the Guilds made it very difficult for any newcomer to practise his art. The records of a police case report that on the 11th of June 1423 some young men, among them, one, Bernabo di San Silvestri, the son of a notary, were observed throwing stones into the painter's room. His assistant, Jacopo Bellini, came out and drove the assailants away with blows, but Bernabo, accusing Jacopo of assault, the latter was committed to prison in default of payment. After six months' imprisonment, a compromise of the fine and a penitential declaration set him at liberty. The accounts declare that Gentile took no steps to be of service to his follower; but Jacopo soon after married a girl from Pesaro, and his first son was christened after his old master, which does not look as though they were on unfriendly terms. Jacopo travelled in the Romagna, and was much esteemed by the Estes of Ferrara, but he was back in Venice in 1430. He has left us only three signed works, and one or two more have lately been attributed to him, but they give very little idea of what an important master he was.

Jacopo Bellini.   AGONY IN GARDEN—DRAWING.   *British Museum.*
(*Photo, Anderson.*)

His Madonna in the Academy has a round, simple type of face, and in the Louvre Madonna, which is attributed but not signed, it is easy to recognise the same arched eyebrows and half-shut, curved eyelids. In this picture, where the Madonna blesses the kneeling Leonello d' Este, we see how Pisanello acted on Jacopo and, through him, on Venetian art. The connection between the two masters has been established in a very interesting way by Professor Antonio Venturi's discovery of a sonnet, written in 1441, which recounts how they painted rival portraits of Leonello, and how Bellini made so lively a likeness that he was adjudged the first place. The landscape in the Louvre picture is advanced in treatment, and with its gilded mountain-tops, its stag and its town upon the hill-side, is full of reminiscences of Pisanello, especially of the "St. George" in S. Anastasia. We come upon such traces, too, in Jacopo's drawings, and it is by his two sketch-books that we can best judge of his greatness. One of these is in the British Museum; the other, in the Louvre, was discovered not many years ago in the granary of a castle in Guyenne. These drawings reveal Jacopo as one of the greatest masters of his day. He is larger, simpler, and more natural than Pisanello, and he apparently cares less for the human figure than for elaborate backgrounds and surroundings. Many of his designs we shall refer to again when we come to speak of his two sons. His "Supper of Herod" reminds us of Masolino's fresco at Castiglione d' Olona. He sketches designs for numbers of religious scenes, treated in an original and interesting manner. A "Crucifixion" has bands of soldiers ranged on either side, an "Adoration of the Magi" has a string of camels coming down the hill, the executioners in a "Scourging" wear Eastern head-dresses. In a sketch for a "Baptism of Christ" tall angels hold the garments in the early traditional way; on one side two play the lute and the violin, while the two on the other side have a trumpet and an organ. He has sketches for the Ascension, Resurrection, Circumcision, and Entombment, repeated over and over again with variations, and one of S. Bernardino preaching in Venice (where he was in 1427). Jacopo delights even more in fanciful and mythological than in sacred subjects. A tournament with spectators, a Faun riding a lion, a "Triumph of Bacchus" with panthers, are among such essays. The fauns pipe, the wine-god bears a vase of fruit. His love of animals is equal to that of Pisanello, and S. Hubert and the stag with the crucifix between its horns is directly reminiscent of the Veronese. His horses, of which there are immense numbers, sometimes look as if copied from ancient bas-reliefs. His treatment of single nude figures is often poor and weak enough, and his rocks have the flat-topped, geological formation of the Paduan School, but no one who so drank in every description of lively scene about him could have been in any danger of becoming a mere archeological type, and it was from this pitfall that he rescued Mantegna. To judge by his drawings, Jacopo did not overlook any source of art open to him; he delights in the rich research of the Paduans as much as in the varieties of wild nature and all the incidents of contemporary life first annexed by Pisanello. He is often very like Gentile da Fabriano, he makes raids into Uccello's domains of perspective, he is frankly mundane and draws a revel of satyrs and centaurs with a real interpretation of the lyrical and pagan spirit of the Greeks, and he has an idealism of the soul, which found its full expression in his son, Giovanni. We cannot call Jacopo Bellini the founder of the Venetian School, for its makings existed already, but it was his influence on his sons which, above all, was accountable for the development of early excellence. His long, flowing lines have a sweep and a fanciful grace which form an absolute antidote to the definite, geometrical Paduan convention. In Jacopo we see the thorough assimilation of those foreign elements which were in sympathy with the Venetian atmosphere, and while up to now Venice had only imbibed influences, she was soon to create for herself an artistic *milieu* and to become the leader of the movement of painting in the north of Italy.

PRINCIPAL WORKS

Jacopo Bellini.

	Brescia.	Annunciation and Predelle.
	Verona.	Christ on Cross.

Venice.	Academy: Madonna.
	Museo Correr: Crucifixion.
London.	British Museum: Sketch-book.
Paris.	Madonna and Leonello d' Este: Sketch-book.

CHAPTER VII
CARLO CRIVELLI

We must turn aside from the main stream when we come to speak of Carlo Crivelli, who, important master as he was, occupies a place by himself. A pupil of the Vivarini and perhaps, as we have noted, of Antonio Negroponte, Crivelli was profoundly influenced by the Paduans, from whom he learned that metallic, finished quality of paint which he carried to perfection. Crivelli shows intellect, individuality, even genius, in the way in which he grapples with his medium and produces his own reading, and the circumstances of his life were such as to throw him in upon himself and to preserve his originality. His little early "Madonna and Child" at Verona is linked with that of Negroponte by the elaborate festoons, strings of beads, and large-patterned brocades used in the surroundings, and has those ugly, foreshortened little *putti*, holding the instruments of the Passion, of the type elaborated by Squarcione and Marco Zoppo, and which, in their improved state, we are accustomed to think of as Mantegnesque.

When Crivelli was thirty-eight years old, he was condemned to six months' imprisonment and to a fine of two hundred lire for an outrage on a neighbour's wife. Perhaps it was to escape from an unenviable reputation that he left Venice soon after and set up painting in the Marches, where he lived from 1468 to 1473. He then went on to Camerino in Umbria, where his great triptych, now in the Brera, was painted, and a few years later he was in Ascoli, with a commission for an Annunciation in the Cathedral. This is the picture now in the National Gallery, in which the Bishop holds a model of the Duomo. After 1490 he worked in little towns in the Marches, and is not mentioned after 1493. He does not seem ever to have come back to Venice.

Shut up in the Marches, where there was little strong local talent, and where he could not keep up with the progress that was taking place in Venice, he was obliged himself to supply the artistic movement. He kept the Squarcionesque traditions to the end, but moulded them by his own love of rich and exuberant decoration. Moreover, he was of a very intense religious bias, and this finds a deeply touching and mystical expression, more especially in his Pietàs. The love of gilded patterns and fanciful detail was deep-seated in all the Umbrian country. His altarpieces were intended as sumptuous additions to rich churches, and were consequently arranged, with many divisions, in the old Muranese manner. His great ancona, in the National Gallery, is a marvel of elaborate ornament and enamel-like painting. The Madonna is delicate, almost affected in her refinement. Her long fingers hold the Child's garment with the extreme of dainty precision, the croziers and rings of the saints and bishops are embossed with gold and real jewels. The flowers in the panel of "The Immaculate Conception," which hangs beside it, are twisted into heads of mythological beasts and grotesques or cherubs; but Crivelli has plenty of strength, and his male saints have vigorous, bony limbs and fierce fanatical eyes. It is, however, in his colour that he charms us most, and though he does not touch the real fount, he is of all the earlier school the most remarkable for subtle tender tones and lovely harmonies of olive-greens and faded rose and cream embossed with gold.

Crivelli continued executing one great ancona after another, limiting his progress to perfecting his technique, and his influence was most deeply felt by such Umbrian painters as Lorenzo di San Severino and Niccola Alunno. The honours paid him testify to the reputation he acquired. He was created a knight and presented with a golden laurel wreath. But though he never, that we can hear of, revisited his native State, he always adds *Venetus* to the signature on his paintings, a fact which tells us that far from Venice and in provincial districts, her prestige was felt and gave his work an enhanced commercial value. He had no after-influence upon the Venetian School, and in this respect is interesting as an example of the tenacity exercised by the Squarcionesque methods, when, unchecked by any counter-attraction, they came to act upon a very different temperament; for in his love of grace and beauty and of rich effects, and especially in his intensity of mystic feeling, Crivelli is a true Venetian and has no natural affinity with the classic spirit of the Paduans.

PRINCIPAL WORKS

Venice.	SS. Jerome and Augustine.
Ascoli.	Duomo: Altarpiece and Pietà.
Berlin.	Madonna and six Saints.
London.	Pietà; The Blessed Ferretti; Madonna and Saints; Annunciation; Ancona in thirteen compartments; The Immaculate Conception.
	Mr. Benson: Madonna.
	Sir Francis Cook: Madonna enthroned.
	Mond Collection: SS. Peter and Paul.
	Lord Northbrook: Madonna; Resurrection; Saints; Crucifixion; Madonna; Madonna and Saints.
Milan.	Brera: SS. James, Bernardino, and Pellegrino; SS. Anthony Abbot, Jerome, and Andrew.
	Poldi-Pezzoli: S. Francis in Adoration.
Rome.	Vatican: Pietà.

CHAPTER VIII
GENTILE BELLINI AND ANTONELLO DA MESSINA

What, then, is the position which art has achieved in Venice a decade after the middle of the fourteenth century, and how does she compare with the Florentine School? The Florentines, Fra Angelico, Andrea del Castagno, and Pesellino were lately dead. Antonio Pollaiuolo was in his prime, Fra Lippo was fifty-four, Paolo Uccello was sixty-three. But though the progress in the north had been slower, art both in Padua and Venice was now in vigorous progress. Bartolommeo Vivarini was still painting and gathering round him a numerous band of followers; Mantegna was thirty, had just completed the frescoes in the Eremitani Chapel and the famous altarpiece in S. Zeno; and Gentile and Giovanni Bellini were two and four years his seniors.

Francesco Negro, writing in the early years of the sixteenth century, speaks of Gentile as the elder son of Jacopo Bellini. Giovanni is thought to have been an illegitimate son, as Jacopo's widow only mentions Gentile and another son, Niccolo, in her will. There is every reason to believe that, as was natural, the two brothers were the pupils and assistants of their father. A "Madonna" in the Mond Collection, the earliest known of Gentile's works, shows him imitating his father's style; but when his sister, Niccolosia, married Mantegna in 1453, it is not surprising to find him following Mantegna's methods for a time, and a fresco of St. Mark in the Scuola di San Marco, an important commission which he received in 1466, is taken direct from Mantegna's fresco at Padua.

As the Bellini matured, they abandoned the Squarcionesque tradition and evolved a style of their own; Gentile as much as his even more famous brother. Gentile is the first chronicler of the men and manners of his time. In 1460 he settled in Venice, and was appointed to paint the organ doors in St. Mark's. These large saints, especially the St. Mark, still recall the Paduan period. They have festoons of grapes and apples hung from the architectural ornaments, and the cast of drapery, showing the form beneath, reminds us of Mantegna's figures. But Gentile soon becomes an illustrator and portrait painter. Much of his work was done in the Scuola of St. Mark, where his father had painted, and this was

15

destroyed by fire in 1485. Early, too, is the fine austere portrait of Lorenzo Giustiniani, in the Academy. In 1479 an emissary from the Sultan Mehemet arrived in Venice and requested the Signoria to recommend a good painter and a man clever at portraits. Gentile was chosen, and departed in September for Constantinople. He painted many subjects for the private apartments of the Sultan, as well as the famous portrait now in the possession of Lady Layard. It would be difficult for a historic portrait to show more insight into character. The face is cold, weary, and sensual, with all the over-refined look of an old race and a long civilisation, and has a melancholy note in its distant and satiated gaze. The Sultan showed Gentile every mark of favour, loaded him with presents, and bestowed on him the title of Bey. He returned home in 1493, bringing with him many sketches of Eastern personages and the picture, now in the Louvre, representing the reception of a Venetian Embassy by the Grand Vizier. Some five years before Gentile's commission to Constantinople Antonello da Messina had arrived in Venice, and the spread and popularisation of oil-painting had hastened the casting off of outworn ecclesiastical methods and brought the painters nearer to the truth of life. Antonello did not actually introduce oils to the notice of Venetian painters, for Bartolommeo Vivarini was already using them in 1473, but he was well known by reputation before he arrived, and having probably come into contact with Flemish painters in Naples, he had had better opportunities of seizing upon the new technique, and was able to establish it both in Milan and in Venice. A large number of Venetians were at this time resident in Messina: the families of Lombardo, Gradenigo, Contarini, Bembo, Morosini, and Foscarini were among those who had members settled there. Many of these were patrons of art, and probably paved the way to Antonello's reception in Venice. At first all the traits of Antonello's early work are Flemish: the full mantles, white linen caps and tuckers, the straight sharp folds and long wings of the angels have much of Van Eyck, but when he gets to Venice in 1475, its colour and life fascinate him, and a great change comes over his work. His portraits show that he grasped a new intensity of life, and let us into the character of the men he saw around him. His "Condottiere," in the Louvre, declares the artist's recognition of that truculent and formidable being, full of aristocratic disdain, the product of a daring, unscrupulous life. The "Portrait of a Humanist," in the Castello in Milan, is classic in its deepest sense; and in the Trivulzio College at Milan an older man looks at us out of sly, expressive eyes, with characteristic eyebrows and kindly, half-cynical mouth. It was not wonderful that these portraits, combined with the new medium, worked upon Gentile's imagination and determined his bent.

The first examples of great canvases, illustrating and celebrating their own pageants, must have mightily pleased the Venetians. Scenes in the style of the reception of the Venetian ambassadors were called for on all hands, and when the excellence of Gentile's portraits was recognised, he became the model for all Venice. When his own and his father's and brother's paintings perished by fire in 1485, he offered to replace them "quicker than was humanly possible" and at a very low price. Giovanni, who had been engaged on the external decorations, was ill at the time, but the Signoria was so pleased with the offer that it was decided to let no one touch the work till the two brothers were able to finish it. Gentile still painted religious altarpieces with the Virgin and Child enthroned with saints, but most of his time was devoted to the production of his great canvases. Some of these have disappeared, but the "Procession" and "Miracle of the Cross," commissioned by the school of S. Giovanni Evangelista, are now in the Academy, and the third canvas, executed for the same school, "St. Mark preaching at Alexandria," which was unfinished at the time of his death, and was completed by his brother, is in the Brera.

Gentile Bellini.   PROCESSION OF THE HOLY CROSS.   *Venice.*
(*Photo, Anderson.*)

These great compositions of crowds bring back for us the Venice of Gentile's day as no verbal description can do. There is no especial richness of colour; the light is that of broad day in the Piazza and among the luminous waterways of the city. We can see the scene any day now in the wide square, making allowance for the difference of costume. The groups are set about in the ample space, with the wonderful cathedral as a background. St. Mark's has been painted hundreds of times, but no one has ever given such a good idea of it as

Gentile—of its stateliness and beauty, of its wealth of detail; and he does so without detracting from the general effect, for St. Mark's, though the keynote of the whole composition, is kept subservient, and is part of the stage on which the scene is enacted. The procession passes along, carrying the relics, attended by the waxlights and the banners. Behind the reliquary kneels the merchant, Jacopo Salò, petitioning for the recovery of his wounded son. Then come the musicians; the spectators crowd round, they strain forward to see the chief part of the cortège, as a crowd naturally does. Some watch with reverence, others smile or have a negligent air. The faces of the candle-bearers are very like those we may see to-day in a great Church procession: some absorbed in their task, or uplifted by inner thoughts; others looking curiously and sceptically at the crowd. Gentile tries in his crowds to bring together all the types of life in Venice, all the officials and the ecclesiastical world, the young and old. With a few strokes he creates the individual and also the type;—the careless rover; the responsible magistrate; the shrewd,practical man of business; the young men, full of their own plans, but pausing to look on at one of the great religious sights of their city. In the "Finding of the Cross" he produces the effect of the whole city *en fête*. It was a sight which often met his eyes. The Doge made no fewer than thirty-six processions annually to various churches of the city, and on fourteen of these occasions he was accompanied by the whole of the nobles dressed in their State robes. Every event of importance was seized on by the Venetian ladies as an opportunity for arraying themselves in the richest attire, cloth of gold and velvet, plumes and jewels. Gentile has massed the ladies of Queen Catherine Cornaro's Court around their Queen upon the left side of the canal. The light from above streams upon the keeper of the School, who holds the sacred relic on high. All round are the old, irregular Venetian houses, and in the crowd he paints the variety of men he saw around him every day in Venice. Yet even in this animated scene he retains his old quattrocento calm. The groups are decorously assisting: only here and there he is drawn off to some small detail of reality, such as an oarsman dexterously turning his boat, or the maid letting the negro servant pass out to take a header into the canal. The spectators look on coolly at one more of the oft-seen, miraculous events. The committee, kneeling at the side, is a row of unforgettable portraits, grave, benign, sour, and austere, with bald head or flowing hair. In this composition he triumphs over all difficulties of perspective; our eye follows the canals, and the boats pass away under the bridge in atmospheric light. All the joy of Venice is in that play of light on broad brick surfaces, light which is cast up from the water and dances and shimmers on the marble façades.

Gentile made his will in 1502, as well as others in 1505 and 1506. He left word that he was to be buried in SS. Giovanni e Paolo, and begged his brother Giovanni to finish the work in the Scuola, in return for which he is to receive their father's sketch-book. The unfinished piece is the "St. Mark preaching at Alexandria," and it shows Gentile still developing his capacity as a painter. It is pale in colour but brilliant in sunlight. The mass of white given by the head-dresses of the Turkish women is cleverly subdued so as not to detract from the effect of the sunlight. The thronged effect of the great square is studied with more than his usual care, and the faces have all the old individuality. The foremost figures in the crowd have a colour and richness which we may attribute to Giovanni's hand.

Gentile was always fully employed, and the detailed paintings of functions became very popular; but he was a far less modern painter than his brother, and, in fact, they represent two distinct artistic generations, though Gentile's work was so much the most elaborate and, as the quattrocento would have thought, the most ambitious.

Gentile is essentially the historic painter, yet his is a grave, sincere art, and he has an unerring instinct for the right incidents to include. He cuts out all unseemly trivialities, his actors are stern, powerful men, the treatment is historic and contemporary, but not gossipy. We realise the look of the Venice of his day, in all its tide of human nature, but we also feel that he never forgot that he was chronicling the doings of a city of strong men, and that he must paint them, even in their hours of relaxation and emotion, so as to convey the real dignity and power which underlay all the events of the Republic.

We gather from his will and that of his wife that they had no children, which perhaps makes the more natural the affectionate terms upon which he remained all through his life with his brother. Their artistic sympathies must have differed widely. Gentile's love for historical research, for costume and for pageants, found no echo in the deeper idealism of Giovanni—indeed, his offer of the famous sketch-book, as an inducement to the latter to finish his last great work, seems to hint that it was an exercise out of his brother's line; but he knew that Giovanni was a great painter, and did not trust it, as we might have expected, to his assistants, Giovanni Mansueti and Girolamo da Santacroce.

PRINCIPAL WORKS

Gentile Bellini.

London.	S. Peter Martyr; Portrait.
Milan.	Brera: Preaching of St. Mark.
Venice.	Doge Lorenzo Giustiniani; Miracle of True Cross; Procession of True Cross; Healing by True Cross.
	Lady Layard. Portrait of Sultan.

Antonello da Messina.

Antwerp.	Crucifixion, 1475.
Berlin.	Three Portraits.
London.	The Saviour, 1465; Portrait; Crucifixion, 1477.
Messina.	Madonna and Saints, 1473.
Paris.	Condottiere.
Milan.	Portrait of a Humanist.
Venice.	Academy: Ecce Homo.
Vicenza.	Christ at the Column.

CHAPTER IX
ALVISE VIVARINI

Contemporary with Giovanni Bellini were artists still firmly attached to the past, who were far from suspecting that he was to outstrip them.

One of Antonio de Murano's sons, Luigi or Alvise Vivarini, grew up to follow his father's profession, and was enrolled in the school of his uncle, Bartolommeo. The latter being an enthusiastic follower of Squarcione, Alvise was at first trained in Paduan principles. Jacopo Bellini's efforts had done something to counteract the hard, statuesque Paduan manner, and had rendered Mantegna's art more human and less stony, but Jacopo could not prevent Squarcionesque painters from importing into Venice the style which he disliked so much. Bartolommeo threw in his lot with the Paduans, and his school, especially when reinforced by Alvise, maintained its reputation as long as it only had to compete with local talent. The Vivarinis had now been firmly established in Venice for two generations, and were the best-known and most popular of her painters. Albert Dürer, on his first visit, admired them more than the Bellini. When, however, Gentile and his brother set up in Venice, a hot rivalry arose between them and the old Muranese School. The Bellini had come with their father from Padua, with all its new and scientific fashions. They had all the prestige of relationship with Mantegna, and they shared the patronage of his powerful employers. The striking historical compositions of Gentile were at once in demand by the great confraternities. Bartolommeo had never been very successful in his dealing with oil-painting, though he had dabbled in it for some years before Antonello da Messina came his way, but the perception with which the Bellini at once grasped the new technique gave them the victory. We have only to compare the formless contours of much of Bartolommeo Vivarini's work, the bladder-like flesh-painting of the Holy Child, with the clear luminous

18

colour and firm delicate touch of Gentile, to see that the one man is leagues ahead of the other.

Alvise Vivarini had more natural affinity with his father than with his uncle. He never becomes so exaggerated in his forms as Bartolommeo. The expression of his faces is much deeper and more inward, and he has something of the devotional sweetness of early art. His first known work is an ancona of 1475 at Montefiorentino, in a lonely Franciscan monastery on the spurs of the Apennines. In the centre of the five panels the Madonna sits with her hands pressed palm to palm, in adoration of the Child asleep across her knees. The painter here follows the tradition of his father and uncle, especially in the Bologna altarpiece, in which they collaborated in 1450. Four saints stand on either side, framed in Gothic panels; it is all in the old way, and it is only by degrees that we see there is more sweetness in the expression, better modelling in the figures, and a slenderer, more graceful outline than the earlier anconæ can show. Only five years after this ancona at Montefiorentino, with its stiff rows of isolated saints, we have the altarpiece in the Academy "of 1480," which was painted for a church in Treviso, and here a great change is immediately apparent. The antiquated division into panels has disappeared, nothing is left of the artificial, Squarcionesque decorations, the attitudes are simple, and the scene is a united one. The Madonna's outstretched hand, the suggestion of "Ecce Agnus Dei," makes an appeal which draws the attention of all the saints to one point, and it is made plain that the one idea pervades the entire assembly. The curtain, which symbolises the sanctuary, still hangs behind the throne, but the gold background is abandoned. Alvise has not indeed, as yet, imagined any landscape or constructed an interior, but he lightens the effect by two arched windows which let in the sky. The forms are characteristic of his idea of drawing the human figure; they have the long thighs with the knees low down, which we are accustomed to find, and he constructs a very fine and sharply contrasted scheme of light and shade. There is no trace of the statuesque Paduan draperies. The Virgin's brocaded mantle is simply draped, and the robes of the saints hang in long straight folds. No doubt Alvise, though nominally the rival of the Bellini, has more affinity with them, particularly with Giovanni, than with the Paduan artists, and as time goes on it is evident that he paints with many glances at what they were doing. In the altarpiece in Berlin he constructs an elaborate cupola above the Virgin, such as Bellini was already using. His saints are full of movement. In the end he begins to attitudinise and to display those artificial graces which were presently accentuated by Lotto.

Alvise Vivarini.   ALTARPIECE OF 1480.   *Venice.*
(Photo, Anderson.)

In 1488 the two Bellini had for some time been employed in the Sala del Gran Consiglio by the Council of Ten. Alvise, with his busy school, had hoped, but hitherto in vain, to be invited to enter into competition with them. At length he wrote the following letter:—

To the Most Serene the Prince and the Most Excellent Signoria—I am Alvise of Murano, a faithful servant of your Serenity and of this most illustrious State. I have long been anxious to exercise my skill before your Sublimity and prove that continued study and labour on my part have not been useless. Therefore offer, as a humble subject, in honour and praise of that celebrated city, to devote myself, without return of payment or reward, to the duty of producing a canvas in the Sala del Gran Consiio, according to the method at present in use by the two brothers Bellinii, and I ask no more for the said canvas than that I should be allowed the expenses of the cloth and colours as well as the wages of the journeymen, in the manner that has been granted to the said Bellinii. When I have done I shall leave to your Serenity of his goodness to give me in his wisdom the price which shall be adjudged to be just, honest, and appropriate, in return for the labour, which I shall be enabled, I trust, to continue to the universal satisfaction of your Serenity and of all the excellent Government, to the grace of which I most heartily commend myself.

The "method at present in use" was presumably the oil-painting established by Antonello, which was now being made use of to replace the decorations in fresco and tempera which Guariento, Pisanello, and Gentile da Fabriano had executed, and which were constantly decaying and suffering from the sea air and the dampness of the climate. The

Council accepted Alvise's offer with little delay, and he was told to paint a picture for a space hitherto occupied by one of Pisanello's, and was given a salary of sixty ducats a year, something less than that drawn by Giovanni Bellini. Unfortunately his work, scenes from the history of Barbarossa, perished in the great fire of 1577.

Venice is rich in works which show us what sort of painter was at the head of the Muranese School at the time when it rivalled that of the Bellini. Alvise has two reading saints on either side of the altarpiece of 1480, and of these the Baptist is one of his best figures, "admirably expressive of tension and of brooding thought." It is large and free in stroke, and particularly advanced in the treatment of the foliage. Close by hangs a character-study of St. Clare; type of a strenuous, fanatical old woman, one which belongs not only to the period, but will be recognised by every student of human nature. Formidable and even cruel is her unflinching gaze; she is such a figure as might have stood for Scott's Prioress, and looks as little likely to show mercy to an erring member of her order. In contrast, there is the exquisite little "Madonna and Child" with the two baby angels, still shown as a Bellini in the sacristy of the Church of the Redentore. It is the most absolutely simple and direct picture of the kind painted in Venice. The baby life is more perfect than anything that Gian. Bellini produced, and if much less intellectual than his Madonnas, there is all the tender charm of the primitives, combined with a freedom of drapery and a softness of form which could not be surpassed. The two little angels are more mundane in spirit than those of the school of Bellini; they have nothing of the mystical quality, though we are reminded of Bellini, and the painting is an exercise in his manner. In the sacristy of San Giobbe is an early Annunciation, which is now definitely assigned to Alvise. It has the old tender sentiment, and the carnations of its draperies are of a lovely tint. The priests of S. Giovanni in Bragora were great patrons of the school of the Vivarini, for here, besides several works by Bartolommeo and his assistants, is a little Madonna in a side chapel, which may be compared with the Redentore picture. The Mother sits inside a room, with the Child lying across her knees in the same pose. The two arched openings in the background of the 1480 altarpiece have become windows, through which we look out on a charming landscape of lake and mountain. In the same church a "Resurrection" is not to be overlooked. It was executed in 1498, and some of the grace and beauty of the sixteenth century has crept into it. Against the pink flush of dawn stands the swaying figure of the risen Christ, and below appear the heads of the two guards, looking up, surprised and joyful. It is perhaps the very earliest example of that soft and sensuous feeling, that rhapsody of sensation which was presently to sweep like a flood over the art of Venice. "What a time must the dawn of the sixteenth century have been when a man of seventy, and not the most vigorous and advanced of his age, had the freshness and youthful courage to greet it; nay, actually to depict its magic and glamour as Alvise does in the 'Resurrection'! Giorgione is here anticipated in the roundness and softness of the figures, and in the effect of light. Titian's Assunta is foreshadowed in the fervour of the guards' expressions." Alvise, if he never thoroughly mastered the structure of the nude, and if his forms keep throughout some touch of the archaic, some awkwardness in the thickness of the figures, with their round heads, long thighs, and uncertain proportions, is yet extraordinarily refined and tender in sentiment, his line has a natural flow and beauty, and the heads of his Madonnas and saints cannot be surpassed in loveliness.

His death came when the noble altarpiece to St. Ambrogio in the Frari was still unfinished, and it was completed by his assistant, Marco Basaiti. The execution is heavy and probably of Basaiti, but the venerable doctor is a grand figure, and the two young soldier saints on his right and left hand are striking examples of the beauty we claim for him. The architectural plan is very elaborate, but altogether successful. The group is set beneath an arched vault supported by columns and cornices. Overhead, behind a balustrade, is placed a coronation of the Virgin. The many figures are grouped so as not to interfere with each other, and the sword of St. George, the crozier of St. Gregory, and the crook of St. Ambrose break up the composition and give length and line. The faces of the saints are extremely beautiful, and the two angels making music below compare well with those of the Bellinesque School.

The portraits Alvise has left add to his reputation, and remind us of those of Antonello da Messina, particularly in the vital expression of the eyes, though they are without Antonello's intense force. The "Bernardo di Salla" and the "Man feeding a Hawk," though some critics still ascribe them to Savoldo, have features which make their attribution to Alvise almost certainly correct. Indeed, the resemblance of Bernardo to the Madonna in the 1480 altarpiece cannot escape the most unscientific observer. There is the same inflated nostril, the peculiarly curved mouth, and vivacious eyes.

Among the followers of Alvise, Marco Basaiti, Bartolommeo Montagna, and Lorenzo Lotto are the most distinguished. Others less direct are Giovanni Buonconsiglio and Francesco Bonsignori, while Cima da Conegliano was for a short time his greatest pupil. We shall return to these later.

PRINCIPAL WORKS

Berlin.	Madonna enthroned, with six Saints.
London.	Portrait of Youth.
Milan.	Bonomi-Cereda Collection: Portrait of a Man.
Naples.	Madonna with SS. Francis and Bernardino.
Paris.	Portrait of Bernardo di Salla.
Venice.	Academy: Seven panels of single Saints; Madonna and six Saints, 1480.
	Frari: S. Ambrose enthroned.
	S. Giovanni in Bragora: Madonna adoring Child; Resurrection and Predelle.
	Redentore: Sacristy: Madonna and Child, with Angels.
Vienna.	Madonna.
Windsor.	Man feeding a Hawk.

CHAPTER X
CARPACCIO

Vittore Carpaccio was Gentile Bellini's most faithful pupil. He and his master stand apart in having, before the arrival of the Venetian School proper, captured an aspect and a charm inspired by the natural beauty of the City of the Sea. Gentile, as we have seen, paints her historic appearance, and Carpaccio gives us something of the delight we feel to-day in her translucent waters and her ample, sea-washed spaces flooded with limpid light. While others were absorbed in assimilating extraneous influences, he goes on his own way, painting, indeed, the scenes that were asked for, but painting them in his own manner and with his own enjoyment.

Pageant-pictures had been the demand of the Venetian State from very early days. The first use of painting had been that made by the Church to glorify religion, and very soon the State had followed, using it to enhance the love which Venetians bore to their city, and to bring home to them the consciousness of its greatness and glory. Pageants and processions were an integral part of Venetian life. The people looked on at them, often as they occurred, with more pride and sense of proprietorship than a Londoner does at a coronation procession or at the King going in state to open Parliament. The Venetian loved splendour and beauty and the story of the city's great achievements, and nothing provided so welcome a subject for the decoration of the great public halls as portrayals of the events which had made Venice famous. Artists had been employed to produce these as early as the end of the fourteenth century, and those of the Bellini and Alvise Vivarini (which perished in the great fire) were a rendering on modern lines of the same subjects, satisfying the more advanced feeling for truth and beauty.

Besides the Church and the public Government, we have already seen the "Schools," as they were called, becoming important employers. These schools were the great organised confraternities in the cause of charity and mutual help, which sprang up in Venice in the fifteenth century. That of St. Mark was naturally the foremost, but others were banded each under their patron saint. Each attracted numbers of rich patrons, for it was the fashion to belong to the confraternities. Riches and endowments rolled in, and halls for meeting and for transacting business were built, and were adorned with pictures setting forth the legends of their patron saints. We have already seen Gentile Bellini employed in the schools of San Marco and San Giovanni, and now the schools of St. Ursula and St. George gave commissions to Carpaccio, or perhaps it would be more correct to say that Gentile, having become pre-eminent in this art, provided employment for his pupil and assistant, and that by degrees Carpaccio became a *maestro* on his own account.

A host of second-rate painters were plying side by side, disciples first of one master, then drawn off to become followers of a second; assimilating the influence first of one workshop and then of another. Carpaccio has been lately identified as a pupil of Lazzaro Bastiani, who had a school in Venice, and the recent attribution to this painter of the "Doge before the Madonna," in the National Gallery, gives some countenance to the contention that he was held to be of great excellence in his time.

Though some historians advance the suggestion that Carpaccio was a native of Capo d'Istria, there is little proof that he was not, like his father Pietro, born a Venetian. He seems to have worked in Venice all his life, his first work being dated 1490 and his last 1520. In 1527 his wife, Laura, declared herself a widow.

The narrative art needed by the confraternities was supplied in perfection by Carpaccio,and one of his earliest independent commissions was the important one of decorating the School of St. Ursula. Devotion to St. Ursula was a monopoly of the school. No one else had a right to collect offerings in her name or to put up an image to her. The legend afforded an opportunity for painting varied and dramatic scenes, of which Carpaccio takes full advantage, and the cycle is one of the freshest and most characteristic things that has come down to us from the quattrocento. Problems are not conspicuous. The mediocre masters who have educated the painter have made little impression on him. He is entirely occupied in delight in his subject and in telling his story. The story of St. Ursula, told briefly, is that she was the daughter of the King of Brittany. The King of England sends his ambassadors to beg her hand for his son, Hereo. Ursula discusses the proposal with her father, and makes the conditions that Hereo, who is a heathen, shall be baptized, and that the betrothed couple must before marriage visit the Pope and the sacred shrines. After taking leave of their parents, the Prince and Princess depart on their expedition, but Ursula has had a vision in her sleep in which an angel has announced her martyrdom. She is accompanied on her journey by 11,000 virgins, and they are received by Pope Cyriacus in Rome. The Pope then makes the return journey with them as far as Cologne, where, however, they are assaulted and massacred by the Huns, after which Ursula is accorded a splendid funeral, and is canonised. The thirteen scenes in which the story is told are arranged on nine canvases, and the painter has not executed them in the chronological order, some of the latest events being the least complete in artistic skill. Professor Leonello Venturi assigns the following dates to the list:

1. The ambassadors of the King of England meet those of the King of Brittany to ask for the hand of Ursula. Probably painted from 1496-98.

2. (On same canvas) Ursula discusses the proposal with her father. 1496-98.

3. The King of Brittany dismisses the ambassadors. 1496-98.

4. The ambassadors return to the King of England. 1496-98.

5. An angel appears to Ursula in her sleep. 1492.

6, 7, 8. The betrothed couple take leave of their respective parents, and the Prince meets Ursula. 1495.

9. The betrothed couple and the 11,000 virgins meet the Pope. 1492.

10. They arrive at Cologne. 1490.

11, 12. The massacre by the Huns. The Funeral. 1495.

13. The saint appears in glory, with the palm of martyrdom, venerated by the 11,000 virgins and received in heaven by the Eternal Father. 1491.

No. 10 is a small canvas, such as might naturally have been chosen for a first experiment. The heads are large with coarse features, and the proportions of the figures are poor. The face of the saint in glory (No. 13), plump and without much expression, is of the type of Bastiani's saints. It may be assumed that such a great scheme of decoration would not have been entrusted to any one who was not already well known as an independent master, but perhaps Carpaccio, who would have been about thirty when the work was begun, was still principally engrossed with the conventional, ecclesiastical subject. The heads of the virgins pressing round the saint appear to be portraits, and were very possibly those of the wives and daughters of members of the confraternity.

The improvement that takes place is so rapid that we can guess how congenial the painter found the task and how quickly he adapted his already trained talent. In No. 5 he takes delight in the opportunity for painting a little domestic scene,—the bedroom of a young Venetian girl, perhaps a sister of his own. The comfortable bed, the dainty furniture, are carefully drawn. The clear morning light streams into the room. The saint lies peacefully asleep, her hand under her head, her long eyelashes resting upon her cheek: the whole is an idyll, full of insight into girlish life. The tiny slippers made, no doubt, one of the details that caught his eye. The crown lying on the ledge of the bed is an arbitrary introduction, as naïf as the angel. In the funeral scene the luminous light is diffused over all, the young saint lies upon her bier and is followed by priest and deacon, the crowd is composed with truth to nature, the draperies and garments are brought into harmony with the sky and background, and in all those that follow we find this quality of light. The landscape behind the massacre has gained in natural character, the city is at some distance, houses and churches are half buried in woods; the setting is much more natural than are the quaint and elegant pages who occupy it, and who are drawing their crossbows and attacking the martyrs with leisurely nonchalance. The panel in which the betrothed couple meet shows a great advance, and this and the succeeding ones of the ambassadors, which were painted between 1495 and 1498, must have crowned Carpaccio's reputation. He paints Venice in its most fascinating aspect; the enamelled beauty of its marbles, its sky and sea, its palaces and ships, the rich and picturesque dresses men wore in the streets, the barge glowing with rich velvets. He evinces a fairy-tale spirit which we may compare with the work of Pintoricchio. His Prince, kneeling in a white and gold dress, with long fair curls, is a real fairy prince; Ursula, in her red dress and puffed sleeves, her rippling, flaxen hair and strings of pearls, is a princess of story. Carpaccio's art is simple and garrulous in feeling, his conception is as unpassionate as the fancies of a child, but he has a true love for these gay crowds; Venice going upon her gallant way—her solid, worthy citizens, men of substance, shrewd and valuable, taking their pleasure seriously with a sense of responsibility. They throng the streets and cross over the bridges, every figure is full of freedom and vitality. The arrival and dismissal of the ambassadors are the best of all the scenes. In the middle of the great stage King Maurus of Brittany sits upon a Venetian terrace. In the colonnade to the left is gathered a group of Venetian personages, members of the Loredano family, which was a special patron of St. Ursula's Guild, and gave this panel. The types are all vividly realised and differentiated: the courtier looking critically at the arrivals; the frankly curious bourgeoisie; the man of fashion passing with his nose in the air, disdaining to stare too closely; the fop with his dogs and their dwarf keeper. Far beyond stretch the lagoons; the sea and air of Venice clear and fresh. What is noticeable even now in an Italian crowd, the absence of women, was then most true to life, for except on special occasions they were not seen in the streets, but were kept in almost Oriental seclusion. The dismissal of the ambassadors affords the opportunity for drawing an interior with the street visible through a doorway. A group at the side, of a man dictating a letter and the scribe taking down his words, writing laboriously, with his shoulders hunched and his head on one side, is excellent in its quiet reality. The same life-like vivacity is displayed in Ursula's consultation with her father. The old nurse crouched upon the steps is introduced to break the line and to throw back the main group. Carpaccio has already used such a figure in the funeral scene, and Titian himself adopts his suggestion.

Carpaccio is not a very great painter, but a charming one. His treatment of light and water, of distant hills and trees, shows a sense of peace and poetry, and though he is influenced by Gentile's splendid realistic heads, the type which appeals to him is gentler and more idealised. His fancy is caught by Oriental details, to which Gentile would naturally have directed his attention, and of which there was no lack in Venice at this time. All his episodes are very clearly illustrated, and his popular brush was kept busily employed. He took a share with other assistants in the series which Gentile was painting in S. Giovanni Evangelista. In 1502 the Dalmatians inhabiting Venice resolved to decorate their school, which had been founded fifty years earlier, for the relief of destitute Dalmatian seamen in Venice. The subjects were to be selected from the lives of the Saviour and the patron saints of Dalmatia and Albania, St. Jerome, St. George of the Sclavonians, and St. Tryphonius. The nine panels and an altarpiece which Carpaccio delivered between 1502 and 1508 still adorn the small but dignified Hall of the school. His "Jerome in his Study" has nothing ascetic, but shows a prosperous Venetian ecclesiastic seated in his well-furnished library among his books and writings. He is less successful in his scenes from the life of Christ; the Gethsemane is an obvious imitation of Mantegna; but when he leaves his own style he is weak and poor, and imaginary scenes are quite beyond him. In the death and interment of St. Jerome he gives a delightful impression of the peace of the old convent garden, and in the scene where the lion introduced by the saint scatters the terrified monks he lets a sense of humour have free play. The monks in their long garments, escaping in all directions, are really comical, and in conjunction with the ingratiating smile of the lion, the scene passes into the region of broad farce. We divine the same sense of the comic in the scene in St. Ursula's history, where the 11,000 virgins are hurrying in single file along a winding road which disappears out of the picture. In the principal scene in the life of St. George, Carpaccio again achieves a masterpiece. The force and vivacity of the saint in armour charging the dragon, lingers long in the memory. The long, decorative lines of lance and war-horse and dragon throw back the whole landscape. The details show an almost childish delight in the realisation of ghoulish horrors. He rather injures his "Triumph of St. George" by his anxiety to bring in the Temple of Solomon at Jerusalem; the flying flags distract the eye, and the whole scene is one of confusion, broken up into different parts, while the dragon is reduced to very unterrifying insignificance. His series for the school of the Albanians dealt with the life of the Virgin, who was their special patron. Its remains are at Bergamo, Milan, and in the Academy. The single figures in the "Presentation," the priest and maiden, are excellent. A child at the side of the steps, leading a unicorn, emblem of chastity, shows once more what a hold this use of a figure had taken of him. In the "Visitation" the figures are too much scattered, and the fantastic buildings attract more attention than the women. He still produced altarpieces, and the Presentation of the Infant Christ in the Temple, which he was called upon to paint for San Giobbe, where one of Bellini's most famous altarpieces stood, challenged him to put forth all his strength. He never produced anything more simple and noble or more worthy of the cinque-cento than this altarpiece (now in the Academy). It surpasses Bellini's arrangement in the way in which the personages are raised upon a step, while the dome overhead and the angel musicians below give them height and dignity. The contrast between the infant and the youthful woman and the old men is purposely marked. Such a contrast between youth and age is a very favourite one. Bellini, in the same church, draws it between SS. Sebastian and Job, and Alvise Vivarini, in his last painting, balances a very youthful Sebastian with St. Jerome. This is the most grandiose, the least of a *genre* picture of all Carpaccio's creations, although he does make Simeon into a pontiff with attendant cardinals bearing his train. One of his last works is the S. Vitale over the high altar of the church of that name, where we forgive the wooden appearance of the horse which the saint rides for the sake of the simple dignity of the rider and the airy effect given by the balcony overhead. Nor must we forget that study of the "Two Courtesans" in the Museo Civico, full of the sarcasm of a deep realism. It conveys to us the matter-of-fact monotony of the long, hot days, and the women and the animals with which they are beguiling their idle hours are painted with the greatest intelligence. It carries us back to another phase of life in

Carpaccio's Venice, seen through his observant, humorous eyes, and if there is nothing in his colour distinctive of the impending Venetian richness, it is still arresting in its brilliant limpidity; it seems drawn straight from the transparent canals and radiant lagoons.

We apprehend the difference at once in Bastiani and in Mansueti, who essay the same sort of compositions. They studied grouping carefully, and it must have seemed easy enough to paint their careful architecture and to place citizens in costume with appropriate action in a "Miracle of the Cross," or the "Preaching of St. Mark"; but these pictures are dry and crowded, they give no illusion of truth, there is none of the careless realism of Carpaccio's crowds,—of incidents taking place which are not essential to the story, and, as in life, are only half seen, but which have their share in producing a full and varied illusion. The scenes want the air and depth in which Carpaccio's pictures are enveloped. We are not stimulated and charmed, taken into the outer air and refreshed by these heavy personages, standing in rows, painted in hot, dry colour, and carrying no conviction in their glance and action.

PRINCIPAL WORKS

Berlin.	Madonna and Saints; Consecration of Stephen.
Ferrara.	Death of Virgin.
Milan.	Presentation of Virgin; Marriage of Virgin; St. Stephen disputing.
Paris.	St. Stephen preaching.
Stuttgart.	Martyrdom of St. Stephen.
Venice.	Academy: The History of St. Ursula and the 11,000 Virgins; Presentation in the Temple.
	Museo Correr: Visitation; Two Courtesans.
	S. Giorgio degli Schiavone: History of SS. George and Tryphonius; Agony in the Garden; Christ in the House of the Pharisee; History of St. Jerome.
	S. Vitale: Altarpiece to S. Vitale.
	Lady Layard. Death of the Virgin; St. Ursula taking leave of her Father.
Vienna.	Christ adored by Angels.

CHAPTER XI
GIOVANNI BELLINI

The difference between Gian. Bellini and his accomplished brother, that which makes us so conscious that the first was the greater of the two and which sets him in a later artistic generation than Gentile, is a difference of mind. Such pageant-pictures as we hear that Giovanni was engaged upon have all been destroyed. We may suspect that their composition was not particularly congenial to him, and that the strictly religious pictures and the small allegorical studies, by which we must judge him, were more after his heart. It is his poetic and ideal feeling which adds so strongly to his claim to be a great artist; it was this which drew all men to him and enabled him so powerfully to influence the art of his day in Venice.

Jacopo's wife, Anna, in a will of 1429, leaves everything to her two sons, Gentile and Niccolo. Giovanni was evidently not her son, but Vasari speaks of him as the elder of the two, so that it is very possible that he was an illegitimate child, brought up, after the fashion that so often obtained, in the full privileges of his father's house. Documents show that Jacopo Bellini was living in Venice in 1437, first near the Piazza, and afterwards in the parish of San Lio. He was a member of S. Giovanni Evangelista, and probably one of the leading artists of the city. His two sons helped him in his great decorative works, and also went with him to Padua, where he painted the Gattamalata Chapel. Their relative position is suggested by a document of 1457, which records that the father received twenty-one ducats for "three figures, done on cloth, put in the Great Hall of the Patriarch," only two of which were to go to the son. In 1459 Gian. Bellini's signature first appears on a document, and at about this time we may suppose that he and his brother began to execute small commissions on their own account. On these visits to Padua the intimacy must have sprung up, which led to Mantegna's marriage in 1453 with Jacopo's daughter. At Padua, too, Bellini, in company with Mantegna, drank in the inspiration left there by Donatello, the greatest master that either of them encountered. It was the humanistic and naturalistic side of Donatello which touched Giovanni Bellini, more than all his classic lore. It chimed in, too, with his father's graceful and fanciful quality, and there is no doubt that the Venetian painters soon exercised a marked influence on Mantegna. They "fought for him to execute small commissions on their Eremitani frescoes he begins to lose his purely statuesque type and to become frankly Renaissance. In the later scenes of the series a pergola with grapes, a Venetian campanile and doorway replace his classic towers and arches of triumph. In the "Martyrdom of St. James" the couple walking by and paying no attention whatever to the tragic event, are very like the people whom Gentile introduces in his backgrounds.

There are few documents more interesting in the history of art than the two pictures of the "Agony in the Garden," executed by the brothers-in-law, about 1455, from a design by Jacopo in the British Museum sketch-book. Jacopo draws the mound-like hill, Christ kneeling before the vision of the Chalice, the figures wrapt in slumber, and the distant town. In few pictures up to this time is the landscape conceived in such sympathy with the figures. As we look at this sketch and examine the two finished compositions, which it is so fortunate to find in juxtaposition in the National Gallery, we surmise that the two artists agreed to carry out the same idea and each to give his version of Jacopo's suggestion, and very curious it is to see the rendering each has produced.

Mantegna has made use of the most formal and Squarcionesque contours in his surroundings. The rocks are of an unnatural, geological structure. The towers of Jerusalem are defined in elaborate perspective, and a band of classic figures fills the middle distance. The sleeping forms of the disciples are laid about like so many draped statues taken from their pedestals. The choir of child angels is solid and leaves nothing to the imagination, and if it were not for the beautifully conceived Christ, the whole composition would leave us quite unmoved. On the other hand, we can never look at Bellini's version without a fresh thrill. He, like Mantegna, has followed Jacopo's scheme of winding roads and the city "set on a hill," and has drawn the advancing band of soldiers; but, independent of all details, he gives us the vision of a poet. The still dawn is breaking over the broadly painted landscape, the rosy shafts of light are colouring the sky and casting their magic over every common object, and, lonely and absorbed, the Sacred Figure kneels, wrapt into the Heavenly Vision, which is hardly more definite than a stronger beam of light upon the radiance. One of the disciples, at least, is a successful and natural study of a tired-out man, whose head has fallen back and whose every limb has relaxed in sleep. Bellini is less assured, less accomplished than Mantegna, but he is able to touch us with the pathos of both natural and spiritual feeling.

Even earlier than this picture, critics place the "Crucifixion" and "Transfiguration" of the Museo Correr and our own "Salvator Mundi." In 1443, when Giovanni was a young man of four or five and twenty, San Bernardino had held a great revival at Padua, and the whole of Venice had thronged to hear him. It is very possible, as Mr. Roger Fry suggests in his *Life of Bellini*, that Giovanni's emotional temperament had been worked upon by the preacher's eloquence, and the very poignant feelings of love and pity which his early art expresses were the deliberate consequence of his sympathy with the deep religious mysteries expounded.

In the two pictures in the Correr, Bellini is still going with the Paduan current. In both we have the winding roads so characteristic of his father, but the rocks in the "Transfiguration" have the jointed, arbitrary character of Mantegna's and the draperies are plastered to the forms beneath; yet the figures here have a beauty and a dignity which no reproduction seems able to convey. The feeling is already more imposing than the execution. Christ and the two prophets tower up against the belt of clouds, the central figure conveying a sense of pathetic isolation; while below, St. John's attitude betrays a state of tension, the feet being drawn up and contorted. This picture prepares us for the overwhelming emotion we find in the "Redeemer" and the group of Pietàs. The treatment of the Christ was a development of the early *motif* of angels flying forward on either side of the Cross, but here the sacred blood pouring into the chalice is also sacramental and connected with the intensified religious fervour which had led to the foundation of the Franciscan and Dominican orders, illustrations of which are met with in the miniatures and wood-engravings of fifteenth-century books of devotion. The accessories, the antique reliefs, the low wall, the distant buildings, have an allegorical meaning underlying each one, and common to trecento and, in a less degree, to quattrocento art. Paradise regained is signified by the paved court with the open door, in contradistinction to the Hortus Clausus, or enclosed court; the type of the old covenant. In one of the bas-reliefs Mucius Scaevola thrusts his hand into the fire, the ancient type of heroic readiness to suffer. The other represents a pagan sacrifice, foreshadowing the sacrifice upon the Cross. Figures in the background are leaving a ruined temple and making their way towards the new Christian city, fortified and crowned with a church tower, and in the midst of all this symbolism, Christ and the attendant angel are placed, vibrating with nervous feeling.

During the next few years, Bellini devoted himself to two subjects of the highest devotional order. These are the Madonna and Child, the great exercise in every age for painters, and the Pietà, which he has made peculiarly his own.

Giovanni Bellini. PIETÀ. *Brera, Milan.*
(Photo, Brogi.)

Close by, at Padua, Giotto had left a rendering of the last subject, so full of passionate sorrow that it is hardly possible that it should not, if only half consciously, have stimulated the artistic sensibilities of the most sensitive of painters; but Bellini's pathos shrinks from all exaggeration. He conceives grief with the tenderest insight. His interest in the subject was so intense that he never left the execution to others, and though not a single one bears his signature, yet each is entirely by his own hand. Besides the Pietà at Milan, which is perhaps the best known, there is one in the Correr Museum, another in the Doge's Palace, and yet others at Rimini and at Berlin. The version he adopts, which places the Body of Christ within the sarcophagus, was a favourite in North Italy. Donatello uses it in a bas-relief (now in the Victoria and Albert Museum), but whether he brought or found the suggestion in Padua nothing exists to show. Jacopo has left sketches in which the whole group is within the tomb, and this rendering is followed by Carpaccio, Crivelli, Marco Zoppo, and others. It is never found in trecento art, and is probably traceable to the Paduan impulse to make use of classic remains.

Giovanni Bellini's Pietàs fall into two groups. In one, the Christ is placed between the Virgin and St. John, who are embodiments of the agony of bereavement. In the other, the dead Redeemer is supported by angels, who express the amazement and grief of immortal beings who see their Lord suffering an indignity from which they are immune.

Mary and St. John *inside* the sarcophagus shows that they are conceived mystically; Mary as the Church, and St. John as the personification of Christian Philosophy—a significance frequently attached to these figures. Such a picture was designed to hang over the altar, at which the mystical sacrifice of the Mass was perpetually offered.

In his treatment of the Brera example Bellini has shaken off the Paduan tradition, and is forming his own style and giving free play to his own feeling. The winding roads and evening sky, barred with clouds, are the accessories he used in the "Agony in the Garden," but the figures are treated much more boldly; the drapery falls in broad masses, and scarcely a trace is left of sculpturesque treatment. Careful as is the study of the nude, everything is subordinated to the emotion expressed by the three figures: the helpless, indifferent calm of the dead, the tender solicitude of the Mother, the wandering, dazed look of the despairing friend. Here there is nothing of beautiful or pathetic symbol; the group is intense with the common sorrow of all the world. Mary presses the corpse to her as if to impart her own life, and gazes with anguished yearning on the beloved face. Bellini seems to have passed to a more complex age in his analysis of suffering, yet here is none of the extravagance which the primitive masters share with the Caracci: his restraint is as admirable as his intensity.

In the Rimini version the tender concern and questioning surprise of the attendant angels contrast with the inert weight of the beautiful dead body they support. Their childish limbs and butterfly wings make a sinuous pattern against the lacquered black of the ground-work, and Mr. Roger Fry makes the interesting suggestion that the effect, reminiscent of Greek vase-painting, and the likeness of the Head of Christ to an old bronze, may, in a composition painted for Sigismondo Malatesta, be no mere accident, but a concession to the patron's enthusiasm for classic art.

In 1470 Bellini received his first commission in the Scuola di San Marco. Gentile had been employed there since 1466 on the history of the Israelites in the desert. Bellini agreed to paint "The Deluge and the Ark of Noah" with all its attendant circumstances, but of these, except from Vasari's descriptions, we can form no idea. These great pageant-pictures had become identified with the Bellini and their following, while the production of altarpieces was peculiarly the province of the Vivarini. Here Bellini effected a change, for sacred subjects best suited the restrained and simple perfection of his style, and afforded the most sympathetic opening for his idealistic spirit. For the next twenty years or more, however, he was unavoidably absorbed in public work, for we hear of his being given the direction of that which Gentile left unfinished in the Ducal Palace when he went to the East in 1479. In 1492, Giovanni being ill, Gentile superintended the work for him, and in that year he was appointed to paint in the Hall of the Grand Council, at an annual salary of sixty ducats. Other commissions were turned out of the *bottega* he had set up with his brother in 1471, and between that year and 1480 he went to Pesaro to paint the important altarpiece that still holds its place there. It is in some ways the greatest and most powerful thing that Bellini ever accomplished. The central figures and the attendant saints have a large gravity and carefully studied individuality. St. Jerome, absorbed in his theological books, an ascetic recluse, is admirably contrasted with the sympathetic, cultured St. Paul. The landscape, set in a marble frame, is a gem of beauty, and proves what an appeal nature was making to the painter. The predella, illustrating the principal scenes in the lives of the saints around the altar, is full of Oriental costumes. The horses are small Eastern horses, very unlike the ponderous Italian war-horse, and the whole is evidently inspired by the sketches which Gentile brought back on his return from Constantinople in 1481.

Looking from one to another of the cycle of Madonna pictures which Bellini produced, and of which so many hang side by side in the Academy, we are able to note how his conception varied. In one of the earliest the Child lies across its Mother's knee, in the attitude borrowed from his father and the Vivarini, from whom, too, he takes the uplifted hands, placed palm to palm. The earlier pictures are of the gentle and adoring type, but his later Madonnas are stately Venetian ladies. He gives us a queenly woman, with full throat and stately poise, in the Madonna degli Alberi, in which the two little trees are symbols of the Old and New Testament; or, again, he paints a lovely intellectual face with chiselled and refined features, and sad dark eyes, and contrasts it dramatically with the bluff St. George in armour; and there is another Madonna between St. Francis and St. Catherine, a picture which has a curious effect of artificial light.

CHAPTER XII
GIOVANNI BELLINI (*continued*)

In 1497 the Maggior Consiglio of the Venetian Republic appointed Bellini superintendent of the Great Hall, and conferred on him the honourable title of State Painter. In this capacity he was the overseer of all public works of painting, and was expected to devote a part of his time to the decoration of the Hall. Sansovino enumerates nine of his historical paintings, which had been painted before the State appointment, all having reference to the visit of Pope Alexander; but though he must have been much engrossed, he seems to have suspended the work from time to time, for between 1485 and 1488 he painted the large altarpiece in the Frari, that at San Pietro in Murano, and the one in the Academy, which was painted for San Giobbe. Of these three, the last shows the greatest advance and is fullest of experiment. The Madonna is a grand ecclesiastical figure. It has been said with truth that it is a picture which must have afforded great support and dignity to the Church. The Infant has an expression of omniscience, and the Mother gazes out of the picture,

28

extending invitation and encouragement to the advancing worshippers. The religious feeling is less profound; the artist has been more absorbed in the contrast between the beautiful, youthful body of St. Sebastian and that of St. Giobbe, older but not emaciated, and with the exquisite surface that his now complete mastery of oil-painting enabled him to produce. This technique has evidently been a great delight, and is here carried to perfection; the skin of St. Sebastian gleams with a gloss like the coat of a horse in high condition. Everything that architecture, sculpture, and rich material can supply is borrowed to enhance the grandeur of the group; but the line of sight is still close to the bottom of the picture, and if it were not for the exquisite grace with which the angels are placed, the Madonna would have a broad, clumsy effect. The Madonna of the Frari is the most splendid in colour of all his works. As he paints the rich light of a golden interior and the fused and splendid colours, he seems to pass out of his own time and gives a foretaste of the glory that is to follow. The Murano altarpiece is quite a different conception; instead of the seclusion of the sanctuary, it is a smiling, *plein air* scene: the Mother benign, the Child soft and playful, the old Doge Barbarigo and the patron saints kneeling among bright birds, and a garden and mediæval townlet filling up the background, for which, by the way, he uses the same sketch as in the Pesaro picture. It says much for his versatility that he could within a short time produce three such different versions.

Among Bellini's most fascinating achievements in the last years of the fifteenth century are his allegorical paintings, known to us by the "Pélerinage de l'Âme" in the Uffizi and the little series in the Academy. The meaning of the first has been unravelled by Dr. Ludwig from a mediæval poem by Guillaume de Guilleville, a Cistercian monk who wrote about 1335, and it is interesting to see the hold it has taken on Bellini's mystic spirit. The paved space, set within the marble rail, signifies, as in the "Salvator Mundi," the Paradise where souls await the Resurrection. The new-born souls cluster round the Tree of Life and shake its boughs. The poem says:

There	is	no	pilgrim	who	is	not	sometimes	sad
Who	has	not	those	who	wound	his		heart,
And	to	whom	it	is	not	often		necessary
To		play		and		be		solaced
And	be		soothed		like		a	child
With			something					comforting.
Know		that			those			playing
There	in	order	to	allay	their			sorrow
Have		found		beneath		that		tree
An	apple	that		great		comfort		gives

To those that play with it.[2]

This may be an allusion to sacramental comfort. St. Peter and St. Paul guard the door, beside which the Madonna and a saint sit in holy conversation. A very beautiful figure on the left, wrapped in a black shawl, requires explanation, and it has been suggested that it is the donor, a woman who may have lost husband and children, and who, still in life, is introduced, watching the happiness of the souls in Paradise. SS. Giobbe and Sebastian, who might have stepped out of the San Giobbe altarpiece, are obviously the patron saints of the family, and St. Catherine, at the Virgin's side, may be the donor's own saint. This picture, with its delicious landscape bathed in atmospheric light, is a forerunner of those Giorgionesque compositions of "pure and unquestioning delight in the sensuous charm of rare and beautiful things" in which the artistic nature is even more engrossed than with the intellectual conception, and within its small space Bellini seems to have enshrined all his artistic creed. The allegories in the Academy are also full of meaning. They are decorative works, and were probably painted for some small cabinet. They seem too small for a cassone. They are ruined by over-painting, but still full of grace and fancy. The figure in the classic chariot, bearing fruit, in the encounter between Luxury and Industry, is drawn from

29

Jacopo's triumphant Bacchus. Fortune floats in her barque, holding the globe, and the souls who gather round her are some full of triumphant success, others clinging to her for comfort, while several are sinking, overwhelmed in the dark waters. "Prudence," the only example of a female nude in Bellini's works, holds a looking-glass. Hypocrisy or Calumny is torn writhing from his refuge. The Summa Virtus is an ugly representation of all the virtues; a waddling deformity with eyes bound holds the scales of justice; the pitcher in its hand means prudence, and the gold upon its feet symbolises charity. The landscape, both of this and of the "Fortune," resembles that which he was painting in his larger works at the end of the century. Soon after 1501 Bellini entered into relations with Isabela d'Este, Marchioness of Gonzaga. That distinguished collector and connoisseur writes through her agent to get the promise of a picture, "a story or fable of antiquity," to be placed in position with the allegories which Mantegna had contributed to her "Paradiso." Bellini agreed to supply this, and received twenty-five ducats on account. He seems, however, to have felt that he would be at a disadvantage in competing with Mantegna on his own ground, and asks to be allowed to choose his subject. Isabela was unwillingly obliged to content herself with a sacred picture, and a "Nativity" was selected. She is at once full of suggestions, desiring to add a St. John Baptist, whom Bellini demurs at introducing except as a child, but in April 1504 the commission is still unaccomplished, and Isabela angrily demands the return of her money. This brings a letter of humble apology from Bellini, and presently the picture is forwarded. Lorenzo of Pavia writes that it is quite beautiful, and that "though Giovanni has behaved as badly as possible, yet the bad must be taken with the good." The joy of its acquisition appeased Isabela, who at once began to lay plans to get a further work out of Bellini, and in 1505 Bembo wrote to her that he would take a fresh commission always providing he might fix the subject. From the catalogue of her Mantovan pictures we gather that the picture "sul asse" (on panel) represented the "B.V., il Putto, S. Giovanni Battista, S. Giovanni Evangelista, S. Girolamo, and Santa Caterina."

The great altarpieces which remain strike us less by their research, their preoccupation with new problems of paint or grouping, than by their intense delight in beauty. Bellini was now nearly eighty years old, and in 1504 the young Giorgione had proclaimed a revolution in art with his Castelfranco Madonna. In composition and detail the Madonna of San Zaccaria is in some degree a protest against the Arcadian, innovating fashion of approaching a religious scene, of which the Church had long since decided on the treatment, yet Bellini cannot escape the indirect suggestion of the new manner. The same leaven was at work in him which was transforming the men of a younger generation. In this altarpiece, in the Baptism at Vicenza, in others, perhaps, which have perished, and above all in the hermit saint in S. Giovanni Crisostomo he is linked in feeling and in treatment with the later Venetian School.

The new device, which he adopts quite naturally, of raising the line of sight, sets the figures in increased depth. For the first time he gives height and majesty to the young Mother by carrying the draperies down over the steps. He realises to the full the contrast between the young, fragile heads of his girl-saints and the dark, venerable countenances of the old men. The head of S. Lucy, detaching itself like a flower upon its stem, reminds us of the type which we saw in his Watcher in the sacred allegory of the Uffizi. The arched, dome-like niche opens on a distance bathed in golden light. Bellini keeps the traditions of the old hieratic art, but he has grasped a new perfection of feeling and atmosphere. Who the saints are matters little; it is the collective enjoyment of a company of congenial people that pleases us so much. The "Baptism" in S. Corona, at Vicenza, painted sixteen years later than Cima's in S. Giovanni in Bragora, is in frank imitation of the younger man. Christ and the Baptist, traditional figures, are drawn without much zest, in a weak, conventional way, but the artist's true interest comes out in the beauty of face and gesture of the group of women holding the garments, and above all in the sombre gloom of the distance, which replaces Cima's charming landscape, and which keys the whole picture to the significance of a portent. In the enthronement of the old hermit, S. Chrysostom himself, painted in 1513, Bellini keeps his love for the golden dome, but he lets us look through its arch, at rolling mountain solitudes, with mists rising between their folds. The geranium robe of the saint, an exquisite, vivid bit of colouring, is caught by the golden sunset rays, the fine ascetic head stands out against the evening sky, and in the faces of the two saints who stand on either side of the aged visionary Bellini has gone back to all his old intensity of religious feeling, a feeling which he seemed for a time to have exchanged for a more pagan tone.

In 1507, at Gentile's death, Giovanni undertook, at his brother's dying request, to finish the "Preaching of St. Mark," receiving as a recompense that coveted sketch-book of his father's, from which he had adopted so many suggestions, and which, though he was the eldest, had been inherited by the legitimate son.

In the preceding year Albert Dürer had visited Venice for the second time, and Bellini had received him with great cordiality. Dürer writes, "Bellini is very old, but is still the best painter in Venice"; and adds, "The things I admired on my last visit, I now do not value at all." Implying that he was able now to see how superior Bellini was to the hitherto more highly esteemed Vivarini.

At the very end of Bellini's life, in 1514, the Duke of Ferrara paid him eighty-five ducats for a painting of "Bacchanals," now at Alnwick Castle; which may be looked upon as an open confession by one who had always considered himself as a painter of distinctively religious works, that such a gay scene of feasting afforded opportunities which he could not resist, for beauty of attitude and colour; but the gods, sitting at their banquet in a sunny glade, are almost fully draped, and there is little of the *abandon* which was affected by later painters. The picture was left unfinished, and was later given to Titian to complete. In his capacity as State Painter to the Republic, it was Bellini's duty to execute the official portraits of the Doges. During his long life he saw eleven reigns, and during four he held the State appointment. Besides the official, he painted private portraits of the Doges, and that of Doge Loredano, in the National Gallery, is one of the most perfect presentments of the quattrocento. This portrait, painted by one old man of another, shows no weakening in touch or characterisation. It is as brilliant and vigorous as it is direct and simple. The face is quiet and unexaggerated; there is no unnatural fire and feeling, but an air of accustomed dignity and thought, while the technique has all the perfection of the painter's prime.

In 1516 Giovanni was buried in the Church of SS. Giovanni and Paolo, by the side of his brother Gentile. To the last he was popular and famous, overwhelmed with attentions from the most distinguished personages of the city. Though he had begun life when art showed such a different aspect, he was by nature so imbued with that temperament, which at the time of his death was beginning to assert itself in the younger school, that he was able to assimilate a really astonishing share of the new manner. He is guided by feeling more than by intellect. All the time he is working out problems, he is dominated by the emotion of his subject, but his emotion, his pathos, are invariably tempered and restrained by the calm moderation of the quattrocento. The golden mean still has command of Bellini, and never allows his feelings, however poignant, to degenerate into sentimentality or violence.

PRINCIPAL WORKS

Bergamo.	Lochis: Madonna (E.).
	Morelli: Two Madonnas.
Berlin.	Pietà (L.); Dead Christ.
Florence.	Uffizi: Allegory; The Souls in Paradise (L.).
London.	Portrait of Doge (L.); Madonna (L.); Agony in Garden (E.); Salvator Mundi (E.).
Milan.	Brera: Pietà (E.); Madonna; Madonna, 1510.
Mond Collection.	Dead Christ; Madonna (E.).
Murano.	S. Pietro: Madonna with Saints and Doge Barbarigo, 1488.
Naples.	Sala Grande: Transfiguration.

31

Pesaro.	S. Francesco: Altarpiece.
Rimini.	Dead Christ (E.).
Venice.	Academy: Three Madonnas; Five small allegorical paintings (L.); Madonna with SS. Catherine and Magdalene; Madonna with SS. Paul and George; Madonna with five Saints.
	Museo Correr: Crucifixion (E.); Transfiguration (E.); Dead Christ; Dead Christ with Angels.
	Palazzo Ducale, Sala di Tre: Pietà (E.).
	Frari: Triptych; Madonna and Saints, 1488.
	S. Giovanni Crisostomo: S. Chrysostom with SS. Jerome and Augustine, 1513.
	S. Maria dell' Orto: Madonna (E.).
	S. Zaccaria: Madonna and Saints, 1505.
Vicenza.	S. Corona: Baptism, 1510.

CHAPTER XIII
CIMA DA CONEGLIANO AND OTHER FOLLOWERS OF BELLINI

The rising tide of feeling, the growing sense of the joy of life and the apprehension of pure beauty, which was strengthening in the people and leading up to the great period of Venetian art, flooded round Bellini and recognised its expression in him. He was more popular and had a larger following among the artists of his day than either Gentile or Carpaccio with their frankly mundane talent. Whatever Giovanni's State works may have been, his religious paintings are the ones which are copied and adapted and studied by the younger band of artists, and this because of their beauty and notwithstanding their conventional subjects. Gentile's pageant-pictures have still something cold and colourless, with a touch of the archaic, while Giovanni's religious altarpieces evince a new freedom of handling, a modern conception of beautiful women, a use of that colour which was soon to reign triumphant. As far as it went indeed, its triumph was alreadyassured; as Giovanni advanced towards old age, it was no longer of any use for the young masters of the day to paint in any way save the one he had made popular, and one artist after another who had begun in the school of Alvise Vivarini ended as the disciple of Giovanni Bellini.

It was the habit of Bellini to trust much to his assistants, and as everything that went out of his workshop was signed by his name, even if it only represented the use of one of his designs, or a few words of advice, and was "passed" by the master, it is no wonder that European collections were flooded with works, among which only lately the names of Catena, Previtali, Pennacchi, Marco Belli, Bissolo, Basaiti, Rondinelli, and others begin to be disentangled.

Only one of his followers stands out as a strong and original master, not quite of the first class, but developing his own individuality while he draws in much of what both Alvise and Bellini had to give. Cima da Conegliano, whose real name was Giovanni Battista, always signs himself *Coneglianensis.* the title of Cima, "the Rock," by which he is now so widely known, having first been mentioned in the seventeenth century by Boschini, and perhaps given him by that writer himself. He was a son of the mountains, who, though he came early to Venice, and lived there most of his life, never loses something of their wild freshness, and to the end delights in bringing them into his backgrounds. He lived with his mother at Conegliano, the beautiful town of the Trevisan marches, until 1484, when he was twenty-five, and then came down to Vicenza, where he fell under the tuition of Bartolommeo Montagna, a Vicentine painter, who had been studying both with Alvise and Bellini. Cima's "Madonna with Saints," painted for the Church of St. Bartolommeo, Vicenza, in 1489, shows him still using the old method of tempera, in a careful, cold, painstaking style, yet already showing his own taste. The composition has something of Alvise, yet that something has been learned through the agency of Montagna, for the figures have the latter's severity and austere character and the colour is clearer and more crude than Alvise's. It is no light resemblance, and he must have been long with Montagna. In the type of the Christ in Montagna's Pietà at Monte Berico, in the fondness for airy porticoes, in the architecture and main features of his "Madonna enthroned" in the Museo Civico at Vicenza, we see characteristics which Cima followed, though he interpreted them in his own way. He turns the heavy arches and domes that Alvise loved, into airy pergolas, decked with vines. He gives increasing importance to high skies and to atmospheric distances. When he got to Venice in 1492, he began to paint in oils, and undertook the panel of S. John Baptist with attendant saints, still in the Church of S. Madonna dell' Orto. The work of this is rather angular and tentative, but true and fresh, and he comes to his best soon after, in the "Baptism" in S. Giovanni in Bragora, which Bellini, sixteen years later, paid him the compliment of copying. It was quite unusual to choose such a subject for the High Altar, and could only be justified by devotion to the Baptist, who was Cima's own name-saint as well as that of the Church. Cima is here at his very highest; the composition is not derived from any one else, but is all the conception of an ingenuous soul, full of intuition and insight. The Christ is particularly fine and simple, unexaggerated in pose and type; the arm of the Baptist is too long, but the very fault serves to give him a refined, tentative look, which makes a sympathetic appeal. The attendant angels look on with an air of sweet interest. The distant mountains, the undulating country, the little town of Conegliano, identified by the castle on its great rock, or *Cima*, are Arcadian in their sunny beauty. The clouds, as a critic has pointed out, are full of sun, not of rain. The landscape has not the sombre mystery of Titian's, but is bright with the joyous delight of a lover of outdoor life. As Cima masters the new medium he becomes larger and simpler, and his forms lose much of their early angularity. A confraternity of his native town ordered the grand altarpiece which is still in the Cathedral there, and in this he shows his connection with Venice; the architecture is partly taken from St. Mark's, the lovely Madonna head recalls Bellini, and a group of Bellinesque angels play instruments at the foot of the throne. Cima is, however, never merged in Bellini. He keeps his own clearly defined, angular type; his peculiar, twisted curls are not the curls of Bellini's saints, his treatment of surface is refined, enamel-like, perfectly finished, but it has nothing of the rich, broken treatment which Bellini's natural feeling for colour was beginning to dictate. Cima's pale golden figures have an almost metallic sharpness and precision, and though they are full of charm and refinement, they may be thought lacking in spontaneity and passion. To 1501 belongs the "Incredulity of St. Thomas," now in the Academy, but painted for the Guild of Masons. It is a picture full of expression and dignity, broad in treatment if a little cold in its self-restraint. Cima seems to have not quite enough intellect, and not quite enough strong feeling. However, the little altarpiece of the Nativity, in the Church of the Carmine in Venice, has a richer, fuller touch, and this foreshadows the work he did when he went to Parma, where his transparent shadows grow broader and stronger, and his figures gain in ease and freedom. He never loses the delicate radiance of his lights, and his types and his architecture alike convey something of a peculiarly refined, brilliant elegance.

Like all these men of great energy and prolific genius, Cima produced an astonishing number of panels and altarpieces, and no doubt had pupils on his own account, for a goodly list could be made of pictures in his style, but not by his own hand, which have been carried by collectors into widely-scattered places. His exquisite surface and finish and his marked originality make him a difficult master to imitate with any success. His latest work is dated 1508, but Ridolfi says he lived till 1517, and it seems probable that he returned to his beloved Conegliano and there passed his last years.

If Cima possessed originality, Vincenzo of Treviso, called Catena, gained an immense reputation by his industry and his power of imitating and adopting the manner of Bellini's School. In those days men did not trouble themselves much as to whether they were original or not. They worked away on traditional compositions, frankly introducing figures from their master's cartoons, modifying a type here, making some little experiment or arrangement there, and, as a French critic puts it, leaving their own personality to "hatch out" in due time, if it existed, and when it was sufficiently ripened by real mastery of their art. It is here that Catena fails; beginning as a journeyman in the Sala del Gran Consiglio, at a salary of three ducats a month, he for long failed to acquire the absolute mastery of drawing which was possessed by the better disciples of the schools. But he is painstaking, determined to get on, and eager to satisfy the continually increasing demand for work. His draperies are confused and unmeaning, his faces round, with small features, inexpressive button mouths, and weak chins, and his flesh tints have little of the glow which is later the prerogative of every second-rate painter. Yet Catena succeeds, like many another careful mediocre man, in securing patronage, and as the sixteenth century opened he gained the distinction from Doge Loredano of a commission to paint the altarpiece for the Pregadi Chapel of the Sala di Tre, in the Ducal Palace. He adapts his group from that of Bellini in the Cathedral of Murano, bringing in a profile portrait of the kneeling Doge, of which he afterwards made numerous copies, one of which was for long assigned to Gentile and one to Giovanni Bellini.

That Catena is not without charm, we discern in such a composition as his "Martyrdom of St. Cristina," in S. Maria Mater Domini, in which the saint, a solid, Bellinesque figure, kneels upon the water, in which she met her death, and is surrounded by little angels, holding up the millstone tied round her neck, and laden with other instruments of her martyrdom. Catena borrows right and left, and tries to follow every new indication of contemporary taste. For instance, he remarks the growing admiration for colour, and hopes by painting gay, flat tints, in bright contrast, to produce the desired effect.

It is evident that he made many friends among the rich connoisseurs of the time, and that his importance was out of proportion to his real merit. Marcantonio Michele, writing an account of Raphael's last days to a friend in Venice, and touching on Michelangelo's illness, begs him to see that Catena takes care of himself, "as the times are unfavourable to great painters." Catena had acquired and inherited considerable wealth; he came of a family of merchants, and resided in his own house in San Bartolommeo del Rialto. He lived in unmarried relations with Dona Maria Fustana, the daughter of a furrier, to whom he bequeaths in his will 300 ducats and all his personal effects. As a careful portrait-painter, with a talent for catching a likeness, he was in constant demand, and in some of his heads— that of a canon dressed in blue and red, at Vienna, and especially in one of a member of the Fugger family, now at Dresden—he attains real distinction. And in his last phase he does at length prove the power that lies behind long industry and perseverance. Suddenly the Giorgionesque influence strikes him, and turning to imbibe this new element, he produces that masterpiece which throws a glamour over all his mediocre performances; his "Warrior adoring the Infant Christ," in the National Gallery, is a picture full of charm, rich and romantic in tone and spirit. The Virgin and the Child upon her knee are of his dull round-eyed type, the form and colours of her draperies are still unsatisfactory, but the knight in armour with his Eastern turban, the romantic young page, holding his horse, are pure Giorgionesque figures. Beautiful in themselves, set in a beautiful landscape glowing with light and air, the whole picture exemplifies what surprising excellence could be suddenly attained by even very inferior artists, who were constantly associating with greater men, at a moment when the whole air was, as it were, vibrating with genius.

Catena was very much addicted to making his will, and at least five testaments or codicils exist, one of them devising a sum of money for the benefit of the School of Painters in Venice, and another leaving to his executor, Prior Ignatius, the picture of a "St. Jerome in his Cell," which may be the one in our national collection, which remained in Venice till 1862. It is painted in his gay tones, imitating Basaiti and Lotto, and brings in the partridge of which he made a sort of sign manual.

Cardinal Bembo writes in 1525 to Pietro Lippomano, to announce that, at his request, he is continuing his patronage of Catena:

Though I had done all that lay in my power for Vincenzo Catena before I received your Lordship's warm recommendation in his favour, I did not hesitate, on receipt of your letter, to add something to the first piece I had from him, and I did so because of my love and reverence for you, and I trust that he will return appropriate thanks to you for having remembered that you could command me.

Marco Basaiti was alternately a journeyman in different workshops and a master on his own account. For long the assistant and follower of Alvise Vivarini, we may judge that he was also his most trusted confidant, for to him was left the task of completing the splendid altarpiece to S. Ambrogio, in the Frari. His heavy hand is apparent in the execution, and the two saints, Sebastian and Jerome, in the foreground, have probably been added by him, for they have the air of interlopers, and do not come up to the rest of the company in form and conception. The Sebastian, with his hands behind his back and his loin cloth smartly tied, is quite sufficiently reminiscent of Bellini's figure of 1473 to make us believe that Basaiti was at once transferring his allegiance to that reigning master. In his earlier phase he has the round heads and the dry precise manner of the Muranese. In his large picture in the Academy, the "Calling of the Sons of Zebedee," he produces a large, important set piece, cold and lifeless, without one figure which arrests us, or lingers in the memory. "The Christ on the Mount" is more interesting as having been painted for San Giobbe, where Bellini's great altarpiece was already hanging, and coming into competition with Bellini's early rendering of the same scene. Painted some thirty years later, it is interesting to see what it has gained in "modernness." The landscape and trees are well drawn and in good colour, and the saints, standing on either side of a high portico, have dignity. In the "Dead Christ," in the Academy, he is following Bellini very closely in the flesh-tints and the *putti*. The *putti*, looking thoughtfully at the dead, is a *motif* beloved of Bellini, but Basaiti cannot give them Bellini's pathos and significance; they are merely childish and seem to be amused.

In 1515 Basaiti has entered upon a new phase. He has felt Giorgione's influence, and is beginning to try what he can do, while still keeping close to Bellini, to develop a fuller touch, more animated figures, and a brilliant effect of landscape. He runs a film of vaporous colour over his hard outlines and makes his figures bright and misty, and though underneath they are still empty and monotonous, it is not surprising that many of his works for a time passed as those of Bellini. Though he is a clever imitator, "his figures are designed with less mastery, his drawing is a little less correct, his drapery less adapted to the under form. Light and shade are not so cleverly balanced, colours have the brightness, but not the true contrast required. In landscape he proceeds from a bleak aridity to extreme gaiety; he does not dwell on detail, but his masses have neither the sober tint nor the mysterious richness conspicuous in his teacher ... he is a clever instrument." Both Previtali and Rondinelli were workers with Basaiti in Bellini's studio. Previtali occasionally signed himself Andrea Cordeliaghi or Cordella, and has left many unsigned pictures. He copies Catena and Lotto, Palma and Montagna; but for a time his work went forth from Bellini's workshop signed with Bellini's name. In 1515, in a great altarpiece in San Spirito at Bergamo, he first takes the title of Previtali, compiling it in the cartello with the monogram already used as Cordeliaghi. There are traces of many other minor artists at this period, all essaying the same manner, copying one or other of the masters, taking hints from each other. The Venetian love of splendour was turning to the collection of works of art, and the work of second-class artists was evidently much in demand and obtained its meed of admiration. Bissolo was a fellow-labourer with Catena in the Hall of the Ducal Palace in 1492; he is soft and nerveless, but he copies Bellini, and has imbibed something of his tenderness of spirit.

It will be seen from this list how difficult it is to unravel the tale of the false Bellinis. The master's own works speak for themselves with no uncertain voice, but away from these it is very difficult to pronounce as to whether he had given a design, or a few touches, or advice, and still more difficult to decide whether these were bestowed on Basaiti in his later manner, or on Previtali or Bissolo, or if the teaching was handed on by them in a still more diluted form to the lesser men who clustered round, much of whose work has survived and has been masquerading for centuries under more distinguished names. It is sometimes affirmed that the loss of originality in the endeavour to paint like greater men has been a symptom of decay in every school in the past. It is interesting to notice, therefore, that in every great age of painting there has always been an undercurrent of imitation, which has helped to form a stream of tradition, and which, as far as we can see, has done no harm to the stronger spirits of the time.

PRINCIPAL WORKS

Cima.

Berlin.	Madonna with four Saints; Two Madonnas.
Conegliano	Duomo: Madonna and Saints, 1493.
Dresden.	The Saviour; Presentation of Virgin.
London.	Two Madonnas; Incredulity of S. Thomas; S. Jerome.
Milan.	Brera: Six pictures of Saints; Madonna.
Parma.	Madonna with Saints; Another; Endymion; Apollo and Marsyas.
Paris.	Madonna with Saints.
Venice.	Academy: Madonna with SS. John and Paul; Pietà; Madonna with six Saints; Incredulity of S. Thomas; Tobias and the Angel.
	Carmine: Adoration of the Shepherds.
	S. Giovanni in Bragora: Baptism, 1494; SS. Helen and Constantine; Three Predelle; Finding of True Cross.
	SS. Giovanni and Paolo: Coronation of the Virgin.
	S. Maria dell' Orto: S. John Baptist and SS. Paul, Jerome, Mark, and Peter.
	Lady Layard. Madonna with SS. Francis and Paul; Madonna with SS. Nicholas of Bari and John Baptist.
Vicenza.	Madonna with SS. Jerome and John, 1489.

Vincenzo Catena.

Bergamo.	Carrara: Christ at Emmaus.
Berlin.	Portrait of Fugger; Madonna, Saints, and Donor (E.).
Dresden.	Holy Family (L.).
London.	Warrior adoring Infant Christ (L.); S. Jerome in his Study (L.); Adoration of Magi (L.).
	Mr. Benson: Holy Family.
	Lord Brownlow: Nativity.
	Mond Collection: Madonna, Saints, and Donors (E.).
Paris.	Venetian Ambassadors at Cairo.
Venice.	Ducal Palace: Madonna, Saints, and Doge Loredan (E.).
	Giovanelli Palace: Madonna and Saints.
	S. Maria Mater Domini: S. Cristina.

S. Trovaso: Madonna.

Vienna.   Portrait of a Canon.

Marco Basaiti.

Bergamo.   The Saviour, 1517; Two Portraits.

Berlin.   Pietà; Altarpiece; S. Sebastian; Madonna (E.).

London.   S. Jerome; Madonna.

Milan.   Ambrosiana: Risen Christ.

Munich.   Madonna, Saints, and Donor (E.).

Murano.   S. Pietro: Assumption.

Padua.   Portrait, 1521; Madonna with SS. Liberale and Peter.

Venice.   Academy: Saints; Dead Christ; Christ in the Garden, 1510; Calling of Children of Zebedee, 1510.

                            Museo Correr: Madonna and Donor; Christ and Angels.

                            Salute: S. Sebastian.

Vienna.   Calling of Children of Zebedee, 1515.

Andrea Previtali.

Bergamo.   Carrara: Pentecost; Marriage of S. Catherine; Altarpiece; Madonna, 1514; Madonna with Saints and Donors.

                            Lochis: Madonna and Saint.

                            Count Moroni: Madonna and Saints; Family Group.

                            S. Alessandro in Croce: Crucifixion, 1524.

                            S. Spirito: S. John Baptist and Saints, 1515; Madonna and four Female Saints, 1525.

Berlin.   Madonna and Saints; Marriage of S. Catherine.

Dresden.   Madonna and Saints.

London.   Madonna and Donor (E.).

Milan.   Brera: Christ in Garden, 1512.

Oxford.   Christchurch Library: Madonna.

Venice.   Ducal Palace: Christ in Limbo; Crossing of the Red Sea.

                            Redentore: Nativity; Crucifixion.

Verona.   Stoning of Stephen; Immaculate Conception.

N. Rondinelli.

Berlin.   Madonna.

Florence.   Uffizi: Madonna and Saints.

Milan.   Brera: Madonna with four Saints and three

37

Angels.

Paris.   Madonna and Saints.

Ravenna.   Two Madonnas with Saints.

                 S. Domenico: Organ Shutters; Madonna and Saints.

Venice.   Museo Correr: Madonna; Madonna with Saints and Donors.

                 Giovanelli Palace: Two Madonnas.

Bissolo.

London.   Mr. Benson: Madonna and Saints.

                 Mond Collection: Madonna and Saints.

Venice.   Academy: Dead Christ; Madonna and Saints; Presentation in Temple.

                 S. Giovanni in Bragora: Triptych.

                 Redentore: Madonna and Saints.

                 S. Maria Mater Domini: Transfiguration.

                 Lady Layard: Madonna and Saints.

PART II

CHAPTER XIV
GIORGIONE

When we enter a gallery of Florentine paintings, we find our admiration and criticism expressing themselves naturally in certain terms; we are struck by grace of line, by strenuous study of form, by the evidence of knowledge, by the display of thought and intellectual feeling. The Florentine gestures and attitudes are expressive, nervous, fervent, or, as in Michelangelo and Signorelli, alive with superhuman energy. But when looking at pictures of the Venetian School we unconsciously use quite another sort of language; epithets like "dark" and "rich" come most freely to our lips; a golden glow, a slumberous velvety depth, seem to engulf and absorb all details. We are carried into the land of romance, and are fascinated and soothed, rather than stimulated and aroused. So it is with portraits; before the "Mona Lisa" our intelligence is all awake, but the men and women of Venetian canvases have a grave, indolent serenity, which accords well with the slumber of thought.

Up to the beginning of the sixteenth century the painters of Venice had not differed very materially from those of other schools; they had gradually worked out or learned the technicalities of drawing, perspective and anatomy. They had been painting in oils for twenty-five years, and they betrayed a greater fondness for pageant-pictures than was felt in other States of Italy. Florence appoints Michelangelo and Leonardo to decorate her public palace, but no great store is set by their splendid achievements; their work is not even completed. The students fall upon the cartoons, which are allowed to perish, instead of being treasured by the nation. Gentile Bellini and Carpaccio and the band of State painters are appreciated and well rewarded. These men have reproduced something of the lucent transparency, the natural colour of Venice, but it is as if unconsciously; they are not fully aiming at any special effect. Year after year the Venetian masters assimilate more or less languidly the influences which reach them from the mainland. They welcome Guariento and Gentile da Fabriano, they set themselves to learn from Veronese or Florentine, the Paduans contribute their chiselled drawing, their learned perspective, their archeological curiosity. Yet even early in the day the Venetians escape from that hard and learned art which is so alien to their easy, voluptuous temperament. Jacopo Bellini cannot conform to it, and his greatest son is ready to follow feeling and emotion, and in his old age is quick to discover the first flavour of the new wine. If Venetian art had gone on upon the lines we have been tracing up to now, there would have been nothing very distinctive about it, for, however interesting and charming Alvise and Carpaccio, Cima and the Bellini may be, it is not of them we think when we speak of the Venetian School and when we rank it beside that of Florence, while Giovanni Bellini alone, in his later works, is not strong enough to bear the burden.

The change which now comes over painting is not so much a technical one as a change of temper, a new tendency in human thought, and we link it with Giorgione because he was the channel through which the deep impulse first burst into the light. We have tried to trace the growth of the early Venetian School, but it does not develop logically like that of Florence; it is not the result of long endeavour, adding one acquisition and discovery to another. Venetian art was peculiarly the outcome of personalities, and it did not know its own mind till the sixteenth century. Then, like a hidden spring, it bubbles irresistibly to the surface, and the spot where it does so is called by the name of a man.

There are beings in most great creative epochs who, with peculiar facility, seem to embody the purpose of their age and to yield themselves as ready instruments to its design. When time is ripe they appear, and are able, with perfect ease, to carry out and give voice to the desires and tendencies which have been straining for expression. These desires may owe their origin to national life and temperament; it may have taken generations to bring them to fruition, but they become audible through the agency of an individual genius. A genius is inevitably moulded by his age. Rome, in the seventeenth century, drew to her in Bernini a man who could with real power illustrate her determination to be grandiose and ostentatious, and, at the height of the Renaissance, Venice draws into her service a man whose sensuous feeling was instilled, accentuated, and welcomed by every element around him.

More conclusively than ever, at this time, Venice, the world's great sea-power, was in her full glory as the centre of the world's commerce and its art and culture. Vasco da Gama had discovered the sea route to India in 1498, but the stupendous effect which this was to exert on the whole current of power did not become apparent all at once. Venice was still the great emporium of the East, linked to it by a thousand ties, Oriental in her love of Eastern richness.

It would be exaggerating to say that the Venetians of the sixteenth century could not draw. As there were Tuscans who understood beautiful harmonies of colour, so there were Venetians who knew a good deal about form; but the other Italians looked upon colour as a charming adjunct, almost, one might say, as an amiable weakness: they never would have allowed that it might legitimately become the end and aim in painting, and in the same way form, though respected and considered, was never the principal object of the Venetians. Up to this time Venice had fed her emotional instincts by pageants and gold and velvets and brocades, but with Giorgione she discovered that there was a deeper emotional vehicle than these superficial glories,—glowing depths of colour enveloped in the mysterious richness of chiaroscuro which obliterated form, and hid and suggested more than it revealed.

Giorgione no longer described "in drawing's learned tongue"; he carried all before him by giving his direct impression in colour. He conceives in colour. The Florentines cared little if their finely drawn draperies were blue or red, but Giorgione images purple clouds, their dark velvet glowing towards a rose and orange horizon. He hardly knows what attitudes his characters take, but their chestnut hair, their deep-hued draperies, their amber flesh, make a moving harmony in which the importance of exact modelling is lost sight of. His scenes are not composed methodically and according to the old rules, but are the direct impress of the painter's joy in life. It was a new and audacious style in painting, and its keynote, and absolutely inevitable consequence, was to substitute for form and for gay, simple tints laid upon it, the quality of chiaroscuro. We all know how the shades of evening are able to transform the most commonplace scene; the dull road becomes a mysterious avenue, the colourless foliage develops luscious depths, the drab and arid plain glows with mellow light, purple shadows clothe and soften every harsh and ugly object, all detail dies, and our apprehension of it dies also. Our mood changes; instead of observing and criticising, we become soothed, contemplative, dreamy. It is the carrying of this profound feeling into a colour-scheme by means of chiaroscuro, so that it is no longer learned and explanatory, but deeply sensuous and emotional, that is the gift to art which found full voice with Giorgione, and which in one moment was recognised and welcomed to the exclusion of the older manner, because it touched the chord which vibrated through the whole Venetian temperament.

And the immediate result was the picture of *no subject*. Giorgione creates for us idle figures with radiant flesh, or robed in rich costumes, surrounded by lovely country, and we do not ask or care why they are gathered together. We have all had dreams of Elysian fields, "where falls not any rain, nor ever wind blows loudly," where all is rest and freedom, where music blends with the plash of fountains, and fruits ripen, and lovers dream away the days, and no one asks what went before or what follows after. The Golden Age, the haunt of fauns and nymphs: there never has been such a day, or such a land: it is a mood, a vision: it has danced before the eyes of poets, from David to Keats and Tennyson: it has rocked the tired hearts of men in all ages: the vision of a resting-place which makes no demands and where the dwellers are exempt from the cares and weakness of mortality. Needless to say, it is an ideal born of the East; it is the Eastern dream of Paradise, and it speaks to that strain in the temperament which recognises that life cannot be all thought, but also needs feeling and emotion. And for the first time in all the world the painter of Castelfranco sets that vague dream before men's eyes. The world, with its wistful yearnings and questionings, such as Leonardo or Botticelli embodied, said little to his audience. Here was their natural atmosphere, though they had never known it before. These deep, solemn tones, these fused and golden lights are what Giorgione grasps from the material world, and as he steeps his senses in them the subject counts but little in the deep enjoyment they communicate. We, who have seen his manner repeated and developed through thousands of pictures, find it difficult to realise that there had been nothing like it before, that it was a unique departure, that when Bellini and Titian looked at his first creations they must have experienced a shock of revelation. The old definite style must have seemed suddenly hard and meagre, and every time they looked on the glorious world, the deep glow of sunset, the mysterious shades of falling night, they must have felt they were endowed with a sense to which they had hitherto been strangers, but which, it was at once apparent, was their true heritage. They had found themselves, and in them Venice found her real expression, and with Giorgione and those who felt his impetus began the true Venetian School, set apart from all other forms of art by its way of using and diffusing and intensifying colour.

When Giorgione, the son of a member of the house of Barbarelli and a peasant girl of Vedelago, came down to Venice, we gather that he had nothing of the provincial. Vasari, who must often have heard of him from Titian, describes him as handsome, engaging, of distinguished appearance, beloved by his friends, a favourite with women, fond of dress and amusement, an admirable musician, and a welcome guest in the houses of the great. He was evidently no peasant-bred lad, but probably, though there is no record of the fact, was brought up, like many illegitimate children, in the paternal mansion. His home was not far from the lagoons, in one of the most beautiful places it is possible to imagine, on a lovely and fertile plain running up to the Asolean hills and with the Julian Alps lying behind. We guess that he received his education in the school of Bellini, for when that master sold his allegory of the "Souls in Paradise" to one of the Medici, to adorn the summer villa of Poggio Imperiale, there went with it the two small canvases now in the Uffizi, the "Ordeal of Moses" and the "Judgment of Solomon," delightful little paintings in Giorgione's rich and distinctive style, but less accomplished than Bellini's picture, and with imperfections in the drawing of drapery and figures which suggest that they are the work of a very young man. The love of the Venetians for decorating the exterior of their palaces with fresco led to Giorgione being largely employed on work which was unhappily a grievous waste of time and talent, as far as posterity is concerned. We have a record of façades covered with spirited compositions and heraldic devices, of friezes with Bacchus and Mars, Venus and Mercury. Zanetti, in his seventeenth-century prints, has preserved a noble figure of "Fortitude" grasping an axe, but beyond a few fragments nothing has survived. Before he was thirty Giorgione was entrusted with the important commission of decorating the Fondaco dei Tedeschi. This building, which we hear of so often in connection with the artists of Venice, was the trading-house for German, Hungarian, and Polish merchants. The Venetian Government surrounded these merchants with the most jealous restrictions. Every assistant and servant connected with them was by law a Venetian, and, in fact, a spy of the Republic. All transactions of buying and selling were carried out by Venetian brokers, of whom some thirty were appointed. As time went on, some of these brokerships must have resolved themselves into sinecure offices, for we find Bellini holding one, and certainly without discharging any of the original duties, and they seem to have become some sort of State retainerships. In 1505 the old Fondaco had been burnt to the ground, and the present building was rising when Giorgione and Titian were boys. A decree went forth that no marble, carving, or gilding were to be used, so that painting the outside was the only alternative. The roof was on in 1507, and from that date Giorgione, Titian, and Morto da Feltre were employed in the adornment of the façade. Vasari is very much exercised over Giorgione's share in these decorations. "One does not find one subject carefully arranged," he complains, "or which follows correctly the history or actions of ancients or moderns. As for me, I have never been able to understand the meaning of these compositions, or have met any one able to explain them to me. Here one sees a man with a lion's head, beside a woman. Close by one comes upon an angel or a Love: it is all an inexplicable medley." Yet he is delighted with the brilliancy of the colour and the splendid execution, and adds, "Colour gives more pleasure in Venice than anywhere else."

Among other early work was the little "Adoration of the Magi," in the National Gallery, and the so-called "Philosophers" at Vienna. According to the latest reading, this last illustrates Virgil's legend that when the Trojan Æneas arrived in Italy, Evander pointed out the future site of Rome to the ancient seer and his son. Giorgione, in painting the scene, is absorbed in the beauty of nature. It is his first great landscape, and all accessories have been sacrificed to intensity of effect. He revels in the glory of the setting sun, the broad tranquil masses of foliage, the long evening shadows, and the effect of dark forms silhouetted against the radiant light.

CHAPTER XV
GIORGIONE (*continued*)

When Giorgione was twenty-six he went back to Castelfranco, and painted an altarpiece for the Church of San Liberale. In the sixteenth century Tuzio Costanza, a well-known captain of Free Companions, who had made his fortune in the wars, where he had been attached to Catherine Cornaro, followed the dethroned queen from Cyprus, and when she retired to Asolo, settled near her at Castelfranco. His son, Matteo, entered the service of the Venetian Republic, and became a leader of fifty lances; but Matteo was killed at the battle of Ravenna in 1504, and Costanza had his son's body embalmed and buried in the family chapel.

Nothing is known of the details of this commission, but we are not straining the bounds of probability by assuming that in a little town like Castelfranco, hardly more than a village, the two youths must have been well known to each other, and that this acquaintance and the familiarity of the one with the appearance of the other may have been the determining cause which led the bereaved father to give the commission to the young painter, while the tragic circumstances were such as would appeal to an ardent, enthusiastic nature. A treasure of our National Gallery is a study made by Giorgione for the figure of San Liberale, who is represented as a young man with bare head and crisp, golden locks, dressed in silver armour, copied from the suit in which Matteo Costanza is dressed in the stone effigy which is still preserved in the cemetery at Castelfranco. At the side of the stone figure lies a helmet, resembling that on the head of the saint in the altarpiece.

In Giorgione's group the Mother and Child are enthroned on high, with St. Francis and St. Liberale on either hand. The Child's glance is turned upon the soldier-saint, a gallant figure with his lance at rest, his dagger on his hip, his gloves in his hand, young, high-bred, with features of almost feminine beauty. The picture is conceived in a new spirit of simplicity of design, and shows a new feeling for restraint in matters of detail. It is the work of a man who has observed that early morning, like late evening, has a marvellous power of eliminating all unessential accessories and of enveloping every object in a delicious scheme

41

of light. Repainted, cleaned, restored as the canvas is, it is still full of an atmosphere of calm serenity. It is not the ecstatic, devotional reverie of Perugino's saints. The painter of Castelfranco has not steeped his whole soul in religious imagination, like the painter of Umbria; he is an exemplar of the lyric feeling; his work is a poem in praise of youth and beauty, and dreams in air and sunshine. He uses atmosphere to enhance the mood, but Giorgione carries his unison of landscape with human feeling much further than Perugino; he observes the delicate effects of light, and limpid air circulates in his distance. The sun rising over the sea throws a glamour and purity of early morning over a scene meant to glorify the memory of a young life. The painter shows his connection with his master by using the figure of the St. Francis in Bellini's San Giobbe altarpiece. What Bellini owed to Giorgione is still a matter for speculation. The San Zaccaria altarpiece was, as we have seen, painted in the year following that of Castelfranco. Something has incited the old painter to fresh efforts; out of his own evolution, or stimulated by his pupil's splendid experiments, he is drawn into the golden atmosphere of the Venetian cinque-cento.

The Venetian painters were distinguished by their love for the kindred art of music. Giorgione himself was an admirable musician, and linked with all that is akin to music in his work, is his love for painting groups of people knit together by this bond. He uses it as a pastime to bring them into company, and the rich chords of colour seem permeated with the chords of sound. Not always, however, does he need even this excuse; his "conversation-pieces" are often merely composed of persons placed with indescribable grace in exquisite surroundings, governed by a mood which communicates itself to the beholder.

With the Florentines, the cartoon was carefully drawn upon the wall and flat tints were superimposed. They knew beforehand what the effect was to be; but the Venetians from this time gradually worked up the picture, imbedding tints, intensifying effects, one touch suggesting another, till the whole rich harmony was gradually evoked. With the Florentines, too, the figures supply the main interest; the background is an arbitrary addition, placed behind them at the painter's leisure, but Giorgione's and Titian's *fêtes champêtres* and concerts could not *be* at all in any other environment. The amber flesh-tints and the glowing garments are so blended with the deep tones of the landscape, that one would not instil the mood the artist desires without the other. Piero di Cosimo and Pintoricchio can place delightful nymphs and fairy princesses in idyllic scenes, and they stir no emotion in us beyond an observant pleasure, a detached amusement; but Giorgione's gloomy blues, his figures shining through the warm dusk of a summer evening, waken we hardly know what of vague yearning and brooding memory.

In the "Fête Champêtre" of the Louvre he acquires a frankly sensuous charm. He becomes riper, richer in feeling, and displays great exuberance of style. The woman filling her pitcher at the fountain is exquisite in line and curve and amber colour. She seems to listen lazily to the liquid fall of the water mingling with the half-heard music of the pipes. The beautiful idyll in the Giovanelli Palace is full of art of composition. It is built up with uprights; pillars are formed by the groups of trees and figures, cut boldly across by the horizontal line of the bridge, but the figures themselves are put in without any attention to subject, though an unconscious humorist has discovered in them the domestic circle of the painter. The man in Venetian dress is there to assist the left-hand columnar group, placed at the edge of the picture after the manner of Leonardo. The woman and child lighten the mass of foliage on the right and make a beautiful pattern. The white town of Castelfranco sings against the threatening sky, the winds bluster through the space, the trees shiver with the coming storm. Here and there leafy boughs are struck in with a slight, crisp touch, in which we can follow readily the painter's quick impression.

The "Knight of Malta" is a grand magisterial figure, majestic, yet full of ardent warmth lying behind the grave, indifferent nobility. The face is bisected with shadow, in the way which Michelangelo and Andrea del Sarto affected, and the cone-shaped head with parted hair is of the type which seems particularly to have pleased the painter. To Giorgione, too, belongs the honour of having created a Venus as pure as the Aphrodite of Cnidos and as beautiful as a courtesan of Titian.

42

Giorgione. FÊTE CHAMPÊTRE. *Louvre.*
(*Photo, Alinari.*)

The death of Giorgione from plague in 1511 is registered by all the oldest authorities. His body was conveyed to Castelfranco by members of the Barbarelli family and buried in the Church of San Liberale. In 1638 an epitaph was placed over his tomb by Matteo and Ercole Barbarelli.

Allowing that he was hardly more than twenty when his new manner began to gain a following, he had only some twelve years in which to establish his deep and lasting influence. We divine that he was a man of strong personality, such a one as warms and stimulates his companions. Even his nickname tells us something,—Great George, the Chief, the George of Georges,—it seems to express him as a leader. And we have no lack of proof that he was admired and looked up to. His style became the only one that found favour in Venice, and the painters of the day did their best to conform to it. Few authentic examples are left from his own hand, but out of his conscious and devoted and more or less successful imitators, there grew up a school, "out of all those fascinating works, rightly or wrongly attributed to him; out of many copies from, or variations on him, by unknown or uncertain workmen, whose drawings and designs were, for various reasons, prized as his; out of the immediate impression he made upon his contemporaries and with which he continued in men's minds; out of many traditions of subject and treatment which really descend from him to our own time, and by retracing which we fill out the original image."

Summing up all these influences, he has left us the Giorgionesque; the art of choosing a moment in which the subject and the elements of colour and design are so perfectly fused and blended that we have no need to ask for any more articulate story; a moment into which all the significance, the fulness of existence has condensed itself, so that we are conscious of the very essence of life. Those idylls of beings wrapped into an ideal dreamland by music and the sound of water and the beauty of wood and mountain and velvet sward, need all our conscious apprehension of life if we are to drink in their full fascination. The dream of the Lotos-eaters can only come with force to those who can contrast it adequately with the experience, the complication, and the thousand distractions of an over-civilised world. Rest and relaxation, the power of the deeply tinted eventide, or of the fresh morning light, and the calm that drinks in the sensations they are able to afford, are among the precious things of life. The instinct upon which Giorgione's work rests is the satisfying of the feeling as well as the thinking faculty, the life of the heart, as compared to the life of the intellect, the solution of life's problems by love instead of by thought. It was the Eastern ideal, and its positive expression is conveyed by means of colour, deep, restful, satisfying, fused and controlled by chiaroscuro rather than by form.

PRINCIPAL WORKS

Berlin.	Portrait of a Man.
Buda-Pesth.	Portrait of a Man.
Castelfranco.	Duomo: Madonna with SS. Francis and Liberale.
Dresden.	Sleeping Venus.
Florence.	Uffizi: Trial of Moses (E.); Judgment of Solomon (E.); Knight of Malta.
Hampton Court.	A Shepherd.
Madrid.	Madonna with SS. Roch and Anthony of Padua.
Paris.	Fête Champêtre.
Rome.	Villa Borghese: Portrait of a Lady.

Venice.	Seminario: Apollo and Daphne.
	Palazzo Giovanelli: Gipsy and Soldier.
	San Rocco: Christ bearing Cross.
Boston.	Mrs. Gardner: Christ bearing Cross.
London.	Sketch of a Knight; Adoration of Shepherds.
	Viscount Allendale: Adoration of Shepherds.
Vienna.	Evander showing Æneas the Future Site of
Rome.	

CHAPTER XVI
THE GIORGIONESQUE

Giorgione had given the impulse, and all the painters round him felt his power. The Venetian painters that is, for it is remarkable, at a time when the men of one city observed and studied and took hints from those of every other, how faint are the signs that this particular manner attracted any great attention in other art centres. Leonardo da Vinci was a master of chiaroscuro, but he used it only to express his forms, and never sacrifices to it the delicacy and fineness of his design. It is the one quality Raphael never assimilates, except for a brief instant at the period when Sebastian del Piombo had arrived in Rome from Venice. It takes hold most strongly upon Andrea del Sarto, who seems, significantly enough, to have had no very pronounced intellectual capacity, but in Venice itself it now became the only way. The old Bellini finds in it his last and fullest ideal; Catena, Basaiti, Cariani do their best to acquire it, and so successfully was it acquired, so congenial was itto Venetian art, that even second- and third-rate Venetian painters have usually something attractive which triumphs over superficial and doubtful drawing and grouping. It is easy to see how much to their taste was this fused and golden manner, this disregard of defined form, and this new play of chiaroscuro. The Venetian room in the National Gallery is full of such examples: the Nymphs and *Amoretti* of No. 1695, charming figures against melting vines and olives; "Venus and Adonis," in which a bewitching Cupid chases a butterfly; Lovers in a landscape, roaming in the summer twilight; scenes in which neither person nor scenery is a pretext for the other, but each has its full share in arousing the desired emotion. Such pictures are ascribed to, or taken from Giorgione by succeeding critics, but have all laid hold of his charm, and have some share in his inspiration.

One of the ablest of his followers, a man whose work is still confounded with the master's, is Cariani, the Bergamasque, who at different times in his life also successfully imitated Palma and Lotto. In his Giorgionesque manner Cariani often creates charming figures and strong portraits, though he pushes his colour to a coarse, excessive tone. His family group in the Roncalli Collection at Bergamo is very close to Giorgione. Seven persons, three women and four men, are grouped together upon a terrace, and behind them stretches a calm landscape, half concealed by a brocaded hanging. The effect of the whole is restful, though it lacks Giorgione's concentration of sensation. Then, again, Cariani flies off to the gayer, more animated style of Lotto. Later on, when he tries to reproduce Giorgione's pastoral reveries, his shepherds and nymphs become mere peasants, herdsmen, and country wenches, who have nothing of the idyllic distinction which Giorgione never failed to infuse. "The Adulteress before Christ" at Glasgow still bears the greater name, but its short, vulgar figures and faulty composition disclaim his authorship, while Cariani is fully capable of such failings, and the exaggerated, red-brown tone is quite characteristic of him.

These painters are more than merely imitative; they are also typical. Giorgione's new manner had appealed to some quality inherent and hereditary in their nature, and the essential traits they single out and dwell upon are the traits which appeal equally to the instincts of both. It is this which makes their efforts more sympathetic than those of other second-rate painters. Colour, or rather the peculiar way in which Giorgione used colour, made a natural appeal to them, and it is a medium which does make an immediate appeal and covers a multitude of shortcomings.

But Giorgione was not to leave his message to the mercy of mere disciples and imitators, however apt. Growing up around him were men to whom that message was an inspiration and a trumpet-call, men who were to develop and deepen it, endowing it with their own strength, recognising that the way which the young pioneer of Castelfranco had pointed out was the one into which they could unhesitatingly pour their whole inclination. The instinct for colour was in their very blood. They turned to it with the heart-whole delight with which a bird seeks the air or a fish the water, and foremost among them, to create and to consolidate, was the mighty Titian.

PRINCIPAL WORKS

Cariani.

	Bergamo.	Carrara: Madonna and Saints.
		Lochis: Woman and Shepherd; Portraits; Saints.
		Morelli: Madonna (L.).
		Roncalli Collection: Family Group.
	Hampton Court.	Adoration of Shepherds (L.); Venus (L.).
	London.	Death of S. Peter Martyr (L.); Madonna and Saints (L.).
	Milan.	Brera: Madonna and Saints (L.); Madonna (L.).
		Ambrosiana: Way to Golgotha.
	Paris.	Madonna, Saints, and Donor (E.); Holy Family and Saints.
	Rome.	Villa Borghese: Sleeping Venus; Madonna and S. Peter.
	Venice.	Holy Family; Portraits.
	Vienna.	Christ bearing Cross; The "Bravo."

School of Giorgione.

	London.	Unknown subject; Adoration of Shepherds; Venus and Adonis; Landscape, with Nymphs and Cupids; The Garden of Love.
		Mr. Benson. Lovers and Pilgrim.

CHAPTER XVII
TITIAN

The mountains of Cadore are not always visible from Venice, but there they lie, behind the mists, and in the clear shining after rain, in the golden eventide of autumn, and on steel-cold winter days they stand out, lapis-lazuli blue or deep purple, or, like Shelley's enchanted peaks, in sharp-cut, beautiful shapes rising above billowy slopes. Cadore is a land of rich chestnut woods, of leaping streams, of gleams and glooms, sudden storms and bursts of sunshine. It is an order of scenery which enters deep into the affections of its sons, and we can form some idea of the hold its mingling of wild poetry and sensuous softness obtained over the mind of Titian from the fact that in after years, while he never exerts himself to paint the city in which he lived and in which all his greatest triumphs were gained, he is uniformly constant to his mountain home, enters into its spirit and interprets its charm with warm and penetrating insight.

The district formed part of the dependencies of the great republic, and relied upon Venice for its safety, its distinction, and in great measure for its employment. The small craftsmen and artists from all the country round looked forward to going down to seek their fortune at her hands. They tacked the name of their native town to their own name, and were drawn into the magnificent life of the city of the sea, and came back from time to time with stories of her art, her power, and beauty.

The Vecelli had for generations held honourable posts in Cadore. The father and grandfather of the young Tiziano were influential men, and with his brother and sisters he must have been brought up in comfort. There are even traditions of noble birth, and it is evident that Titian was always a gentleman, though this did not prevent his being educated as a craftsman, and when he was only ten years old he was sent down to Venice to be apprenticed to a mosaicist.

It was a changing Venice to which Titian came as a boy; changing in its life, its social and political conditions, and its art was faithfully registering its aspirations and tastes. More than at any previous time, it was calculated to impress a youth to whom it had been held up as the embodiment of splendid sovereignty, and the difference between the little hill-town set in the midst of its wild solitudes and the brilliant city of the sea must have been dazzling and bewildering. A new sense of intellectual luxury had awakened in the great commercial centre. The Venetian love of splendour was displaying itself by the encouragement and collection of objects of art, and both ancient and modern works were in increasing request. On Gentile Bellini's and Carpaccio's canvases we see the sort of people the Venetians were, shrewd, quiet, splendour-loving, but business-like, the young men fashionably dressed, fastidious connoisseurs, splendid patrons of art and of religion. Buyers were beginning to find out what a delightful decoration the small picture made, and that it was as much in place in their own halls as over the altar of a chapel. The portrait, too, was gaining in importance, and the idea of making it a pleasure-giving picture, even more than a faithful transcript, was gathering ground. The "Procession of the Relic" was still in Gentile's studio, but the Frari "Madonna and Child" was just installed in its place. Carpaccio was beginning his long series of St. Ursula, and the Bellini and Vivarini were in keen rivalship.

Titian is said to have passed from the *bottega* of Gentile to that of Giovanni Bellini, but nothing in his style reminds us of the former, and even his early work has very little that is really Bellinesque, whereas from the very first he reflects the new spirit which emanated from Giorgione. Titian was a year the elder, and we can divine the sympathy that arose between the two when they came together in Bellini's School. As soon as their apprenticeship was at an end they became partners. Fond of pleasure and gaiety, loving splendour, dress, and amusement, they were naturally congenial companions, and were drawn yet more closely together by their love for their art and by the aptitude with which Titian grasped Giorgione's principles.

And if we ask ourselves why we take for granted that of two young men so closely allied in age and circumstance we accept Giorgione as the leader and the creator of the new style, we may answer that Titian was a more complex character. He was intellectual, and carried his intellect into his art, but this was no new feature. The intellect had had and was having a large share in art. But in that part which was new, and which was launching art upon an untried course, Giorgione is more intense, more one-idea'd than Titian. What he does he does with a fervour and a spontaneity that marks him as one who pours out the language of the heart.

The partnership between the two was probably arranged a few years before the end of the century, for we have seen that young painters usually started on their own account at about nineteen or twenty. For some years Titian, like Giorgione, was engrossed by the decorations of the Fondaco dei Tedeschi. The groups of figures described by Zanetti in 1771 show us that while Giorgione made some attempt at following classic figures, Titian broke entirely with Greek art and only thought of picturesque nature and contemporary costume.

Vasari complains that he never knew what Titian's "Judith" was meant to represent, "unless it was Germania," but Zanetti, who had the benefit of Sebastiano Ricci's taste, declares that from what he saw, both Giorgione and Titian gave proofs of remarkable skill. "While Giorgione showed a fervid and original spirit and opened up a new path, over which he shed a light that was to guide posterity, Titian was of a grander and more equable genius, leaning at first, indeed, upon Giorgione's example, but expanding with such force and rapidity as to place him in advance of his companion, on an eminence to which no later craftsman was able to climb.... He moderated the fire of Giorgione, whose strength lay in fanciful movement and a mysterious artifice in disposing shadows, contrasted darkly with warm lights, blended, strengthened, blurred, so as to produce the semblance of exuberant life." Certain works remain to link the two painters; even now critics are divided as to which of the two to attribute the "Concert" in the Pitti. The figures are Giorgionesque, but the technique establishes it as an early Titian, and it is doubtful whether Giorgione would be capable of the intellectual effort which produced the dreamy, passionate expression of the young monk, borne far out of himself by his own melody, and half recalled to life by the touch on his shoulder. Titian, like Giorgione, was a musician, and the fascination of music is felt by many masters of the Italian schools. In one picture the player feels vaguely after the melody, in another we are asked to anticipate the song that is just about to begin, or the last chords of that just finished vibrate upon the ear, but nowhere else in all art has any one so seized the melody of an instant and kept its fulness and its passion sounding in our ears as this musician does.

Though we cannot say that Titian was the pupil of any one master, the fifteen years, more or less, that he spent with Giorgione left an indelible impression upon him. We have only to look at such a picture as the "Madonna and Child with SS. John Baptist and Antony Abate," in the Uffizi, an early work, to recollect that in 1503 Giorgione at Castelfranco had taken the Madonna from her niche in the sanctuary and had enthroned her on high in a bright and sunny landscape with S. Liberale standing sentinel at her feet, like a knight guarding his liege lady.

Titian in this early group casts every convention aside; a beautiful woman and lovely children are placed in surroundings whose charm is devoid of hieratic and religious significance. The same easy unfettered treatment appears in the "Madonna with the Cherries" at Vienna, and the "Madonna with St. Bridget and S. Ulfus" at Madrid, and while it has been surmised that the example of the precise Albert Dürer, who paid his first visit to Venice in 1506, was not without its effect in preserving Titian from falling into laxity of treatment and in inciting him to fine finish, it is interesting to find that Titian was, in fact, discarding the use of the carefully traced and transferred cartoon, and was sketching his design freely on panel or canvas with a brush dipped in brown pigment, and altering and modifying it as he went on.

The last years of Titian's first period in Venice must have been anxious ones. The Emperor Maximilian was attacking the Venetian possessions on the mainland, in anger at a refusal to grant his troops a free passage on their way to uphold German supremacy in Central Italy. Cadore was the first point of his invasion, and from 1507 Titian's uncle and great-uncle were in the Councils of the State, his father held an important command, and his brother Francesco, who had already made some progress as an artist, threw down his brush and became a soldier. Titian was not one of those who took up arms, but his thoughts must have been full of the attack and defence in his mountain fastnesses, and he must have anxiously awaited news of his father's troops and of the squadrons of Maso of Ferrara, under whose colours Francesco was riding. Francesco made a reputation as a distinguished soldier, and was severely wounded, and when peace was made, Titian, "who loved him tenderly," persuaded him to return to the pursuit of art.

The ratification of the League of Cambray, in which Julius II., Maximilian, and Ferdinand of Naples combined against the power of Venice, was disastrous for a time to the city and to the artists who depended upon her prosperity. Craftsmen of all kinds first fled to her for shelter, then, as profits and orders fell off, they left to look elsewhere for commissions. An outbreak of plague, in which Giorgione perished, went further to make Venice an undesirable home, and at this time Sebastian del Piombo left for Rome, Lotto for the Romagna, and Titian for Padua.

We may believe that Titian never felt perfectly satisfied with fresco-painting as a craft, for when he was given a commission to fresco the halls of the Santo, the confraternity of St. Anthony, patron-saint of Padua, he threw off beautifully composed and spirited drawings, but he left the execution of them chiefly to assistants, among whom the feeble Domenico Campagnola, a painter whom he probably picked up at Padua, is conspicuous. Even where the landscape is best, as in "S. Anthony restoring a Youth," the drawing and composition only make us feel how enchanting the scene would have been in oils on one of Titian's melting canvases. In those frescoes which he executed himself while his interest was still fresh, the "Miracle which grants Speech to an Infant" is the most Giorgionesque. Up to this time he had preserved the straight-cut corsage and the actual dress of his contemporaries, after the practice of Giorgione; he keeps, too, to his companion's plan of design, placing the most important figures upon one plane, close to the frame and behind a low wall or ledge which forms a sort of inner frame and with a distant horizon. In the Paduan frescoes he makes use of this plan, and the straight clouds, the spindly trees, and the youths in gay doublets are all reminiscent of his early comrade, but the group of women to the left in the "Miracle of the Child" shows that Titian is beginning more decidedly to enunciate his own type. The introduction of portraits proves that he was tending to rely largely upon nature, in contradistinction to Giorgione's lyrically improvised figures. He fuses the influence of Giorgione and the influence of Antonello da Messina and the Bellini in a deeper knowledge of life and nature, and he is passing beyond Giorgione in grasp and completeness. When he was able to return to Venice, which he did in 1512, a temporary peace having been concluded with Maximilian, he abandoned the uncongenial medium of fresco for good, and devoted himself to that which admitted of the afterthoughts, the enrichments, the gradual attainment of an exquisite surface, and at this time his works are remarkable for their brilliant gloss and finish.

During the next twelve years we may group a number of paintings which, taken in conjunction with those of Giorgione, show the true Venetian School at its most intense, idyllic moment. They are the works of a man in the pride of youth and strength, sane and healthy, an example of the confident, sanguine, joyous temper of his age, capable of embodying its dominant tendencies, of expressing its enjoyment of life, its worldly-mindedness, its love of pleasure, as well as its noble feeling and its grave and magnificent purpose.

For absolute delight in colour let us turn to a picture like the "Noli me tangere" of the National Gallery. The golden light, the blues and olives of the landscape, the crimson of the Magdalen's raiment, combine in a feast of emotional beauty, emphasising the feeling of the woman, whose soul is breathed out in the word "Master." The colour unites with the light and shadow, is embedded in it; and we can see Titian's delight in the ductile medium which had such power to give material sensation. In these liquid crimsons, these deep greens and shoaling blues, the velvety fulness and plenitudes of the brush become visible; we can look into their depths and see something quite unlike the smooth, opaque washes of the Florentines.

In such a masterpiece as "Sacred and Profane Love," painted during these years for the Borghese, there are summed up all those artistic aims towards which the Venetian painters had been tending. The picture is still Giorgionesque in mood. It may represent, as Dr. Wickhoff suggests, Venus exhorting Medea to listen to the love-suit of Jason; but the subject is not forced upon us, and we are more occupied with the contrast between the two beautiful personalities, so harmoniously related to each other, yet so opposed in type. The gracious, self-absorbed lady, with her softly dressed hair, her loose glove, her silvery satin dress, is a contrast in look and spirit to the goddess whose free, simple attitude and outward gaze embody the nobler ideal. The sinuous and enchanting line of Venus's figure against the crimson cloak has, I think, been the outcome of admiration for Giorgione's "Sleeping Venus," and has the same soft, unhurried curves. Titian's two figures are perfectly spaced in a setting which breathes the very aroma of the early Renaissance. A bas-relief on the marble fountain represents nymphs whipping a sleeping Love to life, while a cupid teases the chaste unicorn. A delicious baby Love splashes in the water, fallen rose-leaves strew the mellow marble rim, around and away stretches a sunny country scene, in which people are placidly pursuing a life of ease and pleasure. What a revelation to Venice these pictures were which began with Giorgione's conversaziones!How little occupied the women are with the story. Venus does not argue, or check off reasons on her fingers, like S. Ursula. Medea is listening to her own thoughts, but the whole scene is bathed in the suggestion of the joy and happiness of love. The little censer burning away in the blue and breathless air might be a philtre diffusing sensuous dreams, and when the rays of the evening sun strike the picture, where it now hangs, and bring out each touch of its glowing radiance, it seems to palpitate with the joy of life and to thrill with the magic of summer in the days when the world was young.

With the influence still lingering of Giorgione's "Knight of Malta," Titian produced some of his finest portraits in the decade that led to the middle of his life. The "Dr. Parma" at Vienna, the noble "Man in Black" and "Man with a Glove" of the Louvre, the "Young Englishman" of the Pitti, with his keen blue eyes, the portrait at Temple Newsam, which, with some critics, still passes as a Giorgione, are all examples in which he keeps the half-length, invented by Bellini and followed by Giorgione.

After the visit to Padua he shows less preference for costume, and his women are generally clothed in a loose white chemise, rather than the square-cut bodice.

We do not wonder that all the leading personages of Italy wished to be painted by Titian. His are the portraits of a man of intellect. They show the subject at his best; grave, cultivated, stately, as he appeared and wished to appear; not taken off his guard in any way. What can be more sympathetic as a personality than the Ariosto of the National Gallery? We can enter into his mind and make a friend of him, and yet all the time he has himself in hand; he allows us to divine as much as he chooses, and draws a thin veil over all that he does not intend us to discover. The painter himself is impersonal and not over-sensitive; he does not paint in his own fancies about his sitter—probably he had none; he saw what he was meant to see. There was what Mr. Berenson calls "a certain happy insensibility" about him, which prevented him from taking fantastic flights, or from looking too deep below the surface.

Titian. ARIOSTO. *London.*
(*Photo, Mansell and Co.*)

CHAPTER XVIII
TITIAN (*continued*)

With the "Assumption," finished in 1518 for the Church of the Frari, Titian rose to the very highest among Renaissance painters. The "Glorious S. Mary" was his theme, and he concentrated all his efforts on the realisation of that one idea. The central figure is, as it were, a collective rather than an individual type. Well proportioned and elastic as it is, it has the abundance of motherhood. Harmonious and serene, it combines dramatic force and profound feeling. Exultant Humanity, in its hour of triumph, rises with her, borne up lightly by that throbbing company of child angels and followed by full recognition and awestruck satisfaction in the adoring gaze of the throng below, yet Titian has contrived to keep some touch of the loving woman hurrying to meet her son. The flood of colour, the golden vault above, the garment of glowing blues and crimsons, have a more than common share in that spirit of confident joy and poured-out life which envelops the whole canvas. In the worthy representation of a great event, the visible assumption of Humanity to the Throne of God, Titian puts forth all his powers and steeps us in that temper of sanguine emotion, of belief in life and confidence in the capacity of man, which was so characteristic of the ripe Renaissance. In looking at this splendid canvas, we must call to mind the position for which Titian painted it. Hung in the dusky recesses of the apse, it was tempered by and merged in its stately surroundings. The band of Apostles almost formed a part of the whispering crowd below, and the glorious Mother was beheld soaring upwards to the golden light and the mysterious vistas of the vaulted arches above.

The patronage of courts had by this time altered the tenor of Titian's life. In 1516 Duke Alfonso d'Este had invited him to Ferrara, where he had finished Bellini's "Bacchanals." It bears the marks of Titian's hand, and he has introduced a well-known point of view at Cadore into the background. In 1518 Alfonso writes to propose another painting, and Titian's acceptance is contained in a very courtier-like letter, in which we divine a touch of irony. "The more I thought of it," he ends, "the more I became convinced that the greatness of art among the ancients was due to the assistance they received from great princes, who were content to leave to the painter the credit and renown derived from their own ingenuity in bespeaking pictures." Alfonso's requirements for his new castle were frankly pagan. Mythological scenes were already popular. Mantegna had adorned Isabela d'Este's "Paradiso" with revels of the gods, Botticelli had given his conception of classic myth in the Medici villa, already Bellini had essayed a Bacchanal, and Titian was to make designs for similar scenes to complete the decorations of the halls of Este. The same exuberant feeling he shows in the "Assumption" finds utterance in the "Garden of Loves" and the "Bacchanals," both painted for Alfonso of Ferrara. The children in the former may be compared with the angels in the "Assumption." Their blue wings match the heavenly blue sky, and they are painted with the most delicate finish.

We can imagine the beauty of the great hall at Ferrara when hung with this brilliant series, which was completed in 1523 by the "Bacchus and Ariadne" of the National Gallery. The whole company of bacchanals is given up to wanton merrymaking. Above them broods the deep blue sky and great white clouds of a summer day. The deep greens of the foliage throw the creamy-white and burning colour of the draperies and the fair forms of the nymphs into glowing relief, while by a convention the satyrs are of a deep, tawny complexion. On a roll of music is stamped the rollicking device, "*Chi boit et ne reboit, ne sçeais que boir soit.*" The purple fruit hangs ripened from the vines, its crimson juice shines like a jewel in crystal goblets and drips in streams over rosy limbs. The influence of such pictures as these was absorbed by Rubens, but though they hardly surpass him in colour, they are more idyllic and less coarse. The perfect taste of the Renaissance is never shown more victoriously than here, where indulgence ceases to be repulsive, and the actors are real flesh and blood, yet more Arcadian than revolting. In the "Bacchus and Ariadne," Titian gives triumphant expression to a mood of wild rejoicing, so gay, so good-tempered, so simple, that we must smile in sympathy. The conqueror flinging himself from his golden chariot drawn by panthers, his deep red mantle fluttering on high, is so full of reckless life that our spirit bounds with him. His rioting band, marching with song and laughter, seems to people that golden country-side with fit inhabitants. The careless satyrs and little merry, goat-legged fauns shock us no more than a herd of forest ponies, tossing their manes and dashing along for love of life and movement.[3] Yet almost before this series was put in place Titian was showing the diversity of his genius by the "Deposition," now in the Louvre, which was painted at the instance of the Gonzaga, Marquis of Mantua and nephew of Alfonso d'Este. Here he makes a great step in the use of chiaroscuro. While it is satisfying in balance and sweeping rhythm, and by the way in which every line follows and intensifies the helpless, slackened lines of the dead Body, it escapes Raphael's academic treatment of the same subject. Its splendid colours are not noisy; they merge into a scene of solemn pathos and tragedy. The scene has a simplicity and unity in its passion, and what above all gives it its intense power is the way in which the flaming hues are absorbed into the twilight shadows. The dark heads stand out against the dying sunset, the pallor of the dead is half veiled by the falling night. It is a picture which has the emotional beauty of a scene in nature, and makes a profound impression by its depth and mystery. This same solemnity and gravity temper the brilliant colouring of the great altarpiece painted for the Pesaro family in the Frari. Columns rise like great tree-trunks, light and air play through the clouds seen between them. The grouping is a new experiment, but the way in which the Mother and Child, though placed quite at one side of the picture, are focussed as the centre of interest, by the converging lines, diagonal on the one hand and straight on theother, crowns it with success. The scheme of colour brings the two figures into high relief, while St. Francis and the family of the donor are subordinated to rich, deep tints. Titian has abandoned, more completely than ever before, any attempt to invest the Child with supernatural majesty. He is a delightful, spoiled baby, fully aware of his sovereignty over his mother, pretending to take no notice of the kneeling suppliants, but occupying himself in making a tent over his head out of her veil. The "Madonna in Glory with six Saints" of the Vatican is another example of the rich and "smouldering" colour in which Titian was now creating his great altarpieces, kneading his pigments into a quality, a solidity, which gives reality without heaviness, and finishing with that fine-grained texture which makes his flesh look like marble endowed with life.

Titian. DIANA AND ACTAEON. *Earl Brownlow.*
(*The Medici Society, Ltd.*)

Venuses, altarpieces, and portraits all tell us how boldly his own style was established. His sacred persons are not different from his pagans and goddesses. Yet though he has gone far, he still reminds us of Giorgione. He has been constant to the earliest influences which surrounded him, and to that temperament which made him accept those influences so instantaneously—and this constancy and unity give him the untroubled ascendancy over art which is such a feature of his position.

With Leonardo and with Titian, painters had sprung to a recognised status in the great world of the Renaissance. They were no longer the patronised craftsmen. They had become the courted guests, the social equals. Titian, passing from the courts of Ferrara to those of Mantua and Urbino, attended by a band of assistants, was a magnificent personage, whose presence was looked upon as a favour, and who undertook a commission as one who conferred a coveted boon. Among those who clustered closest round the popular favourite, no one did more to enhance his position than Aretino, the brilliant unscrupulous debauchee, wit, bully, blackmailer, but a man who, with all his faults, had evidently his own power of fascination, and, the friend of princes, must have been himself the prince of good company. Aretino, as far as he could be said to be attached to any one, was consistent in his attachment to Titian from the time they first met at the court of the Gonzaga. He played the part of a chorus, calling attention to the great painter's merits, jogging the memory of his employers as to payments, and never ceasing to flatter, amuse, and please him. Titian, for his part, shows himself equally devoted to Aretino's interests, and has left various characteristic portraits of him, handsome and showy in his prime, sensual and depraved as age overtook him.

In the spring of 1528 the confraternity of St. Peter Martyr invited artists to send insketches for an altarpiece to their patron-saint, in SS. Giovanni and Paolo, to replace an old one by Jacobello del Fiore. Palma Vecchio and Pordenone also competed, but Titian carried off the prize. The picture was delivered in 1530, and during the autumn of 1529 Sebastian del Piombo had returned to Venice from Rome, and Michelangelo had sought refuge there from Florence and had stayed for some months. A quarrel with the monks over the price had delayed the picture, so that it may quite probably have only been begun after intercourse with the Roman visitors had given a fresh turn to Titian's ideas; for though he never ceases to be himself, it certainly seems as if the genius of Michelangelo had had some effect. From what we know of the altarpiece, which perished by fire in 1867, but of which a good copy by Cigoli remains, Titian embarked suddenly upon forms of Herculean strength in violent action, but there his likeness to the Florentine ended; the figures were, indeed, drawn with a deep, though not altogether successful, attention to anatomy and foreshortening, but the picture obtained its effect and derived its impressiveness from the setting in which the figures were placed—the great trees, bending and straining, the hurrying clouds, as if nature were in portentous harmony with the sinister deed, and overhead the enchanting gleam of light which shot downward and irradiated the face of the martyr and the two lovely winged boys, bathed in a flood of blue æther, who held aloft the palm of victory. Many copies of it remain, and we only regret that one which Rubens executed is not preserved among them.

When we look at the delicious "Madonna del Coniglio" in the Louvre and our own "Marriage of S. Catherine," the first of which certainly, and the second probably, was painted about this time, we cannot doubt that the charm of the idea of motherhood had particularly arrested the painter. About 1525 his first son, Pomponio, was born, and was followed by another son and a daughter. In the S. Catherine he paints that passion of mother-love with an intensity and reality that can only be drawn from life, and on the wheel at her feet he has inscribed his name, Ticianus, F. His feeling for landscape is increasing, and the landscape in these pictures equals the figures in importance and has engrossed the painter quite as much. Every year Titian paid a visit to Cadore, and in the rich woodlands, the distant villages, the great white villa on the hill-side, and, above all, in the far-off blue mountains and the glooms and gleams of storm and sunshine, the sudden dart of rays through the summer clouds, which he has painted here, we see how constant was his study of his native country, and how profoundly he felt its poetry and its charm. He had married Cecilia, the daughter of a barber belonging to Perarolo, a little town near Cadore. In 1530 she died, and he mourned her deeply. He went on working and planning for his children's future, and his sister came from Cadore to take charge of the motherless household; but his friends' letters speak of his being ill from melancholy, and he could not go on living in the old house at San Samuele, which had been his home for sixteen years. He took a new house on the north side of the city, in the parish of San Canciano. The Casa Grande, as it was called, was a building of importance, which the painter first hired and finally bought, letting off such apartments as he did not need. The first floor had a terrace, and was entered by a flight of steps from the garden, which overlooked the lagoons, and had a view of the Cadore mountains. It has been swept away by the building of the Fondamenta Nuove, but the documents of the leases are preserved, and the exact site is well established. Here his children grew up, and he worked for them unceasingly. Pomponio, his eldest son, was idle and extravagant, a constant source of trouble, and Aretino writes him reproachful letters, which he treats with much impertinence. Orazio took to his father's profession, and was his constant companion, and often drew his cartoons; and his beautiful daughter, Lavinia, was his greatest joy and pride. In this house Titian showed constant hospitality, and there are records of the princely fashion in which he entertained his friends and distinguished foreign visitors. Priscianese, a well-known Humanist and *savant* of the day, describes a Bacchanalian feast on the 1st of August, in a pleasant garden belonging to Messer Tiziano Vecellio. Aretino, Sansovino, and Jacopo Nardi were present. Till the sun set they stayed indoors, admiring the artist's pictures. "As soon as it went down, the tables were spread, looking on the lagoons, which soon swarmed with gondolas full of beautiful women, and resounded with music of voices and instruments, which till midnight, accompanied our delightful supper. Titian gave the most delicate viands and precious wines, and the supper ended gaily."

In the year 1532 Titian for the first time sought other than Italian patronage. Charles V., who was then at the height of his power, with all Italy at his feet, passed through Mantua, and among all the treasures that he saw was most struck by Titian's portrait of Federigo Gonzaga. After much writing to and fro, it was arranged that Titian should meet the Emperor at Bologna, where he had just been crowned. He made his first sketch of him, from which he afterwards produced a finished full length. It was the first of many portraits, and Vasari declares that from that time forth Charles would never sit to any other master. He received a knighthood, and many commissions from members of the Emperor's court. It was for one of his nobles, da Valos, Marquis of Vasto, that he painted the allegorical piece in the Louvre, in which Mary of Arragon, the lovely wife of da Valos, is parting with her husband, who is bound on one of the desperate expeditions against the terrible Turks. Da Valos is dressed in armour, and the couple are encircled by Hymen, Victory, and the God of Love. The composition was repeated more than once, but never with quite the same success. We again suspect the influence of Michelangelo in the altarpiece painted before Titian next left Venice, of St. John the Almsgiver, for the Church of that name, of which the Doge was patron. The figures are life-size, the types stern and rugged, daringly foreshortened, and the colours, though gorgeous, are softened and broken by broad effects of light and shade. It is painted in a solemn mood, a contrast to that in which about this time he produced a series of beautiful female portraits, nude or semi-nude, chiefly, it would appear, at the instance of the Duke of Urbino. The Duke at this time was the General-in-Chief of the Venetian forces, a position which took him often to Venice, and Titian's relations with him lasted till the painter's death. At least twenty-five of his works must have adorned the castles of Urbino and Pesaro. Among these were the Venus of the Uffizi, "La Bella di Tiziano," in her gorgeous scheme of blue and amethyst, the "Girl in a Fur Cloak," besides portraits of the Duke and Duchess. Itwould be impossible to enumerate here the numbers of portraits which Titian was now supplying. The reputation he had acquired, not only in Italy, but in Spain, France, and Germany, was greater than had ever been attained by any painter, while his social position was established among the highest in every court. "He had rivals in

Venice," says Vasari, "but none that he did not crush by his excellence and knowledge of the world in converse with gentlemen." There is not a writer of the day who does not acclaim his genius. Titian was undoubtedly very fond of money, and had amassed a good fortune. He was constantly asking for favours, and had pensions and allowances from royal patrons. Lavinia, when she married, brought her husband a dowry of 1400 ducats. He had painted the portraits of the Doges with tolerable regularity, but all through his life complaints were heard of his neglect of the work of the Hall of Grand Council. Occupied as he was with the work of his foreign patrons, he had systematically neglected the conditions enjoined by his possession of a Broker's patent, and the Signoria suddenly called on him to refund the salary amounting to over 100 ducats a year, for the twenty years during which he had drawn it without performing his promise, while they prepared to instal Pordenone, who had lately appeared as his bitter rival, in his stead. Though Titian must have been making large sums of money at this time, his expenses were heavy, and he could not calmly face the obligation to repay such a sum as 2000 ducats at the same time that he lost the annual salary, nor was it pleasant to be ousted by a second-rate rival. His easy remedy was, however, in his own hands; he set to work and soon completed a great canvas of the "Battle of Cadore," which, though it is only known to us from a contemporary print and a drawing by Rubens, evidently deserved Vasari's verdict of being the finest battlepiece ever placed in the hall. The movement and stir he contrives to give with a small number of figures is astonishing. The fortress burns upon the hill-side, a regiment advancing with lances and pennons produces the illusion that it is the vanguard of a great army, the desperate conflict by the narrow bridge realises all the terrors of war. It was an atonement for his long period of neglect, but it was not till 1439 that, Pordenone having suddenly died, the Signoria relented and reinstated Titian in his Broker's patent. One of his later paintings for the State still keeps its place, "The Triumph of Faith," in which Doge Grimani, a splendid, steel-clad form with flowing mantle, kneels before the angelic apparition of Faith, who holds a cross, which angels and cherubs help her to support. Beneath the clouds are seen the Venetian fleet, the Ducal Palace, and the Campanile. It is an allegory of Grimani's life; his defeat and captivity are symbolised by the cross and chalice, and the magnificent figure of St. Mark with the lion is introduced to show that the Doge believes himself to owe his freedom to the saint's intercession. The prophet and standard-bearer at the sides were added by Marco Vecellio.

Though the battlepiece perished in the fire of 1577, another masterpiece of this time marks a climax in Titian's brilliantly coloured and highly finished style. The "Presentation of the Virgin" was painted for the refectory of the Confraternity of the Carità, which was housed in the building now used as the Academy, so that the picture remains in the place for which it was executed. It is one of the most vivid and life-like of all his works. The composition is the traditional one; the fifteen steps of the "Gospel of Mary," the High Priest of the old dispensation welcoming the childish representative of the new. Below is a great crowd, but it is this little figure which first attracts the eye. The contrast between the mass of architecture and the free and glowing country beyond is not without meaning, and a broken Roman torso, lying neglected on the ground, symbolises the downfall of the Pagan Empire. The flight of steps, with the figure sitting below them, is an idea borrowed from Carpaccio, and perhaps taken by him from the sketch-book of Jacopo Bellini. The men on the left are portraits of members and patrons of the confraternity. Most Titianesque are the beautiful women in rich dresses at the foot of the steps. In this stately composition we see what is often noticeable in Titian's scenes; he brings in the bystanders after the manner of a Greek chorus. They all, with one accord, express the same sentiment. There is a certain acceptation of the obvious in Titian, a vein of simplicity flows through his nature. He has not the sensitive and subtle search after the motives of humanity which we find in Tintoretto or Lotto. He has great intellectual power, but not great imagination. It is a temper which helps to keep the unity, the monumental quality of his scenes undisturbed and adds to their effect. In the "Ecce Homo" Christ is shown to the populace by Pilate, who with dubious compliment is a portrait of Aretino, and the contrast of the lonely, broken-down man with the crowd which, with all its lower instincts let loose, thunders back the cry of "Crucify Him," is the more dramatic because of the unanimous spirit which possesses the raging multitude. Other artists would have given more incidental byplay, and drawn off our attention from the main issue.

CHAPTER XIX
TITIAN (*continued*)

While Titian was executing portraits of the Doges, of Aretino and of Isabella of Portugal, and of himself and his daughter Lavinia, he was also striking out a new line in the ceiling pictures for the Church of San Spirito, which have since been transferred to the Salute. Though painted before his journey to Rome, it may be suspected that he had Michelangelo's work in the Sixtine Chapel in mind, and that he was setting himself the task of bold foreshortening and technical problems. The daring of the conception is great, yet we feel sure that this is not Titian's element; his figures in violent movement give a vivid idea of strength and muscular force, but fail both in grace and drawing, and though the colour and light and shade distract our attention from defects of form, he does not possess that mastery over the flowing silhouette which Tintoretto attained.

It was in 1543 that his relations with the Farnese, whose young cardinal he had beenpainting, drew him at last to Rome. Leo X. had tried to attract him there without success, but now at sixty-eight he found himself as far on the road as Urbino. His son Orazio was with him, and Duke Guidobaldo was himself his escort, and sent him on with a band of men-at-arms from Pesaro. He was received in Rome by Cardinal Bembo; Paul III. gave him a cordial welcome and Vasari was appointed his cicerone. It is interesting to inquire what impression Rome, with its treasures of antique statuary and contemporary painting, made upon Titian. "He is filled with wonder and glad that he came," writes Bembo. In a letter to Aretino he regrets that he had not come before. He stayed eight months in Rome, and was made a Roman citizen. He visits the Stanze of Raphael in company with Sebastian del Piombo, and Michelangelo comes to see him at his lodgings, and he receives a long letter from Aretino advising him to compare Michelangelo with Raphael, and Sansovino and Bramante with the sculptors and architects of antiquity. Titian was well established in his own style, and was received as the creator of acknowledged masterpieces, and he never painted a more magnificent portrait-piece than that of Paul III., the peevish old Pope, ailing and humorous, suspicious of the two nephews who are painted with him, and who he guessed to be conspiring against him. The characteristic attitude of the old man of eighty, bent down in his chair, his quick, irritable glance, the steady, determined gaze of the cardinal, the obsequious attitude and weak, wily face of Ottavio Farnese are all immortalised in a broader, more careless technique than Titian has hitherto used. Though he does not seem to have been directly influenced by all he saw in Rome, we undoubtedly find a change coming over his work between 1540 and 1550, which may be in part ascribed to a widening of his artistic horizon and a consciousness of what others were doing, both around him and abroad. In its whole handling and character his late is different from his early manner. It begins at this time to take on a blurred, soft, impressionist character. His delight in rich colouring seems to wane, and he aims at intensifying the power of light. He reaches that point in the Venetian School of painting which we may regard as its climax, when there is little strong local colour, but the canvas seems illumined from within. There are no clear-cut lines, but the shapes are suggested by sombre enveloping shades in which the radiant brightness is embedded. His landscapes alter too; they are no longer blue and smiling, filled with loving detail, but grander, more mysterious. In the "St. Jerome" in Paris the old Saint kneels in wild and lonely surroundings, and the moon, slowly rising behind the dark trees, sends a sharp, silver ray across the crucifix. The "Supper at Emmaus" has the grandiose effect that is given by avoidance of detail and simplification of method.

Titian painted several portraits of himself, and we know what sort of stately figure was presented by the old man of seventy who, at Christmas in 1547, set forth to ride across the Alps in the depths of winter to obey Charles V.'s call to Augsburg. The excitement of the public was great at his departure, and Aretino describes how his house was besieged for the sketches and designs he left behind him. For nearly forty years Titian was employed by the House of Hapsburg. He had been working for Charles since 1530, and when the Emperor abdicated, his employment by Philip II. lasted till his death. The palace inventory of 1686 contained seventy-six Titians, and though probably not all were genuine, yet an immense number were really by him, and the gallery, even now, is richer in his works than any other.

The great hall of the Pardo must have been a wonderful sight, with Titian's finest portrait of himself in the midst, and the magnificent portraits and sacred and allegorical pieces which he continued from this time forward to contribute to it. In this year, which was the last before Charles's abdication, and during this visit to South Germany, he painted the great equestrian portrait of the Emperor on the field of Mühlberg, and two years later came the first of his many portraits of Philip II. The face, in the first sketch, is laid in with a sort of fury of impressionism, and in the parade portrait the sitter is realised as a man of great distinction. Ugly and sensual as he is, we never tire of looking at Titian's conception—a full length of distinguished mien rendered attractive by magnificent colour. Everything in it lives, and the slender, aristocratic hands are, as Morelli says, a whole biography in themselves.

The splendid series of allegorical subjects which Titian contributed to the Pardo, while he was still supplying sacred pictures and altarpieces to Venice and the neighbouring mainland, are among his most mature and important works. Never has his gamut of tones been fuller and stronger than in the "Jupiter and Antiope," or the "Venus of the Pardo" as it is sometimes called. The Venus herself has the attitude of Giorgione's dreaming goddess, with her arm flung up above her head. It is, perhaps, the only time that Titian succeeds in giving anything ideal to one of his Venuses. The famous nudes of the Uffizi and the Louvre are splendid courtesans, far removed from Giorgione's idyllic vision; but Antiope, slumbering on her couch of skins, and her woodland lover, gazing with adoring eyes on her beautiful face, have a whole world of sweet and joyful fancy. The whole scene is full of a *joie de vivre*, which carries us back to the Bacchanals painted so many years before, and in these Titian gives King Philip his most perfect work, every touch of which is his own. This picture, now in the Louvre, was given to Charles I. by the King of Spain, and bought for Cardinal Mazarin in 1650. "Danaë," "Venus and Adonis," "Europa and the Bull," and a "Last Supper" followed in quick succession, but Titian was now employing many assistants, and great parts of the canvases issuing from his workshop show weak, imitative hands, while replicas were made of other works.

His later feeling for the religious in art is expressed in the now bedimmed paintings in San Salvatore in Venice. Vasari describes these in 1566. Painted when Titian was nearly ninety years old, the "Transfiguration" is remarkable for forcible, majestic movement, while in the "Annunciation" he invents quite a new treatment. Mary turns round and raises her veil, while she grasps the book as if she depended on it for stay and support. The four angels are full of life and gaiety, and the whole has much grace and colour, though it is dashed in, in the painter's later style, in broad and sweeping planes without patience of detail. The old man has signed it "Titianus, fecit, fecit," a contemptuous reply to some critics who complained of its want of finish. He knew well what it was in composition and execution, and that all that he had ever known or done lay within the careless strength of his last manner.

A letter written to the King of Spain's secretary in 1574 gives a list "in part" of fourteen pictures sent to Madrid during the last twenty-five years, "with many others which I do not remember." On every hand we hear of lost pictures from the master's brush, and the number produced even during the last ten years of his life must have been enormous, for till the end he was full of great undertakings and achievements. Very late in life he painted a "Shepherd and Nymph" (Vienna), which in its idyllic feeling, its slumberous delight, its mingling of clothed and nude figures, recalls the early days with Giorgione, yet the blurred and smouldering richness, the absolute negation of all sharp lines and lights is in his very latest style, and he has gone past Giorgione on his own ground. Then in strange contrast is the "Christ Crowned with Thorns," at Vienna, a tragic figure stupefied with suffering. His last great work was the "Pietà" in the Academy, which, though unfinished, is nobly designed and very impressive. He places the Virgin supporting the Body in a great dome-shaped niche, which gives elevation. It is flanked by two calm, antique, stone figures, whose impassive air contrasts with the wild pain and grief below. The Magdalen steps out towards the spectator with the wailing cry of a Greek tragedy. It perhaps hardly moves us like the concentrated feeling of Bellini's Madonna, or the hurried, trembling grief of

Tintoretto's Magdalen, but it is monumental in the sweeping grace of its line, and full of nobility of feeling. It is sadly rubbed and darkened and has lost much of Titian's colour, but is still beautiful in its deep greys mingled with a sombre golden glow, as of half-extinguished fires. These late paintings are of the true impressionist order; looked at closely they present a mass of scumbled touches, of incoherent dashes, but if we step farther away, to the right focus, light and dark arrange themselves, order shines through the whole, and we see what the great master meant us to see. "Titian's later creations," says Vasari, "are struck off rapidly, so that when close you cannot see them, but afar they look perfect, and this is the style which so many tried to imitate, to show that they were practised hands, but only produced absurdities." Titian was preparing the picture for the Frari, in payment for the grant of a tomb for himself, when in August 1576 the plague broke out in Venice, and on the 27th the great painter died of it in his own house. The stringent regulations concerning infection were relaxed to do honour to one of the greatest sons of Venice, and he was laid to rest in the Frari, borne there in solemn procession, through a city stricken by terror and panic, and buried in the Chapel of the Crucified Saviour, for which his last work was ordered. The "Assumption" of his prime looked down upon him, and close at hand was the "Madonna of Casa Pesaro." His son Orazio caught the plague and died immediately after, and the painter's house was sacked by thieves and many precious things stolen.

The great personality of Titian stands out as that which of all others established and consolidated the school of Venice. He is its central figure. The century of life, of which eighty years were passed in ceaseless industry of production, left its deep impression on the art of every civilised country of Europe. Every great man of the day who was a lover of art and culture fell under Titian's spell. His influence on his contemporaries was enormous, and he had everything: genius, industry, personal distinction, character, social charm. He is, perhaps, of too intellectual a cast of mind to be quite typical of the Venetian spirit, in the way that Tintoretto is; it is conceivable that in another environment Titian might have developed on rather different lines, but this temper gave him greater domination. He was free from the eccentricities which beset genius. He possessed the saving salt of practical common sense, so that the golden mean of sanity and healthful joy in his works commended them to all men, and they are not difficult to understand. Yet while all can see the beauty of his poetic instinct for colour, his interesting and original technique, his grasp and scope, his mastery and certainty have gained for him the title of "the painter's painter." There is no one from whom men feel that they can so safely learn so much, and the grand breadth and power of elimination of his later years is justified by the way in which in his earlier work he has carried exquisite finish and rich impasto to perfection.

PRINCIPAL WORKS

Ancona.	Crucifixion (L.).
	S. Domenico: Madonna with Saints and Donor, 1520.
Antwerp.	Pope Alexander VI. presenting Jacopo Pesaro.
Berlin.	Infant Daughter of Strozzi, 1542; Portrait of Himself (L.); Lavinia bearing Charges.
Brescia.	SS. Nazaro e Celso: Altarpiece, 1522.
Dresden.	Madonna with Saints (E.); Tribute Money (E.); Lavinia as Bride, 1555; Lavinia as Matron (L.); Portrait, 1561; Lady with Vase (L.); Lady in Red Dress.
Florence.	Pitti: La Bella; Aretino, 1545; Magdalen; The Young Englishman; The Concert (E.); Philip II.; Ippolito de Medici, 1533; Tomaso Mosti.
	Uffizi: Eleanora Gonzaga, Duchess of Urbino,

1537; Francesco della Rovere, Duke of Urbino, 1537; Flora; Venus, the head a portrait of Lavinia; Venus, the head a portrait of Eleanora Gonzaga; Madonna with S. Anthony Abbot.

London.
Holy Family and Shepherd; Bacchus and Ariadne (E.); Noli me tangere (E.); Madonna with SS. John and Catherine.

Bridgewater House: Holy Family (E.); Venus of the Shell; Three Ages of Man; Diana and Actaeon, 1559; Callisto, 1559.

Earl Brownlow: Diana and Actaeon (L.).

Sir F. Cook: Portrait of Laura de Dianti.

Madrid.
Madonna with SS. Ulfus and Bridget (E.); Bacchanal; The Garden of Loves; Danaë, 1554; Venus and Youth playing Organ (L.); Salome (portrait of Lavinia); Trinity, 1554; Entombment, 1559; Prometheus; Religion succoured by Spain (L.); Sisyphus (L.); Alfonso of Ferrara; Charles V. at the Battle of Mühlberg, 1548; Charles V. and his Dog, 1533; Philip II., 1550; Philip II.; The Infant; Don Fernando and Victory; Portrait; Portrait of Himself; Duke of Alva; Venus and Adonis; Fall of Man; Empress Isabella.

Medole.
(near Brescia) Christ appearing to His Mother.

Munich.
Vanitas; Portrait of Charles V., 1548; Madonna and Saints; Man with Baton.

Naples.
Paul III. and Cardinals, 1545; Danaë.

Padua.
Scuola del Santo: Frescoes; S. Anthony granting Speech to an Infant; The Youth who cut off his Leg; The Jealous Husband, 1511.

Paris.
Madonna with Saints (E.); La Vierge au Lapin; Madonna with S. Agnes; Christ at Emmaus (L.); Crowning with Thorns (L.); Entombment; S. Jerome (L.); Jupiter and Antiope (L.); Francis I.; Allegory; Marquis da Valos and Mary of Arragon; Alfonso of Ferrara and Laura Dianti; L'Homme au Gant (E.); Portraits.

Rome.
Villa Borghese: Sacred and Profane Love (E.); St. Dominio (L.); Education of Cupid (L.).

Capitol: Baptism (E.).

Doria: Daughter of Herodias.

Vatican: Madonna in Glory and six Saints, 1523.

Treviso.
Duomo: Annunciation.

Urbino.
Resurrection (L.); Last Supper (L.).

Venice.
Academy: Presentation of Virgin, 1540; S. John in the Desert; Assumption, 1518; Pietà, 1573.

Palazzo Ducale Staircase: S. Christopher, 1523.

Sala di Quattro Porte: Doge Giovanni before Faith, 1555.

Frari: Pesaro Madonna, 1526.

S. Giovanni Elemosinario: S. John the Almsgiver, 1523.

Scuola di San Rocco: Annunciation (E.).

Salute Sacristy: Descent of the Holy Spirit; St. Mark enthroned with Saints; David and Goliath; Sacrifice of Isaac; Cain and Abel.

S. Salvatore: Annunciation (L.); Transfiguration (L.).

Verona.	Duomo: Assumption.
Vienna.	Gipsy Madonna (E.); Madonna of the Cherries (E.); Ecce Homo, 1543; Isabela d'Este, 1534; The Tambourine Player; Girl in Fur Cloak; Dr. Parma (E.); Shepherd and Nymph (L.); Portraits; Doge Andrea Gritti; Jacopo Strada; Diana and Callisto; Madonna and Saints.
Wallace Collection.	Perseus and Andromeda. (In collaboration with his nephew, Francesco Vecellio.)
Louvre.	Madonna and Saints. (The same by Francesco alone.)
Glasgow.	Madonna and Saints.

CHAPTER XX
PALMA VECCHIO AND LORENZO LOTTO

Among the many who clustered round Titian's long career, Palma attained to a place beside him and Giorgione which his talent, which was not of the highest order, scarcely warranted. But he was classed with the greatest, and influenced contemporary art because his work chimed in so well with the Venetian spirit. A Bergamasque by birth, he came of Venetian parentage, and learnt the first elements of his art in Venice. He never really mastered the inner niceties of anatomy in its finest sense, and the broad generalisation of his forms may be meant to conceal uncertain drawing, but his large-bosomed, matronly women and plump children, his round, soft contours, his clean brilliancy, and the clear golden polish in which his pictures are steeped, made a great appeal to the public. His invention is the large Santa Conversazione, as compared with those in half-length of the earlier masters. The Virgin and saints and kneeling or bending donors are placed underthe spreading trees of a rich and picturesque landscape. It is Palma's version of the Giorgionesque ideal, which he had his share in establishing and developing. The heavy tree-trunk and dark foliage, silhouetted almost black against the background, are characteristic of his compositions. As his life goes on, though he still clings to his full, ripe figures and to the same smooth fleshiness in his women, the features become delicate and chiselled, and the more refined type and subtler feeling of his middle stage may be due to his companionship with Lotto, with whom he was in Bergamo when they were both about twenty-five. He touches his highest, and at the same time keeps very near Giorgione, in the splendid St. Barbara, painted for the company of the *Bombadieri* or artillerists. Their cannon guard the pedestal on which she stands; it was at her altar that they came to commend themselves on going forth to war, and where they knelt to offer thanksgiving for a safe return; and she is a truly noble figure, regal in conception and fine and firm in execution, attired in sumptuous robes of golden brown and green, with splendid saints on either hand. Palma was often approached by his patrons who wanted mythological scenes, gods, and goddesses; but though he produced a Venus, a handsome, full-blown model, he never excels in the nude, and his tendency is to seize upon the homely. His scenes have a domestic, familiar flavour. With all his golden and ivory beauty he lacks fire, and his personages have a sluggish, plethoric note. In his latest stage he hides all sharpness in a sort of scumble or haze. It would, however, be unfair to say he is not fine, and his portraits especially come very near the best. Vienna is rich in examples in half-lengths of one beautiful woman after another robed in the ample and gorgeous garments in which he is always interested. Among them is his handsome daughter, Violante, with a violet in her bosom, and wearing the large sleeves he admires. The "Tasso" of the National Gallery has been taken from him and given first to Giorgione and then to Titian, but there now seems some inclination to return it to its first author. It has a more dreamy, intellectual countenance than we are accustomed to associate with Palma; but he uses elsewhere the decorative background of olive branches, and the waxen complexion, tawny colouring, and the pronounced golden haze are Palmesque in the highest degree. The colouring is in strong contrast to the pale ivory glow of the Ariosto of Titian, which hangs near it.

Palma Vecchio. HOLY FAMILY. *Colonna Gallery, Rome.*
(Photo, Anderson.)

No one could be more unlike Palma than his contemporary, Lorenzo Lotto, who has for long been classed with the Bergamasques, but who is proved by recently discovered documents to have been born in Venice. It was for long an accepted fact that Lotto was a pupil of Bellini, and his earliest altarpiece, to S. Cristina at Treviso, bears traces of Bellini's manner. A Pietà above has child angels examining the wounds with the grief and concern which Bellini made so peculiarly his own, and the St. Jerome and the branch of fig-leaves silhouetted against the light remind us of the altarpiece in S. Crisostomo. Lotto seems to have clung to quattrocento fashions. The ancona had long been rejected by most of his contemporaries, but he painted one of the last for a church in Recanati, in carved and gilt compartments, and he painted predellas long after they had become generally obsolete. We ask ourselves how it was that Lotto, who had so susceptible and easily swayed a nature, escaped the influence of Giorgione, the most powerful of any in the Venice of his youth— an influence which acted on Bellini in his old age, which Titian practically never shook off, and which dominated Palma to the exclusion of any earlier master.

It would take too long to survey the train of argument by which Mr. Berenson has established Alvise Vivarini as the master of Lotto. Notwithstanding that Bellini's great superiority was becoming clear to the more cultured Venetians, Alvise, when Lotto was a youth, was still the painter *par excellence* for the mass of the public. In the S. Cristina altarpiece the Child standing on its Mother's knee is in the same attitude as the Child in Alvise's altarpiece of 1480, and the Mother's hand holds it in the same way. Other details which supply internal evidence are the shape of hands and feet, the round heads and the way the Child is often represented lying across the Mother's knees. Lotto carries into old age the use of fruit and flowers and beads as decoration, a Squarcionesque feature beloved of the Vivarini, but which was never adopted by Bellini.

About 1512 Lotto comes into contact with Palma, and for a short time the two were in close touch. A "Santa Conversazione," of which a good copy exists in Villa Borghese, Rome, and one at Dresden, with the Holy Family grouped under spreading trees, is saturated with Palma's spirit, but it soon passes away, and except for an occasional touch, disappears entirely from Lotto's work.

Lotto may have had relations in Bergamo, for when in 1515 a competition between artists was set on foot by Alessandro Martino, a descendant of General Colleone, for an altarpiece for S. Stefano, he competed and carried off the prize. This was the first of the series of the great works for Bergamo, which enrich the little city, where at this period he can best be studied. The great altarpiece (now removed to San Bartolommeo) is a most interesting human document, a revelation of the painter's personality. He does not break away from hieratic conventions, like the rival school; his Madonna is still placed in the apse of the church with saints grouped round her, a form from which the Vivarini never departed, but the whole is full of intense movement, of a lyric grace and ecstasy, a desire to express fervent and rapturous devotion. The architectural background is not in happy proportion in relation to the figures, but the effect of vista and space is more remarkable than in any North Italian master. The vivid treatment of light and shade, and the gaiety and delicacy of the flying angels, who hold the canopy, and of the putti, who spread the carpet below, the shapes of throne and canopy and the decorations have led to the idea that Lotto drew his inspiration from Correggio, whom he certainly resembles in some ways; but at this time Correggio was only twenty, and had not given any examples of the style we are accustomed to call Correggiesque. We must look back to a common origin for those decorative details, which are so conspicuous in Crivelli and Bartolommeo Vivarini, which came to Lotto through the Vivarini and to Correggio through Ferrarese painters, and of which the fountain-head for both was the school of Squarcione. For the much more striking resemblances of composition and spirit, the explanation seems to be that Lotto on one side of his nature was akin to Correggio; he had the same lyrical feeling, the same inclination to exuberance and buoyancy. To both, painting was a vehicle for the expression of feeling, but Lotto had also common sense and a goodly share of that humour that is allied to pathos.

Till the year 1526 Lotto was much in Bergamo, where the first altarpiece gained him orders for others. The reputation of a member of the school of Venice was a sure passport to employment. We trace Alvise's tradition very plainly in the altarpiece in San Bernardino, where the gesture of the Madonna's hand as she expounds to the listening saints recalls Alvise's of 1480. The little gathered roses, which Lotto makes use of to the end of his life, lie scattered on the step; angels, daringly foreshortened, sweep aside the curtain of the sanctuary. The colour is in Lotto's scarlet, light blues, and violet. He soon shows himself fond of genre incidents, and in "Christ taking leave of His Mother" gives a view into a bedroom and a cat running across the floor. The donor kneels with her hair fashionably dressed and wearing a pearl necklace. In the "Marriage of S. Catherine" at Bergamo the saint is evidently a portrait, with hair pearl-wreathed. She kneels very simply and naturally before the Child, and the exquisitely lovely and elaborately gowned young woman who represents the Madonna, looks out towards the spectator with a mundane and curiously modern air. It was probably the recognition of Lotto's success with portraits that led to their being so often introduced into his sacred pieces. In the one we have just noticed, the donor, Niccolas Bonghi, is brought in, and is on rather a larger scale than the rest, but Lotto has evidently not found him interesting. The portraits of the brothers della Torre, and that of the Prothonotary Giuliano in the National Gallery, inaugurate that wonderful series of characterisations which are his greatest distinction. A series of frescoes in village churches round Bergamo must also be noticed. They are remarkable for spontaneous and original decoration, and may compare with the ceremonial groups of Gentile Bellini and Carpaccio. Lotto's personages, as they chatter in the market-places, are full of natural animation and gaiety, and we realise what a step had been made in the painting of actual life.

Owing to the unsettled state of the rest of Italy, the years from 1530 to 1540, which Lotto spent in Venice, found that city the gathering-ground of many of the most distinguished scholars and deepest thinkers of the day. Men of all shades of religious thought were engaged in learned discussion, and Lotto's ardent and inquiring temperament must have been stimulated by such an environment. During these years, too, he became intimate with Titian, and experimented in Titian's style, with the result that his painting gets thicker and richer, more fused and solid, and his figures are better put together. He imitates Titian's colour, too, but it makes him paint in deeper, fiercer tints, and he soon finds it does not suit him, and returns to his own scheme. His colour is still rather too dazzling, but the distances are translucent and atmospheric. He continues to introduce portraits. In his altarpiece in SS. Giovanni and Paolo the deacons giving alms and receiving petitions curiously resemble in type and expression the ecclesiastics we see to-day.

Lotto was now an accepted member of Titian's set, and Aretino, in a letter dated 1548, writes that Titian values his taste and judgment as that of no other; but Aretino, with his usual mixture of connoisseurship and clever spite, goes on to insinuate accidentally, as it were, what he himself knew perfectly well, that Lotto was not considered on a par with the masters of the first rank. "Envy is not in your breast," he says, "rather do you delight to see in other artists certain qualities which you do not find in your own brush, ... holding the second place in the art of painting is nothing compared to holding the first place in the duties of religion."

An interesting codex or commentary tells us that Lotto never received high prices for his work, and we hear of him hawking pictures about in artistic circles, putting them up in raffles, and leaving a number with Jacopo Sansovino in the hope that he might hear of buyers. His work ended as it had begun, in the Marches. He undertook commissions at Recanati, Ancona, and Loreto, and in September 1554 he concluded a contract with the Holy House at Loreto, by which, in return for rooms and food, he made over himself and all his belongings to the care of the fraternity, "being tired of wandering, and wishing to end his days in that holy place." He spent the last four years of his life at Loreto as a votary of the Virgin, painting a series of pictures which are distinguished by the same sort of apparent looseness and carelessness which we noticed in Titian's late style; a technique which, as in Titian's case, conceals a profound knowledge of plastic modelling.

Though Lotto executed an immense number of important and very beautiful sacred works, his portraits stand apart, and are so interesting to the modern mind that one is tempted to linger over them. Other painters give us finer pictures; in none do we feel so anxious to know who the sitters were and what was their story. Lotto has nothing of the Pagan quality which marks Giorgione and Titian; he is a born psychologist, and as such he witnesses to an attitude of mind in the Italy of his day which is of peculiar interest to our own. Lotto's bystanders, even in his sacred scenes, have nothing in common with Titian's "chorus"; they have the characterisation of distinct individuals, and when he is concerned with actual portraits he is intensely receptive and sensitive to the spirit of his sitters. He may be said to "give them away," and to take an almost unfair advantage of his perception. The sick man in the Doria Gallery looks like one stricken with a death sentence. He knows at least that it is touch and go, and the painter has symbolised the situation in the little winged genius balancing himself in a pair of scales. In the Borghese Gallery is the portrait of a young, magnificently dressed man, with a countenance marked by mental agitation, who presses one hand to his heart, while the other rests on a pile of rose-petals in which a tiny skull is half-hidden. The "Old Man" in the Brera has the hard, narrow, but intensely sad face of one whose natural disposition has been embittered by the circumstances of his life, just as that of our Prothonotary speaks of a large and gentle nature, mellowed by natural affections and happy pursuits. We smile, as Lotto does, with kindly mischief at "Marsilio and his Bride;" the broad, placid countenance of the man is so significantly contrasted with the clever mouth and eyes of the bride that it does not need the malicious glance of the cupid, who is fitting on the yoke, to "dot the i's and cross the t's" of their future. Again, the portrait of Laura di Pola, in the Brera, introduces us to one of those women who are charming in every age, not actually beautiful, but harmonious, thoughtful, perfectly dressed, sensible, and self-possessed, and the "Family Group" in our own gallery holds a history of a couple of antagonistic temperaments united by life in common and the clasping hands of children. Lotto does not keep the personal expression out of even such a canvas as his "Triumph of Chastity" in the Rospigliosi Gallery. His delightful Venus, one of the loveliest nudes in painting, flies from the attacking termagant, whose virtue is proclaimed by the ermine on her breast, and sweeps her little cupid with her with a well-bred, surprised air, suggestive of the manners of mundane society.

Lorenzo Lotto. PORTRAIT OF LAURA DI POLA. *Brera.*
(Photo, Anderson.)

The painter who was thus able to unveil personality had evidently a mind that was aware of itself, that looked forward to a wider civilisation and a more earnest and intimate religion. His life seems to have been one of some sadness, and crowned with only moderate success. He speaks of himself as "advanced in years, without loving care of any kind, and of a troubled mind." His will shows that his worldly possessions were few and poor, and that he had no heir closer than a nephew; but he leaves some of his cartoons as a dowry to "two girls of quiet nature, healthy in mind and body, and likely to make thrifty housekeepers," on their marriage to "two well-recommended young men," about to become painters. His sensitive and introspective temperament led him to prefer the retirement and the quiet beauty of Loreto to the brilliant society of which he was made free in Venice. "His spirit," says Mr. Berenson, "is more like our own than is perhaps that of any other Italian painter, and it has all the appeal and fascination of a kindred soul in another age."

PRINCIPAL WORKS

Palma Vecchio.

Bergamo.	Lochis: Madonna and Saints (L.).
Cambridge	Fitzwilliam Museum: Venus (L.).
Dresden.	Madonna; SS. John, Catherine; Three Sisters; Holy Family; Meeting of Jacob and Rachel (L.).
London.	Hampton Court: Santa Conversazione; Portrait of a Poet.
Milan.	Brera: SS. Helen, Constantine, Roch, and Sebastian; Adoration of Magi (L.), finished by Cariani.
Naples.	Santa Conversazione with Donors.
Paris.	Adoration of Shepherds.
Rome.	Villa Borghese: Lucrece (L.); Madonna with Saints and Donor.
	Capitol: Christ and Woman taken in Adultery.
	Palazzo Colonna: Madonna, S. Peter, and Donor.
Venice.	Academy: St. Peter enthroned and six Saints; Assumption.
	Giovanelli: Sposalizio (L.).
	S. Maria Formosa: Altarpiece.
Vienna.	Santa Conversazione; Violante (L.); Five Portraits of Women.

Lorenzo Lotto.

Ancona.	Assumption, 1550; Madonna with Saints (L.).
Asolo.	Madonna in Glory, 1506.
Bergamo.	Carrara: Marriage of S. Catherine; Predelle.
	Lochis: Holy Family and S. Catherine; Predelle; Portrait.
	S. Bartolommeo: Altarpiece, 1516.
	S. Alessandro in Colonna: Pietà.
	S. Bernardino: Altarpiece.
	S. Spirito: Altarpiece.
Berlin.	Christ taking leave of His Mother; Portraits.
Brescia.	Nativity.

Cingoli.	S. Domenico: Madonna and Saints and fifteen Small Scenes.
Florence.	Uffizi: Holy Family.
London.	Hampton Court: Portrait of Andrea Odoni, 1527; Portrait (E.); Portraits of Agostino and Niccolo della Torre, 1515; Family Group; Portrait of Prothonotary Giuliano.
	Bridgewater House: Madonna and Saints (E.).
Loreto.	Palazzo Apostolico: Saints; Nativity; S. Michael and Lucifer (L.); Presentation (L.); Baptism (L.); Adoration of Magi (L.).
Recanati.	Municipio: Altarpiece, 1508; Transfiguration (E.).
	S. Maria Sopra Mercanti: Annunciation.
Rome.	Villa Borghese: Madonna with S. Onofrio and a Bishop, 1508.
	Rospigliosi: Love and Chastity.
Venice.	Carmine: S. Nicholas in Glory, 1529.
	S. Giacomo dall' Orio: Madonna with Saints, 1546.
	SS. Giovanni e Paolo: S. Antonino bestowing Alms, 1542.
Vienna.	Santa Conversazione, etc.

CHAPTER XXI
SEBASTIAN DEL PIOMBO

It was very natural that Rome should wish for works of the masters of the new Venetian School, but the first-rate men were fully employed at home. All the efforts made to secure Titian failed till nearly the end of his career. On the other hand, Venice was full of less famous masters following in Giorgione's steps. When Sebastian Luciani was a young man, Giorgione was paramount there, and no one could have foretold that his life would be of such short duration. It was to be expected, therefore, that a painter who consulted his own interests should leave the city where he was overshadowed by a great genius and go farther afield. The influence of the Guilds was withdrawn in the sixteenth century, so that it was a simpler matter for painters to transfer their talents, and painting was beginning to appeal strongly to the *dilettanti*, who rivalled one another in their offers.

Only one work of Sebastian's is known belonging to this earlier time in Venice. It is the "S. Chrysostom enthroned," in S. Giovanni Crisostomo, and its majesty and rich colouring, and more especially the splendid group of women on the left, so proud and soft in their Venetian beauty, make us wonder if Sebastian might not have risen to greater heights if he had remained in his natural environment. He responded to the call to Rome of Agostino Chigi, the great painter, art collector, and patron, the friend of Leo X. Chigi had just completed the Farnesina Villa, and Sebastian was employed till 1512 on its decoration, and at once came under the influence of Michelangelo. The "Pietà" at Viterbo shows that influence very strongly; in fact, Vasari says that Michelangelo himself drew the cartoon for the figure of Christ, which would account for its extraordinary beauty. Sebastian embarked on a close intimacy with the Florentine painter, and, according to Vasari, the great canvas of the "Raising of Lazarus," in the National Gallery, was executed under the orders and in part from the designs of Michelangelo. This colossal work was looked on as one of the most important creations of the sixteenth century, but there is little to make us wish to change it for the altarpiece of S. Crisostomo. The desire for scientific drawing and the search after composition have produced a laboured effect; the female figures are cast in a masculine mould, and it lacks both the severe beauty of the Tuscan School and the emotional charm of Sebastian's native style. We cannot, however, avoid conjecturing if in the figure of Lazarus himself we have not a conception of the great Florentine. It is so easy in pose, so splendid in its, perhaps excessive, length of limb, that our thoughts turn involuntarily to the *Ignudi* in the Sixtine Chapel. The picture has been dulled and injured by repainting, but the distance still has the sombre depth of the Venetians. All through Sebastian's career he seeks for form and composition, but, great painter as he undoubtedly is, he is great because he possesses that inborn feeling for harmony of colour. This is what we value in him, and he excels in so far as he follows his Venetian instincts.

The death of Raphael improved Sebastian's position in Rome, and though Leo X. never liked or employed him, he did not lack commissions. The "Fornarina" in the Uffizi, with the laurel-wreathed head and leopard-skin mantle, still reveals him as the Venetian, and it is curious that any critic should ever have assigned its rich, voluptuous tone and its coarse type to Raphael. Sebastian obtained commissions for decorating S. Maria del Popolo in oils and S. Pietro in Montorio in fresco, but in the latter medium, though he is ambitious of acquiring the force of Michelangelo, he lacks the Tuscan ease of hand. Colour, for which he possessed so true an aptitude, the deep, fused colour of Giorgione, is set aside by him; his tints become strong and crude, his surfaces grow hard and polished, and he thinks, above all, of bold action, of drawing and modelling. The Venetian genius for portraiture remains, and he has left such fine examples as the "Andrea Doria" of the Vatican, or the "Portrait of a Man in the Pitti," a masterly picture both in drawing and execution, with grand draperies, a fur pelisse, and damask doublet with crimson sleeves. In the National Gallery we possess his own portrait by himself, in company with Cardinal de Medici. The faces are well contrasted, and we judge from Sebastian's that his biographer describes him justly, as fat, indolent, and given to self-indulgence, but genial and fond of good company.

After an absence of twenty years he returned to Venice. There he came in contact with Titian and Pordenone, and struck up a friendship with Aretino, who became his great ally and admirer. The sack of Rome had driven him forth, but in 1529, when the city was beginning partially to recover from that time of horror, he returned, and was cordially welcomed by Clement VII., and admitted into the innermost ecclesiastical circles. The Piombo, a well-paid, sinecure office of the Papal court, was bestowed on him, and his remaining years were spent in Rome. He was very anxious to collaborate with Michelangelo, and the great painter seems to have been quite inclined to the arrangement.The "Last Judgment," in the Sixtine Chapel, was suggested, and Sebastian had the melancholy task of taking down Perugino's masterpieces; but he wished to reset the walls for oils, and Michelangelo stipulated for fresco, saying that oils were only fit for women, so that no agreement was arrived at.

Sebastian's mode of work was slow, and he employed no assistants. He seems to have been inordinately lazy, fond of leisure and good living, and his character shows in his work, which, with a few exceptions, has something heavy and common about it, a want of keenness and fire, an absence of refinement and selection.

PRINCIPAL WORKS

Florence.	Uffizi: Fornarina, 1512; Death of Adonis.
	Pitti: Martyrdom of S. Agatha, 1520; Portrait (L.).
London.	Resurrection of Lazarus, 1519; Portraits.
Naples.	Holy Family; Portraits.
Paris.	Visitation, 1521.
Rome.	Portrait of Andrea Doria (L.).

Farnesina: Frescoes, 1511.

S. Pietro in Montorio. Frescoes.

| Treviso. | S. Niccolo: Incredulity of S. Thomas (E.). |
| Venice. | Academy: Visitation (E.). |

S. Giovanni Chrisostomo: S. Chrysostom enthroned (E.).

| Viterbo. | Pietà (L.). |

CHAPTER XXII
BONIFAZIO AND PARIS BORDONE

Some uncertainty has existed as to the identity of the different members of the family of Bonifazio. All the early historians agree in giving the name to one master only. Boschini, however, in 1777 discovered the register of the death of a second, and a third bearing the name was working twenty years later. Upon this Dr. Morelli came to the conclusion that we must recognise three, if not four, masters bearing the name of Bonifazio, but documents recently discovered by Professor Ludwig have in great measure destroyed Morelli's conjectures. There may have been obscure painters bearing the name, but they were mere imitators, and it is doubtful if any were related to the family of de Pitatis.

Bonifazio Veronese is really the only one who counts. As Ridolfi says, he was born in Verona in the most beautiful moment of painting. He came to Venice at the age of eighteen, and became a pupil of Palma Vecchio, with whom his work has sometimes beenconfused. After Palma's death Bonifazio continued in friendly relations with his old master's family, and his niece married Palma's nephew. Bonifazio himself married the daughter of a basket-maker, and appears to have had no children, for he and his wife by their wills bestowed their whole fortune on their nephews. Antonio Palma, who married Bonifazio's niece, was a painter whose pictures have sometimes been attributed to the legendary third Bonifazio. Bonifazio's life was passed peacefully in Venice. He received many important commissions from the Republic, and decorated the Palace of the Treasurers. His character and standing were high, and he was appointed, in company with Titian and Lotto, to administer a legacy which Vincenzo Catena had left to provide a yearly dower for five maidens. After a long life spent in steady work, Bonifazio withdrew to a little farm amidst orchards—fifteen acres of land in all—at San Zenone, near Asolo; but he still kept his house in San Marcuola, where he died. He was buried in S. Alvise in Venice.

A son of the plains and of Venetian stock, his work is always graceful and attractive, though inclined to be hot in colour. It has a very pronounced aristocratic character, and bears no trace of the rough, provincial strain of such men as Cariani or Pordenone. It is very fine and glowing in colour, but lacks vigour and energy in design. Nowhere do we get more worldly magnificence or such frank worship of wealth as on Bonifazio's joyous canvases. He represents Christian saints and Eastern kings alike, as gentlemen of princely rank. There is a note of purely secular art about his Adorations and Holy Families. In the "Adoration of the Magi," in the Academy, the Madonna is a handsome, prosperous lady of Bonifazio's acquaintance. The Child, so far from raising His hand in benediction, holds it out for the proffered cup. He does not, as usual, distinguish the eldest king, but singles out the cup held by the second, who, in a puffed velvet dress, is an evident portrait, probably that of the donor of the picture, who is in this way paid a courtier-like compliment. The third king is such a Moor as Bonifazio must often have seen embarking from his Eastern galley on the Riva dei Schiavoni. A servant in a peaked hood peers round the column to catch sight of what is going on. The groups of animals in the background are well rendered. In the "Rich Man's Feast," where Lazarus lies upon the step, we have another scene of wealthy and sumptuous Venetian society, an orgy of colour. And, again, in the "Finding of Moses" (Brera) he paints nobles playing the lute, making love and feasting, and lovely fair-haired women listening complacently. We are reminded of the way in which they lived: their one preoccupation the toilet, the delight ofappearing in public in the latest and most magnificent fashions. And in these paintings Bonifazio depicts the elaborate striped and brocaded gowns in which the beautiful Venetians arrayed themselves, made in the very fashions of the year, and their thick, fair hair is twisted and coiled in the precise mode of the moment. The deep-red velvet he introduces into nearly all his pictures is of a hue peculiar to himself. As Catena often brings in a little white lap-dog, so Bonifazio constantly has as an accessory a liver-and-white spaniel.

Vasari speaks of Paris Bordone as the artist who most successfully imitated Titian. He was the son of well-to-do tradespeople in Treviso, and received a good education in music and letters, before being sent off to Venice and placed in Titian's studio. Bordone does not seem to have been on very friendly terms with Titian. He was dissatisfied with his teaching, and Titian played him an ill turn in wresting from him a commission to paint an altarpiece which had been entrusted to him when he was only eighteen. He was, above all, in love with the manner of the dead Giorgione, and it was upon this master that he aspired to form his style. His masterpiece, in the Academy, was painted for the Confraternity of St. Mark, and made his reputation. The legend it represents may be given in a few words:

In the days of Doge Gradenigo, one February, there arose a fearful storm in Venice. During the height of the tempest, three men accosted a poor old fisherman, who was lying in his decayed old boat by the Piazza, and begged that he would row them to S. Niccolo del Lido, where they had urgent business. After some demur they persuaded him to take the oars, and in spite of the hurricane, the voyage was accomplished. On reaching the shore they pointed out to him a great ship, the crew of which he perceived to consist of a band of demons, who were stirring up the waves and making a great hubbub. The three passengers laid their commands on them to desist, when immediately they sailed away and there was a calm. The passengers then made the oarsman row them, one to S. Niccolo, one to S. Giorgio, and the third was rowed back to the Piazza. The fisherman timidly asked for his fare, and the third passenger desired him to go to the Doge and ask for payment, telling him that by that night's work a great disaster had been averted from the city. The fisherman replied that he should not be believed, but would be imprisoned as a liar. Then the passenger drew a ring from his finger. "Show him this for a sign," he said, "and know that one of those you have this night rowed is S. Niccolas, the other is S. George, and I am S. Mark the Evangelist, Protector of the Venetian Republic." He then disappeared. The next day the fisherman presented the ring, and was assigned a provision for life from the Senate.

There has, perhaps, never been a richer and more beautiful subject-picture painted than this glowing canvas, or one which brings more vividly before us the magnificence of the pageants which made such a part of Venetian life in the golden age of painting. It is all strength and splendour, and escapes the hectic colour and weaker type which appear in Bordone's "Last Supper" and some of his other works. In 1538 he went to France and entered the service of Francis II., painting for him many portraits of ladies, besides works for the Cardinals of Guise and of Lorraine. The King of Poland sent to him for a "Jupiter and Antiope." At Augsburg he was paid 3000 crowns for work done for the great Fugger family.

No one gives us so closely as Bordone the type of woman who at this time was most admired in Venice. The Venetian ideal was golden haired, with full lips, fair, rosy cheeks, large limbed and ample, with "abundant flanks and snow-white breast." A type glowing with health and instinct with life, but, to say the truth, rather dull, without deep passions, and with no look that reveals profound emotions or the struggle of a soul. From what we see of Bordone's female portraits and from some of the mythological compositions he has left, he might have been among the most sensually minded of men. His beautiful courtesan, in the National Gallery, is an almost over-realistic presentment of a woman who has just parted from her lover. His women, with their carnation cheeks and expressionless faces, are like beautiful animals; but, as a matter of fact, their painter was sober and temperate in his life, very industrious, and devoted to his widowed mother. About 1536 he married the daughter of a Venetian citizen, and had a son, who became one of the many insignificant painters of the end of the sixteenth century. Most of his days were divided between his little Villa of Lovadina in the district of Belluno, and his modest home in the Corte dell' Cavallo near the Misericordia. "He lives comfortably in his quiet house," writes Vasari, who certainly knew Bordone in Venice, "working only at the request of princes, or his friends, avoiding all rivalry and those vain ambitions which do but disturb the repose of man, and seeking to avert any ruffling of the serene tranquillity of his life, which he is accustomed to preserve simple and upright."

Many of his pictures show an intense love of country solitudes. His poetic backgrounds, lonely mountains, leafy woods, and sparkling water are in curious contrast to the sumptuous groups in the foreground.

His "Three Heads," in the Brera, is a superb piece of painting and an interesting characterisation. The woman is ripe, sensual, and calculating, feeling with her fingers for the gold chain, a mere golden-fleshed, rose-flushed hireling, solid and prosaic. The go-between is dimly seen in the background, but the face of the suitor is a strange, ironic study: past youth, worn, joyless, and bitter, taking his pleasure mechanically and with cynical detachment. The "Storm calmed by S. Mark" (Academy) was, in Mr. Berenson's opinion, begun by Giorgione.

Rich, brilliant, and essentially Venetian as is the work of these two painters, it does not reach the highest level. It falls short of grandeur, and has that worldly tone that borders on vulgarity. As we study it we feel that it marks the point to which Venetian art might have attained, the flood-mark it might have touched, if it had lacked the advent of the three or four great spirits, who, appearing about the same time, bore it up to sublimer heights and developed a more distinguished range of qualities. Bonifazio and Bordone lack the grandeur and sweetness of Titian, the brilliant touch and imaginative genius of Tintoretto, the matchless feeling for colour, design, and decoration of Veronese, but they continue Venetian painting on logical lines, and they form a superb foundation for the highest.

PRINCIPAL WORKS

Bonifazio Veronese.

	Dresden.	Finding of Moses.
	Florence.	Pitti: Madonna; S. Elizabeth and Donor (E.); Rest in Flight into Egypt; Finding of Moses.
	Hampton Court.	Santa Conversazione.
	London.	Santa Conversazione (E.).
	Milan.	Brera: Finding of Moses.
	Paris.	Santa Conversazione.
	Rome.	Villa Borghese: Mother of Zebedee's Children; Return of the Prodigal Son.
		Colonna: Holy Family with Saints.
	Venice.	Academy: Rich Man's Feast; Massacre of Innocents; Judgment of Solomon, 1533; Adoration of Kings.
		Giovanelli: Santa Conversazione.
	Vienna.	Santa Conversazione; Triumph of Love; Triumph of Chastity; Salome.

Paris Bordone.

	Bergamo.	Lochis: Vintage Scenes.
	Berlin.	Portrait of Man in Black; Chess Players; Madonna and four Saints.
	Dresden.	Apollo and Marsyas; Diana; Holy Family.
	Florence.	Pitti: Portrait of Woman.

Genoa.	Brignole Sale: Portraits of Men; Santa Conversazione.
Hampton Court.	Madonna and Donors.
London.	Daphnis and Chloe; Portrait of Lady.
	Bridgewater House: Holy Family.
Milan.	Brera: Descent of Holy Spirit; Baptism; S. Dominio presented to the Saviour by Virgin; Madonna and Saints; Venal Love.
	S. Maria pr. Celso: Madonna and S. Jerome.
Munich.	Portrait; Man counting Jewels.
Paris.	Portraits.
Rome.	Colonna: Holy Family and Saints.
Treviso.	Madonna and Saints.
	Duomo: Adoration of Shepherds; Madonna and Saints.
Venice.	Academy: Fisherman and Doge; Paradise; Storm calmed by S. Mark.
	Palazzo Ducale Chapel: Dead Christ.
	Giovanelli: Madonna and Saints.
	S. Giovanni in Bragora; Last Supper.
Vienna.	Allegorical Pictures; Lady at Toilet; Young Woman.

CHAPTER XXIII
PAINTERS OF THE VENETIAN PROVINCES

It has become usual to include in the Venetian School those artists from the subject provinces on the mainland, who came down to try their luck at the fountain-head and to receive its hallmark on their talent. The Friulan cities, Udine, Serravalle, and small neighbouring towns, had their own primitive schools and their scores of humble craftsmen. Their art wavered for some time in its expression between the German taste, which came so close to their gates, and the Italian, which was more truly their element.

Up to 1499 Friuli was invaded seven times in thirty years by the Turks. They poured in large numbers over the Bosnian borders, crossed the Isonzo and the Tagliamenta, and massacred and carried off the inhabitants. These terrible periods are marked by the cessation of work in the provinces, but hope always revived again. The break caused by such a visitation can be distinctly traced in the Church of S. Antonino, at the little town of San Daniele. Martino da Udine obtained the epithet of Pellegrino da San Daniele in 1494 when he returned from an early visit to Venice, where he had been apprenticed to Cima. He was appointed to decorate S. Antonino. His early work there is hard and coarse, ill-drawn, the figures unwieldy and shapeless, and the colour dusky and uniform; but owing to the Turkish raid, he had to take flight, and it was many a year before the monks gained sufficient courage and saved enough money to continue the embellishment of their church. In the meantime, Pellegrino's years had been spent partly in Venice and partly, perhaps, in Ferrara, for the reason Raphael gave for refusing to paint a "Bacchus" for the Duke, was that the subject had already been painted by Pellegrino da San Daniele. When Pellegrino resumed his work, it demonstrated that he had studied the modern Venetians and had come under a finer, deeper influence. A St. George in armour suggests Giorgione's S. Liberale at Castelfranco; he specially shows an affinity with Pordenone, who was his pupil and who was to become a better painter than his old master. As Pellegrino goes on he improves consistently, and adopts the method, so peculiarly Venetian, of sacrificing form to a scheme of chiaroscuro. He even, to some extent, succeeds in his difficult task of applying to wall painting the system which the Venetians used almost exclusively for easel pictures. He was an ambitious, daring painter, and some of his church standards were for long attributed to Giorgione. The church of San Antonino remains his chief monument; but for all his travels Pellegrino remains provincial in type, is unlucky in his selection, cares little for precision of form, and trusts to colour for effect.

The same transition in art was taking place in other provinces. Morto da Feltre, Pennacchi, and Girolamo da Treviso have all left work of a Giorgionesque type, and some painters who went far onward, began their career under such minor masters. Giovanni Antonio Licinio, who takes his name from his native town of Pordenone, in Friuli, was one of these. All the early part of his life was spent in painting frescoes in the small towns of the Friulan provinces. At first they bear signs of the tuition of Pellegrino, but it soon becomes evident that Pordenone has learned to imitate Giorgione and Palma. Quite early, however, one of his chief failings appears, and one which is all his own, the disparity in size between his various figures. The secondary personages, the Magi in a Nativity, the Saints standing round an altar, are larger and more athletic in build and often more animated in action than the principal actors in the scene. What pleased Pordenone's contemporaries was his daring perspective and his instinctive feeling for movement. He carried out great schemes in the hill-towns, till at length his reputation, which had long been ripe in his native province, reached Venice. In 1519 he was invited to Treviso to fresco the façade of a house for one of the Raviguino family. The painter, as payment, asked fifty scudi, and Titian was called in to adjudicate, but he admired the work so much that he hinted to Raviguino that he would be wise not to press him for a valuation. As a direct consequence of this piece of business, Pordenone was employed on the chapel at Treviso, in conjunction with Titian. At this time the Assumption and the Madonna of Casa Pesaro were just finished, and it is probable that Pordenone paid his first visit to Venice, hard by, and saw his great contemporary's work. With his characteristic distaste for fresco, Titian undertook the altarpiece and painted the beautiful Annunciation which still holds its place, and Pordenone covered the dome with a foreshortened figure of the Eternal Father, surrounded by angels. Among the remaining frescoes in the Chapel, an Adoration of the Magi and a S. Liberale are from his brush. Fired by his success at Treviso, Pordenone offered his services to Mantua and Cremona, but the Mantovans, accustomed to the stately and restrained grace of Mantegna, would have nothing to say to what Crowe and Cavalcaselle call his "large and colossal fable-painting." He pursued his way to Cremona, and that he studied Mantegna as he passed through Mantua is evident from the first figures he painted in the cathedral. In Cremona every one admired him, and all the artists set to work to imitate his energetic foreshortening, vehement movement and huge proportions.

Pordenone, with his love for fresco, was all his life an itinerant painter. In 1521 he was back at Udine and wandered from place to place, painting a vast distemper for the organ doors at S. Maria at Spilimbergo, the façade of the Church of Valeriano, an imposing series at Travesio, and in 1525, the "Story of the True Cross" at Casara. At the last place he threw aside much of his exaggeration, and, ruined and restored as the frescoes are, they remain among his most dignified achievements. He may be studied best of all at Piacenza, in the Church of the Madonna di Campagna, where he divides his subjects between sacred and pagan, so that we turn from a "Flight into Egypt" or a "Marriage of S. Catherine," to the "Rape of Europa" or "Venus and Adonis." At Piacenza he shows himself the great painter he undoubtedly is, having achieved some mastery over form, while his colour has the true Venetian quality and almost equals oils in its luscious tones and vivid hues, which he lowers and enriches by such enveloping shadows as only one whose spirit was in touch with the art of Giorgione would have understood how to use. Very complete records remain of Pordenone's life, full details of a quarrel with his brother over property left by his father in 1533, and accounts of the painter's negotiations to obtain a knighthood, which he fancied would place him more on a par with Titian when he went to live in Venice. The coveted honour was secured, but from this time he seems to have been very jealous of Titian and to have aimed continually at rivalling him. Pordenone was a punctual and rapid decorator, and on being given the ceiling of the Sala di San Finio to decorate in the summer of 1536, he finished the whole by March 1538. We have seen how Titian annoyed the Signoria by his delays, how anxious they were to transfer his commission to Pordenone, and what a narrow escape the Venetian had of losing his Broker's patent. Pordenone was engaged by the nuns of Murano to paint an Annunciation, after they had rejected one by Titian on account of its price, and though it seems hardly possible that any one could have compared the two men, yet no doubt the pleasure of getting an altarpiece quickly and punctually and for a moderate sum, often outweighed the honour of the possible painting by the great Titian.

No one has left so few easel-paintings as Pordenone; fresco was so much better suited to his particular style. The canvas of the "Madonna of Mercy" in the Venice Academy, was painted about 1525 for a member of the house of Ottobono, and introduces seven members of the family. It is very free from his colossal, exaggerated manner; the attendant saints are studied from nature, and in his journals the painter mentions that the St. Roch is a portrait of himself. The "S. Lorenzo enthroned," in the same gallery, shows both his virtues and failings. The saints have his enormous proportions. The Baptist is twisting round, to display the foreshortening which Pordenone particularly affects. The gestures are empty and inexpressive, but the colour is broad and fluid; there is a large sense of decoration in the composition, and something simple and austere about the figure of S. Lorenzo. As is so often the case with Pordenone, the principal actor of the scene is smaller and more sincerely imagined than the attendant personages, who are crowded into the foreground, where they are used to display the master's skill.

Pordenone died suddenly at Ferrara, where he had been summoned by its Duke to undertake one of his great schemes of decoration. He was said to have been poisoned, but though he had jealous rivals there seems no proof of the truth of the assertion, which was one very commonly made in those days. He is interesting as being the only distinguished member of the Venetian School whose frescoes have come down to us in any number, and as being the only one of the later masters with whom it was the chosen medium.

His kinsman, Bernardino Licinio, is represented in the National Gallery by a half-lengthof a young man in black, and at Hampton Court by a large family group and by another of three persons gathered round a spinet. His masterpiece is a Madonna and Saints in the Frari, which shows the influence of Palma. His flesh tints, striving to be rich, have a hot, red look, but his works have been constantly confounded with those of Giorgione and Paris Bordone.

A long list might be given of minor artists who were industriously turning out work on similar lines to one or other of these masters: Calderari, who imitates Paris Bordone as well as Pordenone; Pomponio Amalteo, Pordenone's son-in-law, a spirited painter in fresco; Florigerio, who practised at Udine and Padua, and of whom an altarpiece remains in the Academy; Giovanni Battista Grassi, who helped Vasari to compile his notices of Friulan art, and many others only known by name.

At the close of the fifteenth century the revulsion against Paduan art extended as far as Brescia, and Girolamo Romanino was one of the first to acquire the trick of Venetian painting. He probably studied for a time under Friulan painters. Pellegrino is thought to have been at Brescia or Bergamo during the Friulan disturbances of 1506-12, and about 1510 Romanino emerges, a skilled artist in Pellegrino's Palmesque manner. His works at this time are dark and glowing, full of warm light and deep shadow; the scene is often laid under arches, after the manner of the Vivarini and Cima; a gorgeous scheme of accessory is framed in noble architecture.

Brescia was an opulent city, second only to Milan among the towns of northern Italy, and Romanino obtained plenty of patronage; but in 1511 the city fell a prey to the horrors of war, was taken and lost by Venice, and in 1512 was sacked by the French. Romanino fled to Padua, where he found a home among the Benedictines of S. Giustina. Here he was soon well employed on an altarpiece with life-size figures for the high altar, and a "Last Supper" for the refectory. It is also surmised that he helped in the series for the Scuola del Santo, for several of which Titian in 1511 had signed a receipt, and the "Death of St. Anthony" is pointed out as showing the Brescian characteristics of fine colour, but poor drawing.

Romanino returned to Brescia when the Venetians recovered it in 1516, but before doing so he went to Cremona and painted four subjects, which are among his most effective, in the choir of the Duomo.

He is not so daring a painter as Pordenone, from whom he sometimes borrows ideas, but he is quite a convert to the modern style of the day, setting his groups in large spaces and using the slashed doublets, the long hose, and plumed headgear which Giorgione had found so picturesque. Romanino is often very poor and empty, and fails most in selection and expression at the moments when he most needs to be great, but he is successful in the golden style he adopted after his closer contact with the Venetians, and his draperies and flesh tints are extremely brilliant. He is, indeed, inclined to be gaudy and careless in execution, and even the fine "Nativity" in the National Gallery gives the impression that size is more regarded than thought and feeling.

Moretto is perhaps the only painter from the mainland who, coming within the charmed circle of Venetian art and betraying the study of Palma and Titian and the influence of Pordenone, still keeps his own gamut of colour, and as he goes on, gets consistently cooler and more silvery in his tones. He can only be fully studied in Brescia itself, where literally dozens of altarpieces and wall-paintings show him in every phase. His first connection was probably with Romanino, but he reminds us at one time of Titian by his serious realism, and finished, careful painting, at another of Raphael, by the grace and sentiment of his heads, and as time goes on he foreshadows the style of Veronese. In the "Feast in the House of Simon" in the organ-loft of the Church of the Pietà in Venice, the very name prepares us for the airy, colonnaded building, with vistas of blue sky and landscape, and the costly raiment and plenishing which might have been seen at any Venetian or Brescian banquet. In his portraits Moretto sometimes rivals Lotto. His personages are always dignified and expressive, with pale, high-bred faces, and exceedingly picturesque in dress and general arrangement. He loved to paint a great gentleman, like the Sciarra Martinengo in the National Gallery, and to endow him with an air of romantic interest.

One of those who entered so closely into the spirit of the Venetian School that he may almost be included within it, is Savoldo. His pictures are rare, and no gallery can show more than one or two examples. The Louvre has a portrait by him of Gaston de Foix, long thought to be by Giorgione. His native town can only show one altarpiece, an "Adoration of Shepherds," low in tone but intense in dusky shadow with fringes of light. He is grey and slaty in his shadows, and often rough and startling in effect, but at his best he produces very beautiful, rich, evening harmonies; and a letter from Aretino bears witness to the estimation in which he was held.

It is not easy to say if Brescia or Vicenza has most claim to Bartolommeo Montagna, the early master of Cima. Born of Brescian parents, he settled early in Vicenza, and he is by far the most distinguished of those Vicentine painters who drank at the Venetian fount. He must have gone early to Venice and worked with the Vivarini, for in his altarpiece in the Brera he has the vaulted porticoes in which Bartolommeo and Alvise Vivarini delighted. His "Madonna enthroned" in the gallery at Vicenza has many points of contact with that of Alvise at Berlin. Among these are the four saints, the cupola, and the raised throne, and he is specially attracted by the groups of music-making angels; but Montagna has more moral greatness than Alvise, and his lines are stronger and more sinewy. He keeps faithful to the Alvisian feeling for calm and sweetness, but his personages have greater weight and gravity. He essays, too, a "Pietà" with saints, at Monte Berico, and shows both pathos and vehemence. He has evidently seen Bellini's rendering, and attempts, if only with partial success, to contrast in the same way the indifference of death with the contemplation and anguish of the bereaved. Hard and angular as Montagna's saints often are, they show power and austerity. His colour is brilliant and enamel-like; he does not arrive at the Venetian depth, yet his altarpieces are very grand, and once more we are struck by the greatness of even the secondary painters who drew their inspiration from Padua and Venice.

Among the other Vicentines, Giovanni Speranza and Giovanni Buonconsiglio were imbued with characteristics of Mantegna. Speranza, in one of his few remaining works, almost reproduces the beautiful "Assumption" by Pizzolo, Mantegna's young fellow-student, in the Chapel of the Eremitani. He employs Buonconsiglio as an assistant, and they imitate Montagna to such an extent that it is difficult to distinguish between their works. Buonconsiglio's "Pietà" in the Vicenza gallery, is reminiscent of Montagna's at Monte Berico. The types are lean and bony, the features are almost as rugged as Dürer's, the flesh earthy and greenish. About 1497 Buonconsiglio was studying oils with Antonello da Messina; he begins to reside in Venice, and a change comes over his manner. His colours show a brilliancy and depth acquired by studying Titian; and then, again, his bright tints remind us of Lotto. His name was on the register of the Venetian Guild as late as 1530.

After Pisanello's achievement and his marked effect on early Venetian art, Veronese painting fell for a time to a very low ebb; but Mantegna's influence was strongly felt here, and art revived in Liberale da Verona, Falconetto, Casoto, the Morone and Girolamo dai Libri, painters delightful in themselves, but having little connection with the school of Venice. Francesco Bonsignori, however, shook himself free from the narrow circle of Veronese art, where he had for a time followed Liberale, and grows more like the Vicentines, Montagna and Buonconsiglio. He is careful about his drawing, but his figures, like those of many of these provincial painters, are short, bony and vulgar, very unlike the slender, distinguished type of the great Paduan. Under the name of Francesco da Verona, Bonsignori works in the new palace of the Gonzagas, and several pictures painted for Mantua are now scattered in different collections. At Verona he has left four fine altarpieces. He went early to Venice, where he became the pupil of the Vivarini. His faces grow soft and oval, and the very careful outlines suggest the influence of Bellini.

Girolamo Mocetto was journeyman to Giovanni Bellini; in fact, Vasari says that a "Dead Christ" in S. Francesco della Vigna, signed with Bellini's name, is from Mocetto's hand. His short, broad figures have something of Bartolommeo Vivarini's character.

Francesco Torbido went to Venice to study with Giorgione, and we can trace his master's manner of turning half tones into deep shades; but he does not really understand the Giorgionesque treatment, in which shade was always rich and deep, but never dark, dirty and impenetrable, nor in the lights can he produce the clear glow of Giorgione. Another Veronese, Cavazzola, has left a masterpiece upon which any painter might be happy to rest his reputation; the "Gattemalata with an Esquire" in the Uffizi, a picture noble in feeling and in execution, and one which owes a great deal to Venetian portrait-painters.

PRINCIPAL WORKS

Pordenone.

Casara.	Old Church: Frescoes, 1525.	
Colatto.	S. Salvatore: Frescoes (E.).	
Cremona.	Duomo: Frescoes; Christ before Pilate; Way to Golgotha; Nailing to Cross; Crucifixion, 1521; Madonna enthroned with Saints and Donor, 1522.	
Murano.	S. Maria d. Angeli: Annunciation (L.).	
Piacenza.	Madonna in Campagna: Frescoes and Altarpiece, 1529-31.	
Pordenone.	Duomo: Madonna of Mercy, 1515; S. Mark enthroned with Saints, 1535.	
	Municipio: SS. Gothard, Roch, and Sebastian, 1525.	
Spilimbergo.	Duomo: Assumption; Conversion of S. Paul.	

Sensigana.	Madonna and Saints.	
Torre.	Madonna and Saints.	
Treviso.	Duomo: Adoration of Magi; Frescoes, 1520.	
Venice.	Academy: Portraits; Madonna, Saints, and the Ottobono Family; Saints.	
	S. Giovanni Elemosinario: Saints.	
	S. Rocco: Saints, 1528.	

Pellegrino.

San Daniele.	Frescoes in S. Antonio.
Cividale.	S. Maria: Madonna with six Saints.
Venice.	Academy: Annunciation.

Romanino.

Bergamo.	S. Alessandro in Colonna: Assumption.
Berlin.	Madonna and Saints; Pietà.
Brescia.	Galleria Martinengo: Portrait; Christ bearing Cross; Nativity; Coronation.
	Duomo: Sacristy: Birth of Virgin; Visitation.
	S. Francesco: Madonna and Saints; Sposalizio.
Cremona.	Duomo: Frescoes.
London.	Polyptych; Portrait.
Padua.	Last Supper; Madonna and Saints.
Sato, Lago di Garda.	Duomo: Saints and Donor.
Trent.	Castello: Frescoes.
Verona.	St. Jerome. S. Giorgio in Braida: Organ shutters.

Moretto.

Bergamo.	Lochis: Holy Family; Christ bearing Cross; Donor.
Brescia.	Galleria Martinengo: Nativity and Saints; Madonna appearing to S. Francis; Saints; Madonna in Glory with Saints; Christ at Emmaus; Annunciation.
	S. Clemente: High Altar and four other Altarpieces.
	S. Francesco: Altarpiece.
	S. Giovanni Evangelista: High Altar; Third Altar.
	S. Maria in Calchera: Dead Christ and Saints; Magdalen washing Feet of Christ.
	S. Maria delle Grazie: High Altar.

SS. Nazaro and Celso: Two Altarpieces;
Sacristy: Nativity.

Seminario di S. Angelo: High Altar.

London.   Portrait of Count Sciarra Martinengo; Portrait;
Madonna and Saints; Two Angels.

Milan.   Brera: Madonna and Saints; Assumption.

Castello: Triptych; Saints.

Rome.   Vatican: Madonna enthroned with Saints.

Venice.   S. Maria della Pietà: Christ in the House of
Levi.

Verona.   S. Giorgio in Braida: Madonna and Saints.

Bartolommeo Montagna.

Bergamo.   Lochis: Madonna and Saint, 1487.

Berlin.   Madonna, Saints, and Donors, 1500.

Milan.   Brera: Madonna, Saints, and Angels.

Padua.   Scuola del Santo: Fresco; Opening of S.
Antony's Tomb.

Pavia.   Certosa: Madonna, Saints, and Angels.

Venice.   Academy: Madonna and Saints; Christ with
Saints.

Verona.   SS. Nazaro e Celso: Saints; Pietà; Frescoes,
1491-93.

Vicenza.   Holy Family; Madonna enthroned; Two
Madonnas with Saints; Three Madonnas.

Duomo: Altarpiece; Frescoes.

S. Corona: Madonna and Saints.

Monte Berico: Pietà, 1500; Fresco.

CHAPTER XXIV
PAOLO VERONESE

Paolo Veronese, though perhaps he is not to be placed on the very highest pinnacle of the Venetian School, must be classed among those few great painters who rose far above the level of most of his contemporaries and who brought in a special note and flavour of his own. His art is an independent art, and he borrows little from predecessors or contemporaries. His free and joyous temperament gave relief at a moment when the Venetian scheme of colour threatened to become too sombre, and when Sebastian del Piombo, Pordenone, Titian himself, and above all Tintoretto, were pushing chiaroscuro to extremes. Veronese discards the deepest bronzes and mulberries and crimsons and oranges, and finds his range among cream and rose and grey-greens. Titian concentrated his colours and intensified his lights, Tintoretto sacrifices colour to vivid play of light and dark, but Veronese avoids the dark; the generous light plays all through his scenes. He has no wish to secure strong effects but delights in soft, faded tints; old rose and *turquoise morte*. In his colour and his subjects he is a personification of the robust, proud, joy-loving Republic, in which, as M. Yriarte says, a man produced his works as a tree produces its fruit. We get very near him in those vast palaces and churches and villas, where his heroic figures expand in the azure air, against the white clouds, and yet he is one of the artists of the Renaissance about

74

whom we know least. Here and there, in contemporary biography, we come across a mention of him and learn that he was sociable and lively, quick at taking offence, fond of his family and anxious to do his best by them. He was, too, very generous with his work—a great contrast in this respect to Titian—and contracts with convents and confraternities show that he often only stipulated for payment for bare time. Yet he was fond of personal luxury, loved rich stuffs, horses and hounds, and, says Ridolfi, "always wore velvet breeches."

His first masters, according to Mr. Berenson, were Badile and Brusasorci, masters of Verona, but before he was twenty, he was away working on his own account. His first patron was Cardinal Gonzaga, who brought several painters from Verona to Mantua; but Mantua was no longer what it had been in the days of Isabela d'Este, and Paolo Caliari soon returned to his own town. Before he was twenty-three he had decorated Villa Porti, near Vicenza, in collaboration with Zelotti, a Veronese, portraying feasting gods and goddesses, framed in light architectural designs in monochrome. The two painters went on to other villas, mixing mortal and mythical figures in a happy, light-hearted medley.

Zelotti having received a commission at Vicenza, Paolo decided to seek his fortune in Venice. The Prior of the Convent of San Sebastiano, on the Zattere, was a Veronese, and Caliari wrote to him before arriving in Venice in 1555. Thanks to the good Prior, who played a considerable part in his destiny, he obtained a commission for a "Coronation of the Virgin and four other Saints." He first painted the sacristy, but his success was instantaneous, and many orders followed. The ceiling of the church was devoted to the history of Esther. The whole of these paintings are marvellously well preserved, and, inset in the carved and gilt framework, make a *coup d'œil* of surprising beauty. They had an immense effect. Every one was able to appreciate these joyous pictures of Venice, the loveliness of her skies, the pomp of her ceremonies, the rich Eastern stuffs and the glorious architecture of her palaces. It was an auspicious moment for a painter of Veronese's temper; the so-called Republic, now, more than ever, an oligarchy, was at the height of its fortunes, redecorating was going forward everywhere, the merchant-nobility was rich and spending magnificently, the Eastern trade was flourishing, Venice was in all her glory. The patrons Caliari came to work for, preferred the ceremonial to the imaginative treatment of sacred themes, and he does not choose the tragedies of the Bible for illustration. He paints the history of Esther, with its royal audiences, banquets, and marriage-feasts. His Christs and Maries and Martyrs are composed, courtly personages, who maintain a dignified calm under misfortune, and have very little violent feeling to show.

At the time of his arrival in Venice, Palma Vecchio was just dead, Tintoretto was absorbed by the Scuola di San Rocco, Paris Bordone was with Francis I. As rivals, Caliari had Salviati, Bonifazio, Schiavone, and Zelotti, all rendering homage to Titian who was eighty years old, but still in full vigour. Titian's opinions in matters of art were dictates, his judgment was a law. He immediately recognised Veronese's genius, which was of a kind to appeal to him, and together with Sansovino, who at this time was Director of Buildings to the Signoria, he received the young painter with an approval which ensured him a good start. Five years after Veronese's arrival he was retained to decorate the Villa Barbaro at Maser, which is a type of those patrician country-houses to which the Venetians were becoming more attached every year. Daniele Barbaro, Patriarch of Aquileia, whose magnificent portrait by Veronese is in the Pitti, was himself an artist and designed the ceiling of the Hall of the Council of Ten. Palladio, Alessandro Vittoria, and Veronese were associated to build him a dwelling worthy of a Prince of the Church. In style the villa is a total contrast to the gorgeous Venetian palaces; it is sober and simple, and well adapted to leisure and retirement. Its white stucco walls and decorations are devoid of gilding and colour, and the rooms adorned by Veronese's brush show him in quite a new light. His visit to Rome did not take place till four years later, but he has been influenced here by the feeling for the antique, and he thinks much of line and style. He leaves on one side the gorgeous brocades and gleaming satins, in which he usually delights, and his nymphs are only clothed in their own beauty. And here Veronese shows his admirable taste and discretion; his patrons, the Barbaro family, are his friends, men and women of the world, who put no restraint on his fancy, and are not prone to censure, and Veronese, with the bridle on his neck, so to speak, uses his opportunities fully, yet never exceeds the limits of good taste. He is not gross and sensual like Rubens, but proud, grave and sweet, seductive, but never suggestive or vulgar. After having placed single figures wherever he can find a nook, he assembles all the gods of Olympia at a supper in the cupola. Immortality is a beautiful young woman seated on a cloud. Mercury gazes at her, caduceus in hand; Diana caresses her great hound; Saturn, an old man, rests his head on his hand; Mars, Apollo, Venus, and a little cupid are scattered in the Empyrean, and Jupiter presides over the party. Below, a balcony rail runs round the cupola, and looking over it, an old lady, dressed in the latest fashion, points out the company to a beautiful young one and to a young man in a doublet who holds a hound in a leash. They are evidently family portraits, taken from those who looked on at the artist, and on the other side he has introduced members of his own family who were helping him. These decorations have a gaiety, an absence of pedantry, a sound and sane sympathy with the spirit of the Renaissance which tell of a happy moment when art was at its height and in touch with its environment. From about 1563 we may begin to date his great supper pictures. The Marriage of Cana (Louvre), one of his most famous works, was painted for the refectory in Sammichele, the old part of S. Giorgio Maggiore. The treaty for it is still in existence, dated June 1562. The artist asks for a year; the Prior is to furnish canvas and colours, the painter's board, and a cask of wine. The further payment of 972 ducats illustrates the prices received by the greatest artists at the height of the Renaissance: £280 for work which occupied quite eight months.

Veronese must have delighted in painting this work. Needless to say, it is not in the leastreligious. He has united in it all the most varied personages who struck his imagination. So we see a Spanish grandee, Francis I., Suleiman the Sultan, Charles V., Vittoria Colonna, and Eleanor of Austria. In the foreground, grouped round a table, are Veronese himself, playing the viol, Tintoretto accompanying him, Jacopo da Ponte seated by them, and Paolo's brother, the architect, with his hand on his hip, tossing off a full glass; and in the governor of the feast, opulent and gorgeously attired, we recognise Aretino. Under the marble columns of a Grimani or a Pesaro, he brings in all the illustrious actors of his own time and leaves us an odd and informing document. We can but accept the scene and admire the originality of its design and the freedom of its execution, its boldness and fancy, the way in which the varied incidents are brought into harmony, and the grace of the colonnade, peopled with spectators, standing out against the depth of distant sky.

The celebrated suppers, of which this is the first example, are dispersed in different galleries and some have disappeared, but from this time Veronese loved to paint these great displays, repeating some of them, but always introducing variety.

Paolo Veronese. MARRIAGE IN CANA. *Louvre.*
(*Photo, Mansell and Co.*)

In 1564 he accompanied Girolamo Grimani, procurator of St. Mark's, who was appointed ambassador to the Holy See, and for the first time saw the works of Raphael and Michelangelo and the treasures of antiquity. For a time, the sight of the antique had some effect upon his work; in his famous ceiling in the Louvre, "Jupiter destroying the Vices," the influence of Michelangelo is apparent and its large gestures are inspired by sculpture. Ridolfi says that Veronese brought home casts from Rome, and statues of Amazons and the Laocoon seem to have inspired the Jupiter. He did not go on long in this path; he does not really care for the nude—it is too simple for him. He prefers that his saints and divinities should appear in the gorgeous costumes of the day, and that his Venus and Diana and the nymphs should trail in rich brocades. But few documents are left concerning his work for the Ducal Palace up to 1576; much of it was destroyed in the great fire, but the Signoria then gave him a number of fresh commissions. The most important was the immense oval of the "Triumph of Venice," or, as it is sometimes called, the "Thanksgiving for Lepanto"; the Republic crowned by victory and surrounded by allegorical figures, Glory, Peace, Happiness, Ceres, Juno and the rest. The composition shows the utmost freedom: the fair Queen leans back, surrounded by laughing patricians, who look up from their balconies, as if they were attending a regatta on the Grand Canal. The horses of the Free Companions, the soldiers who go afar to carry out the will of the Republic, prance in a crowd of personages, each of whom represents a town or colony of her domain. Like all Veronese's creations, this will always be pre-eminently a picture of the sixteenth century, dated by a thousand details of costume, architecture, and armour. Venice, the Venice of Lepanto and the Venier, of Titian, Aretino, and Veronese himself, makes a deep impression upon us, and the artist reflects his age with sympathetic spontaneity.

Hardly a hall of the Ducal Palace but can show a canvas of Veronese or the assistants by whom he was now surrounded. From time to time he resumed the decorations of S. Sebastiano, and his incessant production betrays no trace of fatigue or languor. The martyrdom of the saint is a triumph of the beauty of the silhouette against a radiant sky. He goes back to Verona and paints the "Martyrdom of St. George." He pours light into it. The saints open a shining path, down which a flower-crowned Love flutters with the diadem and palm of victory. The whole air and expression of St. George is full of strength and that look of goodness and serenity which is the painter's nearest approach to religious feeling. Veronese was created a Chevalier of St. Mark; every one was asking for his services, but he was a stay-at-home by nature and fond of living with his family. Philip II. longed to get him to cover his great walls in the Escurial, but he very civilly declined all his invitations and sent Federigo Zucchero in his stead.

It was on account of the "Feast in the House of Levi" that in 1573 he was hauled before the tribunal of the Inquisition, and the document concerning this was only discovered a few years ago. The Signoria had never allowed any tribunal to chastise works of literature; on the contrary, Venice, though comparatively poor herself in geniuses of the mind, was the refuge of freedom of thought, and, in fact, had made a sort of compact with Niccolas V., which allowed her to set aside or suspend the decisions of the Holy Office, from which she could not quite emancipate herself. Veronese, however, was denounced by some "aggrieved person," to whom his way of treating sacred subjects seemed an outrage on religion. The members of the tribunal demanded "who the boy was with the bleeding nose?" and "why were halberdiers admitted?" Veronese replied that they were the sort of servants a rich and magnificent host would have about him. He was then asked why he had introduced the buffoon with a parrot on his hand. He replied that he really thought only Christ and His Apostles were present, but that when he had a little space over, he adorned it with imaginary figures. This defence of the vast and crowded canvas did not commend itself, and he was asked if he really thought that at the Last Supper of our Saviour it was fitting to bring in dwarfs, buffoons, drunken Germans, and other absurdities. Did he not know that in Germany and other places infested with heresy, they were in the habit of turning the things of Holy Church into ridicule, with intent to teach false doctrine to the ignorant? Paolo for his defence cited the Last Judgment, where Michelangelo had painted every figure in the nude, but the Inquisitor replied crushingly, that these were disembodied spirits, who could not be expected to wear clothing. Could Veronese uphold his picture as decent? The painter was probably not very much alarmed. He was a person of great importance in Venice, and the proceedings of the Inquisition were always jealously watched by members of the Senate, who would not have permitted any unfair interference with the liberties of those under the protection of the State. The real offence was the introduction of the German soldiers, who were peculiarly obnoxious to the Venetians; but Veronese did not care what the subject was as long as it gave him an excuse for a great *spectacle*. Brought to bay, he gave the true answer: "My Lords, I have not considered all this. I was far from wishing to picture anything disorderly. I painted the picture as it seemed best to me and as my intellect could conceive of it." It meant that Veronese painted in the way that he considered most artistic, without even remembering questions of religion, and in this he summed up his whole æsthetic creed. He was set at liberty on condition that he took out one or two of the most offending figures. The "Feast in the House of Levi" (as he named it after the trial) is the finest of all his great scenic effects. The air circulates freely through the white architecture, we breathe more deeply as we look out into the wide blue sky, and such is the sensation of expansion, that it is hardly possible to believe we are gazing at a flat wall. Titian's backgrounds are a blue horizon, a burning twilight. Veronese builds marble palaces, with rosy shadows, or columns blanched in the liquid light. His personages show little violent action. He places them in noble poses in which they can best show off their magnificent clothes, and he endows his patricians, his goddesses, his sacred persons, with a uniform air of majestic indolence.

After his "trial," Veronese proceeded more triumphantly than ever. Every prince wished to have something from his brush; the Emperor Rudolph, at Prague, showed with pride the canvases taken later by Gustavus Adolphus. The Duke of Modena, carrying on the traditions of Ferrara, added Veronese's works to the treasures of the house of Este. The last ten years of his life were given up to visiting churches on the mainland and on the little islands round Venice, all covetous to possess something by the brilliant Veronese, whose name was in every mouth. Torcello, Murano, Treviso, Castelfranco, every convent and monastery loaded him with commissions, and it is significant of the spirit of the time, that in spite of the disapproval of the Holy See, his most ardent patrons, those who delighted most in his robust, uncompromising worldliness, were to be found in the religious houses. Then, when he went to rest in the summer heats in some villa on the Brenta, he left delightful souvenirs here and there. It was on such an occasion, for the Pisani, that he painted the "Family of Darius," which was sold to England by a member of the house in 1857. The royal captives, who are throwing themselves at the feet of the conqueror, are, with Paolo's usual frank naïveté and disregard of anachronisms, dressed in full Venetian costume—all the chief personages are portraits of the Pisani family. The freedom and rapidity of execution, the completeness and finish, the charm of colour, the beauty of the figures (especially the princely ones of Alexander and Hephaestion), and its extraordinary energy, make this one of the finest of all his works. The critic, Charles Blanc, says of it, "It is absurd and dazzling."

In the "Rape of Europa," he recurred again to one of those legends of fabled beings who have outlasted dynasties and are still fresh and living. Veronese was surrounded by men like Aretino and Bembo, well versed in mythology, and with his usual zest he makes the tale an excuse for painting lovely, blooming women, rich toilets, and a delightful landscape. The wild flowers spring, and the little Loves fly to and fro against a cloud-flecked sky of the wonderful Veronese turquoise. It is the work of a man who is a true poet of colour and for whom colour represents all the emotions of joy and pleasure.

Veronese died comparatively young, of chill and fever, and all his family survived him. He lies buried in San Sebastiano. From contemporary memoirs we know that he lived and dressed splendidly. He kept immense stores of gorgeous stuffs to paint from in his studio, and drew everything from life,—the negroes covered with jewels, the bright-eyed pages, the models who, robed in velvets, brocades and satins, became queens or courtesans or saints. The pearls which bedecked them were from his own caskets. Though we know little of his private life, his work is so alive that he seems personified in it. He is saved from what might have been a prosaic or a sordid style by the delicious, ever-changing colour in which he revels; his silks and satins are less modelled by shadows than tinted by broken reflections, his embroidered and striped and arabesqued tissues are so harmoniously combined that the eye rests, wherever it falls, on something exquisite and subtle in tint. This is where his genius lies, "the decoration does not add to the interest of the drama; it replaces it"; in short, it *is* the drama itself, for his types show little selection, and his ideal of female beauty is not a very sympathetic one. His personages are cold and devoid of expression, their gestures are rather meaningless, but by means of light and air and exquisite colour he gives the poetical touch which all great art demands.

On account of their size few examples of Veronese's work are to be found in private collections, but the galleries of the different European capitals are rich in them. Numbers of paintings, too, which are by his assistants are dignified by his name, and directly after his death spurious works were freely manufactured and sold as genuine.

PRINCIPAL WORKS

Dresden.	Madonna with Cuccina Family; Adoration of Magi; Marriage of Cana.
Florence.	Pitti: Portrait of Daniele Barbaro.

	Uffizi: Martyrdom of S. Giustina; Holy Family (E.).
London.	Consecration of S. Niccolas; The Family of Darius before Alexander; Adoration of the Magi.
Maser.	Villa Barbaro: Frescoes.
Padua.	S. Giustina: Martyrdom of S. Giustina.
Paris.	Christ at Emmaus; Marriage of Cana.
Venice.	Academy: Battle of Lepanto; Feast in the House of Levi; Madonna with Saints.
	Ducal Palace: Triumph of Venice; Rape of Europa; Venice enthroned.
	S. Barnabà: Holy Family.
	S. Francesco della Vigna: Holy Family.
	S. Sebastiano: Madonna and Saints; Crucifixion; Madonna in Glory with S. Sebastian and other Saints; others in part; Frescoes; Saints and Figure of Faith; Sibyls.
Verona.	Portrait of Pasio Guadienti, 1556.
	S. Giorgio: Martyrdom of S. George.
Vicenza.	Monte Berico: Feast of St. Gregory, 1572.
Vienna.	Christ at the House of Jairus.

CHAPTER XXV
TINTORETTO

It does not seem likely that many new discoveries will be made about Tintoretto's life. It was an open and above-board one, and there is practically no time during its span that we are not able to account for, and to say where he was living and how he was occupied. The son of a dyer, a member of one of the powerful guilds of Venice, the "little dyer," *il tentoretto*, appears as an enthusiastic boy, keen to learn his chosen art. He was apprenticed to Titian and, immediately after, summarily ejected from that master's workshop, on account, it seems probable, of the independence and innovation of his style, which was of the very kind most likely to shock and puzzle Titian's courtly, settled genius. After this he painted when and where he could, pursuing his artistic studies with the headlong ardour which through life characterised his attitude towards art. Mr. Berenson thinks he may have worked in Bonifazio's studio. He formed a close friendship with Andrea Schiavone,[4] he imported casts of Michelangelo's statues, he studied the works of Titian and Palma. Over his door was written "the colour of Titian and the form of Michelangelo." All his energies were for long devoted to the effort to master that form. Colour came to him naturally, but good drawing meant more to him than it had ever done to any Venetian. Long afterwards, to repeated inquiries as to how excellence could be best ensured, he would give no other advice than the reiterated, "study drawing." He practised till the human form in every attitude held no difficulties for him. He suspended little models by strings, and drew every limb and torso he could get hold of over and over again. He was found in every place where painting was wanted, getting the builders to let him experiment upon the house-fronts. To master light and shade he constructed little cardboard houses, in which, by means of sliding shutters, lamplight and skylight effects could be arranged. It is particularly interesting to hear of this part of his education, as in the end the love of shine and shadow was the most victorious of all his inspirations.

The chief events in Tintoretto's life are art-events. For some years he frescoed the outside of houses at a nominal price, or merely for his expenses. He decorated household furniture and everything he could lay hands on. Then came a few small commissions, an altarpiece here, organ-doors there, for unimportant churches. No one in Venice talked of any one save Palma, Bonifazio, and, above all, Titian, and it was difficult enough for an outsider, who was not one of their clique, to get employment. But by the time Tintoretto was twenty-six his talent was becoming recognised; he had painted the two altarpieces for SS. Ermagora and Fortunato, and the offer he made to decorate the vast church of his parish brought him conspicuously into notice. In the first ardour of youth he completed the "Last Judgment" for the choir. From time to time, during fourteen years, he redeemed his early promises and executed the "Golden Calf" and the "Presentation of the Virgin." Within two years of his offer to the Prior, came his first great opportunity of achieving distinction. This was a commission from the Confraternity of St. Mark, and with the "Miracle of the Slave" he sprang at once to the highest place.

The picture was universally admired, and was followed by three more dealing with the patron saint. At forty he married happily a beautiful young girl, Faustina dei Vescovi, or Episcopi, as it is indifferently given, the daughter of a noble family of the mainland. Tradition has always pointed to the girl in blue in the "Golden Calf" as her portrait, while it is easy to recognise Tintoretto himself in the black-bearded giant, who helps to carry the idol. His house at this time was somewhere in the Parrocchia dell' Orto, and there, during the next fourteen years, eight children were born, of whom the two eldest, Domenico and Marietta, attained distinction in their father's profession. Another great event, which profoundly influenced his life, was the beginning of his connection in 1560 with the Scuola di San Rocco, the great confraternity which was devoted to combating the ravages of the plague and to succouring the families of its victims. His work for this lasted to the end of his life and is his most distinguished memorial.

The palace to which the Robusti family moved in 1574, and which was inhabited by his descendants so late as 1830, can still be identified in the Calle della Sensa. It is broken up into two parts, but it is evident that it was a dwelling of some importance, a good specimen of Venetian Gothic. It still bears marks of considerable decoration; the walls are sheathed in marble plaques, and the first floor has rows of Gothic windows in delicately carved frames and little balconies of fretted marble. Zanetti, in 1771, gives an etching of a magnificent bronze frieze cast from the master's design, which ran round the Grand Sala. The family must have occupied the *piano nobile* and let off the floors they did not require.

Descriptions of the life led by the painter and his family are given by Vasari, who knew him personally, and by Ridolfi, whose book was published in 1646, and who must have known his children, several of whom were still alive and proud of their father's fame. We hear of pleasant evenings spent in the little palace, of the enthusiastic love of music, Tintoretto himself and his daughter being highly gifted. Among the *habitués* were Zarlino, for twenty-five years chapel-master of St. Mark's, one of the fathers of modern music; Bassano; and Veronese, who, in spite of his love for magnificent entertainments, was often to be found in Tintoretto's pleasant home. Poor Andrea Schiavone was always welcome, and as time went on the house became the haunt of all the cultured gentlemen and *litterati* of Venice.

It is not difficult from the materials available to form a sufficiently lively idea of this Venetian citizen of the sixteenth century, as father and husband, host and painter. Ridolfi has collected a number of anecdotes, which space forbids me to use, but which are all very characteristic. We gather that he was a man of strong character, generous, sincere and simple, decided in his ways, caring little for the great world, but open-handed and hospitable under his own roof, observant of men and manners, and sometimes rather brusque in dealing with bores and offensive persons. Full of dry quiet humour and of good-natured banter of his wife's little weaknesses. A man, too, of upright conduct and free, as far as it can be ascertained, from any of those laxities and infidelities, so freely quoted of celebrated men and so easily condoned by his age. Art was Tintoretto's main preoccupation; but he seems to have been a man of strong religious bias, making a close study of the Bible, and turning naturally in his last days to those truths with which his art had made him familiar, truths which he had represented with that touch of mystic feeling which was the deepest part of his nature.

His relations with the State commenced in 1574, when his offer to present a superb painting of the Victory of Lepanto was made to and accepted by the Council of Ten. Tintoretto was rewarded by a Broker's patent, and between this and the "Paradiso," the work of his old age, he executed a number of pictures for the Signoria. The only record of any travels are confined to two journeys paid to Mantua, where he went in the 'sixties and again in 1579 to see to the hanging of paintings done for the Gonzaga, and of which the documents have been kept, though the pictures have vanished. Tintoretto's last years were saddened by the death of his beloved daughter, who had always been his constant companion. He died in 1579 after a fortnight's illness and left a will, which, together with that of his son, throws a good deal of light upon the family history.

It is not easy to select from the vast quantity of work left by Tintoretto. He is one of those painters whose whole life was passed in his native city and who can only be adequately studied in that city. Perhaps the first place in which to seek him, is the great church which was the monument of his early prime. The "Last Judgment" was probably inspired by that of Michelangelo, of which descriptions and sketches must have reached the younger master, over whom the Florentine had exercised so strong a fascination. Tintoretto's version impresses one as that of a mind boiling with thoughts and visions which he pours out upon the huge space. It depicts a terrible catastrophe, a scene of rushing destruction, of forms swept into oblivion, of others struggling to the light, of many beautiful figures and of a flood of air and light behind the rushing water,—water which makes us almost giddy as we watch it. The "Golden Calf" is a maturer production and includes some of the loveliest women Tintoretto ever painted. We see too plainly the planning, the device of concentrating interest on the idol by turning figures and pointing fingers, but nothing can be imagined more supple and queenly than the woman in blue, and the way the light falls on her head and perfectly foreshortened arm shows to what excellence Tintoretto had attained. The "Presentation" is a riper work. The drawing of the flight of steps and of the groups upon them could not be bettered. The little figure of the Virgin, prototype of the new dispensation, as she advances to meet the representative of the old, thrills with mystic feeling, yet the painter has contrived to retain the sturdy simplicity of a child. The "St. Agnes," with its contrast of light and shade, of strength made perfect in weakness, is of later date and was the commission of Cardinal Contarini.

It is interesting to realise how Tintoretto, especially in the "Presentation," has contrived, while using the traditional episodes, to infuse so strong an imaginative sense. The contrast of age and youth, the joy of the Gentiles, the starlike figure of the child surrounded by shadows, convey an emotional feeling, in harmony with the nature of the scene.

Next let us group together the miracles in the history of St. Mark. One of the qualities which strikes us most in the "Miracle of the Slave" is its strong local colour. It tells of Titian and Bonifazio and is unlike Tintoretto's later style. The colours are glowing and gem-like; carnations, orange-yellows, deep scarlet, and turquoise-blue. The crimson velvet of the judge's dress is finely relieved against a blue-green sky, and Tintoretto has kept that instinctive fire and dash which culminates at once and without effort in perfect action, "as a bird flies, or a horse gallops." It startled the quiet members of the Guild, and at the first moment they hesitated to accept it. The "Rescue of the Saracen" and the "Transportation of the Body" are more in the golden-brown manner to which he was moving, but it is in the "Finding of the Body" (Brera) that he rises to the highest emotional pitch. The colossal form of the saint, expanding with life and power as he towers in the spirit above his own lifeless clay, draws all eyes to him and seems to fill the barrel-roofed hall with ease and energy. Every part of the vault is flooded by his life-giving energy, and here Tintoretto deals with light and shade with full mastery.

As we follow Tintoretto's career, it is borne in upon us how little positive colour it takes to make a great colourist. The whole Venetian School, indeed, does not deal with what we understand as bright colour. Vivid tints are much more characteristic of the Flemish and the Florentine, or, let us say, of the painters of to-day. Strong, crude colours are to be seen on all sides in the Salon or the Royal Academy, but they are absent from the scheme of sombre splendour which has given the Venetians their title to fame. This is especially true of Tintoretto, and it becomes more so as he advances. His gamut becomes more golden-brown and mellow; the greys and browns and ivories combine in a lustrous symphony more impressive than gay tints, flooded with enveloping shadow and illumined by flashes of iridescent light. Another noticeable feature is the way in which he puts on his oil-colour, so that it bears the direct impression of the painter's hand. The Florentines had used flat tints, opaque and with every brush-mark smoothed away; but as the later Venetians covered large spaces with oil-colour, they no longer sought to dissimulate the traces of the brush, and light, distance, movement, were all conveyed by the turns and twists and swirls with which the thin oil-colour was laid on. Look at the power of touch in such a picture as the "Death of Abel"; we see this spontaneity of execution actually forming part of the emotion with which the picture is charged. The concentrated hate of the one figure, the desperate appeal of the other, the lurid note of the landscape, gain their emotion as much from the impetuous brush-work as from the more studied design. We come closest to the painter's mind in the Scuola di San Rocco. He had already been employed in the church, and there remains, darkened and ruined by damp, the series illustrative of the career of S. Roch, patron saint of sufferers from the plague. When the great Halls of Assembly were to be decorated in 1560, the confraternity asked a conclave of painters, among whom were Veronese and Andrea Schiavone, to prepare sketches for competition. When they assembled to display their designs, Tintoretto swept aside a cartoon from the ceiling of the refectory and discovered a finished picture, the "S. Roch in Glory," which still holds its place there. Neither the other artists nor the brethren seem to have approved of this unconventional proceeding, but he "hoped they would not be offended; it was the only way he knew." Partly from the displeased withdrawal of some of the rest, but partly also from the excellence of the work, the commission fell to Tintoretto, and after two years' work he was received into the order, and was assigned an annual provision of 100 ducats (£50) a year for life, being bound every year to furnish three pictures.

CHAPTER XXVI
TINTORETTO (*continued*)

The first portion of the vast building that was finished was the Refectory, but in examining the scheme, it is perhaps more convenient to leave it to its proper place, which is the climax. Before beginning, Tintoretto must have had the whole thing planned, and we cannot doubt that he was influenced by the Sixtine Chapel and recalled its plan and significance; the old dispensation typifying the new, the Old Testament history vivified by the acts of Christ. The main feature of the harmony which it is only reasonable to suppose governs the whole building, is its dedication to S. Roch, the special patron of mercy. The principal paintings of the Upper Hall are therefore concerned with acts of divine mercy and deliverance, and even the monochromes bear upon the central idea. On the roof are the three most important miracles of mercy performed on behalf of the Chosen People. The paintings on roof and walls are linked together. The "Fall of Man" at one end of the Hall, the disobedient eating, corresponds with the obedient eating of the Passover at the other, and is interdependent with the Manna in the Wilderness, the Last Supper, and the Miracle of the Loaves. The Miracles of satisfied thirst are represented by "Moses striking the Rock," Samson drinking from the jawbone and the waters of Meribah. The Baptism and other signs of the Advent of Christ and the Divine preparation, balance events in the early life of Moses. In the Refectory which opens from the Great Hall, we come to the "Crucifixion," the crowning act of mercy, surrounded by the events which immediately succeeded it, and typified immediately above in the Central Hall, by the lifting up of the Brazen Serpent. The miracles include six of refreshment and succour, two of miraculous restoration to health, and two of deliverance from danger. The whole scheme has been worked out in detail in my book on "Tintoretto."

In the working out of his great scheme, Tintoretto is impatient of hackneyed and traditional forms; he must have a reading of his own, and one which appeals to his imagination. We see that passion for movement which distinguishes his early work. "Moses striking the Rock" is a figure instinct with purpose and energy. The water bounds forth, living, life-giving, the people strain wildly to reach it. His figures are sometimes found fault with, as extravagant in gesture, but the attitudes were intended to be seen and to arrest attention from far below, and we must not forget that the painter's models were drawn from a Southern race, to whom emphasis of action is natural. Tintoretto, it may be conceded, is on certain occasions, generally when dealing with accessory figures, inclined to excess of gesture; it is the defect of his temperament, but when he has a subject that carries him away he is sincere and never violent in spirit. Titian is cold compared to him; his colour, however effective, is calculated, whereas Tintoretto's seems to permeate every object and to soak the whole composition. To quote a recent critic: "He chose to begin, if possible, with a subject charged with emotion. He then proceeded to treat it according to its nature, that is to say, he toned down and obscured the outlines of form and mapped out the subject instead in pale or sombre masses of light and shade. Under the control of this powerful scheme of chiaroscuro, the colouring of the composition was placed, but its own character, its degree of richness and sobriety, was determined by the kind of emotion belonging to the subject. To use colour in this way, not only with emotional force, but with emotional truth, is to use it to perform one of the greatest functions of art."[5]

So in the Crucifixion it is not so much the aspect of the groups, the pathos of the faces or gestures, that tells, but it is the mystery and gloom in which the whole scene is muffled, the atmosphere into which we are absorbed, the sense of livid terror conveyed by the brooding light and shadow, that makes us feel how different the rendering is from any other. In the "Christ before Pilate" the head and figure of Christ are not particularly impressive in themselves, but the brilliant light falling on the white robes and coursing down the steps supplies dignity and poetry; the slender white figure stands out like a shaft of light against the lurid and troubled background. Again, in the "Way to Golgotha" the falling evening gleam, the wild sky, the deep shadow of the ravine, throw into relief the quiet form, detached in look and feeling, as of one upborne by the spirit far above the brutal throng. Nowhere does that spiritual emotion find deeper expression than in the "Visitation." The passion of thanksgiving, the poignancy of mother-love, throb through the two women, who have been travelling towards one another, with a great secret between them, and who at length reach the haven of each other's love and knowledge. Here, too, the dying light, the waving tree, the obliteration of form, and the feeling of mystery make a deep appeal to the sensuous apprehension. We find it again and again; the great trees sway and whisper in the gathering darkness as the Virgin rides through the falling evening shadows, clasping her Babe, and in that most moving of all Tintoretto's creations, the "S. Mary of Egypt," the emotional mood of Nature's self is brought home to us. The trees that dominate the landscape are painted with a few "strokes like sabre cuts"; the landscape, given with apparent carelessness, yet conveying an indescribable sense of space and solemnity, unfolds itself under the dying day; and in solitary meditation, thrilling with ecstasy, sits that little figure, whose heart has travelled far away to commune with the Spirit, "whose dwelling is the light of setting suns."

It is not possible in a short space to touch, even in passing, on all the many scenes in these halls: the "Annunciation," with its marvellous flight of cherubs, reminding us of the flight of pigeons in the Piazza, and how often the old painter must have watched them; the "Temptation," contrasting the throbbing evil, the flesh that *must* be fed, with the calm of absolute purity; the "Massacre of the Innocents," for which the horrors of sacked towns could have supplied many a parallel,—we have not time to dwell on these, but we may notice how the artist has overcome the difficulty of seeing clearly in the dark halls, by choosing strong and varied effects of light for the most shadowed spaces, and we can picture what the halls must have been like when they first glowed from his hand, adorned with gilded fretwork and moulding, and hung with opulent draperies, with the rose-red and purple of bishops' and cardinals' robes reflected in the gleaming pavement.

Tintoretto. Scuola di San Rocco.
S. MARY OF EGYPT.
(Photo, Anderson.)

Leonardo, by one supreme example, Tintoretto, by many renderings, have made the "Last Supper" peculiarly their own in the domain of art. It shows how strongly the mystic strain entered into the man's character, that often as Tintoretto treated the subject, it never lost its interest for him, and he never failed to find a fresh point of view. In that in S. Polo, Christ offers the sacred food with a gesture of vehement generosity. Placed as the picture is, to appeal to all comers to the Mass, to afford them a welcome as they pass to the High Altar, it tells of the Bread of Life given to all mankind. Tintoretto himself, painted in the character of S. Paul, stands at one side, absorbed in meditation. We need not insist again on the emotional value of the deep colours, the rich creams and crimsons and the chiaroscuro. In his latest rendering, in S. Giorgio Maggiore, he touches his highest point in symbolical treatment. Some people are only able to see a theatrical, artificial spirit in this picture, but at least, when we consider what deep meditation Tintoretto had bestowed on his subjects, we may believe that he himself was sincere and that he let himself go over what commended itself as an entirely new rendering. "The Light shined in the Darkness, and the Darkness comprehended it not." The supernatural is entering on every side, but the feast goes on; the serving men and maids busy themselves with the dishes; the disciples are inquiring, but not agitated; none see that throng of heavenly visitants, pouring in through the blue moonlight, called to their Master's side by the supreme significance of His words. The painter has taken full advantage of the opportunity of combining the light of the cresset lamp, pouring out smoky clouds, with the struggling moonlight and the unearthly radiance, in divers, yet mingling streams which fight against the surrounding gloom. In the scene in the Scuola di S. Rocco the betrayal is the dominating incident, and in San Stefano all is peace, and the Saviour is alone with the faithful disciples.

Tintoretto. BACCHUS AND ARIADNE. *Ducal Palace, Venice.*
(*Photo, Anderson.*)

Though several of the large compositions ascribed to Tintoretto in the Ducal Palace are only partly by him, or entirely by followers and imitators, its halls are still a storehouse of his genius. There is much that is fine about the great state pieces. In the "Marriage of St. Catherine," the saint, in silken gown and long transparent veil, is an exquisite figure. Tintoretto bathes all his pageantry in golden light and air, and yet we feel that these huge official subjects, with the prosaic old Doges introduced in incongruous company, neither stimulated his imagination nor satisfied his taste. It is on the smaller canvases that he finds inspiration. He never painted anything more lovely, more perfect in design, or more gay and tender in idea, than the cycle in the Ante-Collegio. The glowing light and exquisitely graded shadows upon ivory limbs have a sensuous perfection and a refined, unselfconscious joy such as is felt in hardly any other work, except the painter's own "Milky Way" in the National Gallery. In all these four pictures the feeling for design, a branch of art in which Tintoretto was past master, is fully displayed. In the Bacchus and Ariadne all the principal lines, the eyes and gestures, converge upon the tiny ring which is the symbol of union between the goddess and her lover, between the queenly city and the Adriatic sea. Or take "Pallas driving away Mars": see how the mass into which the figures are gathered on the left adds strength to the thrust of the goddess's arm, and what steadiness is given by that short straight lance of hers, coming in among all the yielding curves. The whole four are linked together in meaning: the call to Venice to reign over the seas, her triumphant peace, with Wisdom guiding her council, and her warriors forging arms in case of need. In conjunction with these pictures are two small ones in the chapel, hardly less beautiful—St. George with St. Margaret, and SS. Andrew and Jerome. It is difficult to say whether the exultant St. George, the dignified young bishop, or the two older saints are the more sympathetic creations, or the more admirable, both in drawing and colour. The sense of space in both settings is an added charm, and every scrap of detail, the leafy boughs, the cross and crozier, is important to the composition.

There are many other striking examples, ranging all through Tintoretto's life, of his untiring imagination. In the Salute is that "Marriage of Cana," in which all the actors seem to swim in golden light. The sharp silhouettes bring out an effect of radiant sunshine with which the hall is flooded, and all the architectural lines lead our eyes towards the central figure, placed at a distance. On that long canvas in the Academy, kneel the three treasurers, pouring out their gold and bending in homage before the Madonna and Child, who sit enthroned upon a broad piazza, through the marble pillars of which a blue and distant landscape shines. Grave senators in mulberry velvet and ermine kneel before the Child, or hold counsel on Paduan affairs under the patronage of S. Giustina. The "Crucifixion" (in S. Cassiano) is another triumph of the painter's imaginative conception. The bold lines of the crosses, the ladder, and the figures detach against a glorious sky, and the presence of the moving, murmuring throng, of which, by the placing of the line of sight, the spectator is made to form a part, is conveyed by the swaying and crossing of the lances borne by the armed men who keep the ground. There is a series, too, which deals with the Magdalen. She mourns her dead in that solemn, restrained "Entombment," where the enfolding shadows frame the cross against the sad dawn, which adorns the mortuary chapel of S. Giorgio Maggiore; and the Pietà in the Brera, the long lines of which add to the impression of tender repose, has its peace broken by the passionate cry of the woman who loved much. Tintoretto's ideas are exhaustless; he can paint the same scene in a dozen different ways, and, in fact, the book of sketches lately acquired by the British Museum shows as many as thirty trials dashed off for one subject, and after all he uses one composed for something quite different. It is this habit of throwing off red-hot essays, fresh from his brain, that has led to the common but superficial judgment that Tintoretto was merely a great improvisatore, whose successes came more or less by good luck. He could, indeed, paint pictures at a pace at which many great masters could only sketch, but he had already designed and considered and rejected, doing with oil, ink, and paper what many of his contemporaries did mentally. Such achievements as the Ante-Collegio cycle, the "House of Martha and Mary," the "Marriage of Cana," the "Temptation of S. Anthony," to name only a few, show a finish and perfection and a balance of design which preclude the idea of their being lightly painted pictures. When he was actually engaged, Tintoretto let himself go with impetuous ardour, but we may feel assured he leftnothing to chance, though he had his own way of making sure of the result.

It is strange to hear people, as one does now and then, talking of the "Paradiso" as "a splendid failure." It may be granted that the subject is an impossible one for human art to realise, yet when all allowance has been made for a lamentable amount of drying and blackening, it is difficult to agree that Ruskin was all wrong in his admiration of that thronging multitude, ordered and disciplined by the tides of light and shadow, which roll in and out of the masses, resolving them into groups and single figures of almost matchless beauty and melting away into a sea of radiant ether, which tells us of the boundless space which surrounds the serried ranks of the Blessed.

Tintoretto was seventy-eight when it was allotted to him, and it was the last great effort of his mind and hand. Studies for it are preserved both at the Louvre and at Madrid, and it is evident that the painter has framed it upon the thought of Dante's mystic rose. The circles and many of the figures can be traced in the poem, and the idea of the Eternal Light streaming through the leaves of the rose dominates the composition. It is appropriate that it should have been his last great work, as it was also the greatest attempt at composition ever made by a master of the Venetian School.

There is no room here to study Tintoretto as a painter of battlepieces, though from the time he painted the "Battle of Lepanto," for the Council of Ten, he often returned to such subjects. His two series for the Gonzaga included several, and the Ducal Palace still possesses examples. The impetuosity of his style stood him in good stead, and he never fails to bring in graceful and striking figures.

His portraits are hardly equal to Titian's intellectual grasp or fine-grained colour, but they are extraordinarily characteristic. He prefers to paint men rather than women, and he painted hundreds—all the great persons of his time who lived in and visited Venice. The Venetian portrait by this time was expected to be more than a likeness and more than a problem. It was to please the taste as a picture, to interest and to satisfy criticism. Tintoretto, like Lotto, gets behind the scenes, and we see some mood, some aspect of the sitter that he hardly expected to show. His penetration is not equal to Lotto's, but he deals with his sitters with an observation which pierces below the surface.

In criticising Tintoretto, men seem often unable to discriminate between the turgid and melodramatic, and the spontaneous and temperamental. The first all must abhor, but the last is sincere and deserves to be respected. It is by his best that we must judge a man, and taking his best and undoubtedly authentic work, no one has left a larger amount which will stand the test of criticism. As an exponent of lofty and elevated central ideas, which unify all parts of his composition, Tintoretto stands with the greatest imaginative minds. The intellectual side of life was exemplified in Florentine art, but the Renaissance would have been a one-sided development if there had not arisen a body of men to whom emotion and the gift of sensuous apprehension seemed of supreme value, and at the very last there arose with him one who, to their philosophy of feeling and the mastery of their chosen medium, added the crowning glory of the imaginative idea.

PRINCIPAL WORKS

Augsburg.	Christ in the House of Martha and Mary.
Berlin.	Portraits; Madonna and Saints; Luna and the Hours; Procurator before S. Mark.
Dresden.	Lady in Black; The Rescue; Portraits.
Florence.	Pitti: Portraits of Men; Luigi Cornaro; Vincenzo Zeno.
	Uffizi: Portrait of Himself; Admiral Venier; Portrait of Old Man; Jacopo Sansovino; Portrait.
Hampton Court.	Esther before Ahasuerus; Nine Muses; Portrait of Dominican; Knight of Malta.
London.	S. George and the Dragon; Christ washing Feet of Disciples; Origin of Milky Way.
	Bridgewater House: Entombment; Portrait.
Madrid.	Battle on Land and Sea; Solomon and the Queen of Sheba; Susanna and the Elders; Finding of Moses; Esther before Ahasuerus; Judith and Holofernes.
Milan.	Brera: S. Helena, Saints and Donors; Finding of the Body of S. Mark (E.).
Paris.	Susanna and the Elders; Sketch for Paradise; Portrait of Himself.
Rome.	Capitol: Baptism; Ecce Homo; The Flagellation.
	Colonna: Adoration of the Holy Spirit; Old Man playing Spinet; Portraits.
Turin.	The Trinity.
Venice.	Academy: S. Giustina and Three Senators; Madonna with Saints and Treasurers, 1566; Portraits of Senators; Deposition; Jacopo Soranzo, 1564 (still attributed to Titian); Andrea Capello (E.); Death of Abel; Miracle of S. Mark, 1548; Adam and Eve; Resurrected Christ blessing Three Senators; Madonna and Portraits; Crucifixion; Resurrection; Presentation in Temple.
	Palazzo Ducale: Doge Mocenigo commended

to Christ by S. Mark; Doge da Ponte before the Virgin; Marriage of S. Catherine; Doge Gritti before the Virgin.

Ante-Collegio: Mercury and Three Graces; Vulcan's Forge; Bacchus and Ariadne; Pallas resisting Mars, abt. 1578.

Ante-room of Chapel: SS. George, Margaret, and Louis; SS. Andrew and Jerome.

Senato: S. Mark presenting Doge Loredano to the Virgin.

Sala Quattro Porte: Ceiling. Ante-room: Portraits; Ceiling, Doge Priuli with Justice. Passage to Council of Ten: Portraits; Nobles illumined by Holy Spirit.

Sala del Gran Consiglio: Paradise, 1590.

Sala dello Scrutino: Battle of Zara.

Palazzo Reale: Transportation of Body of S. Mark; S. Mark rescues a Shipwrecked Saracen; Philosophers.

Giovanelli Palace: Battlepiece; Portraits.

S. Cassiano: Crucifixion; Christ in Limbo; Resurrection.

S. Giorgio Maggiore: Last Supper; Gathering of Manna; Entombment (in Mortuary Chapel).

S. Maria Mater Domini: Finding of True Cross.

S. Maria dell' Orto: Last Judgment (E.); Golden Calf (E.); Presentation of Virgin (E.); Martyrdom of S. Agnes.

S. Polo: Last Supper; Assumption of Virgin.

S. Rocco: Annunciation; Pool of Bethesda; S. Roch and the Beasts; S. Roch healing the Sick; S. Roch in Campo d' Armata; S. Roch consoled by an Angel.

Scuola di S. Rocco: Lower Hall, all the paintings on wall. Staircase: Visitation. Upper Hall: all the paintings on walls and ceiling. Refectory: Crucifixion, 1565; Christ before Pilate; Ecce Homo; Way to Golgotha; Ceiling, 1560.

Salute: Marriage of Cana, 1561; Martyrdom of S. Stephen.

S. Silvestro: Baptism.

S. Stefano: Last Supper; Washing of Feet; Agony in Garden.

S. Trovaso: Temptation of S. Anthony.

Vienna.   Susanna and the Elders; Sebastian Venier; Portraits of Procurators, Senators, and Men (fifteen in all); Old Man and Boy; Portrait of Lady.

CHAPTER XXVII
BASSANO

We wonder how many of those sightseers who pass through the Ante-Collegio in the Ducal Palace, and stare for a few moments at Tintoretto's famous quartet and at Veronese's "Rape of Europa," turn to give even such fleeting attention to the long, dark canvas which hangs beside them, "Jacob's Journey into Canaan," by Jacopo da Ponte, called Bassano.

Yet from the position in which it is placed the visitor might guess that it is considered to be a gem, and it gains something in interest when we learn from Zanetti that it was ordered by Jacopo Contarini at the same time as the "Rape of Europa," as if the great connoisseur enjoyed contrasting Veronese's light, gay style with the vigorous brush of da Ponte.

If attention is arrested by the beauty of the painting, and the visitor should be inspired to seek the painter in his native city, he will be well repaid. Bassano once held an important position on the main road between Italy and Germany, but since the railroad was made across the Brenner Pass, few people ever see the little town which lies cradled on the spurs of the Italian Alps, where the gorge of Valsugana opens. It is surrounded by chestnut woods, which sweep up to the blue mountains, the wide Brenta flows through the town, and the houses cluster high on either side, and have gardens and balconies overhanging the water. The façades of many of the houses are covered with fading frescoes, relics of da Ponte's school of fresco-painters, which, though they are fast perishing, still give a wonderful effect of warmth and colour.

Jacopo da Ponte was the son and pupil of his father, Francesco, who in his day had been a pupil of the Vicentine, Bartolommeo Montagna. Francesco da Ponte's best work is to be found at Bassano, in the cathedral and the church of San Giovanni, and has many of the characteristics, such as the raised pedestal and vaulted cupola, which we have noticed that Montagna owed to the Vivarini. Francesco's son went when very young to Venice, and was there thrown at once among the artists of the lagoons, and attached himself in particular to Bonifazio. In Jacopo's earliest work, now in the Museum at Bassano, a "Flight into Egypt," Bonifazio's tuition is markedly discernible in the build of the figures and, above all, in the form of the heads. A comparison of the very peculiarly shaped head of the Virgin in this picture with that of the Venetian lady in Bonifazio's "Rich Man's Feast," in the Venetian Academy, leaves us in no doubt on this score. Jacopo's "Adulteress before Christ" and the "Three in the Fiery Furnace" have Bonifazio's manner in the architecture and the staging of the figures. Only five examples are known of this early work of da Ponte, and it is all in Bonifazio's lighter style, not unlike his "Holy Family" in the National Gallery.

The house in which the painter lived when he returned to his native town, still stands in the little Piazza Monte Vecchio, and its whole façade retains the frescoes, mouldy and decaying, with which he decorated it. The design is in four horizontal bands. First comes a frieze of children in every attitude of fun and frolic. Then follows a long range of animals—horses, oxen, and deer. Musical instruments and flowers make a border, with allegorical representations of the arts and crafts filling the spaces between the windows. The principal band is decorated with Scriptural subjects, most of which are now hardly discernible, but which represent "Samson slaying the Philistines," "The Drunkenness of Noah," "Cain and Abel," "Lot and his Daughters," and "Judith with the Head of Holofernes." Between the two last there formerly appeared a drawing of a dead child, with the motto, "Mors omnia aequat," which was removed to the Museum in 1883, in comparatively good preservation.

Jacopo da Ponte lived a busy life at Bassano, where, with the help of his four sons, who were all painters, he poured out an inexhaustible stream of works, which, it is said, were put up to auction at the neighbouring fairs, if no other market was forthcoming. From time to time he and his sons went down to Venice, and with the help of the eldest, Francesco, Bassano (as he is generally known) painted the "Siege of Padua" and five other works in the Ducal Palace. His mature style was founded mainly upon that of Titian, and it is to this second manner that he owes his fame. He makes use of fewer colours, and enhances his lights by deepening and consolidating his shadows, so that they come into strong contrast, and his technique gains a richer impasto. He has a marvellous faculty for keeping his colour pure, and his greens shine like a beetle's wing. A nature-lover in the highest degree, his painting of animals and plants evinces a mind which is steeped in the magic of outdoor life. A subject of which he was particularly fond, and which he seems to have undertaken for half the collectors of Europe, was the "Four Seasons." Here was found united everything that Bassano most loved to paint: beasts of the farmyard and countryside, agriculturists with their implements, scenes of harvest-time and vintage, rough peasants leading the plough, cutting the grass, harvesting the grain, young girls making hay, driving home the cattle, taking dinner to the reapers. When he was obliged to paint for churches he chose such subjects as the Adoration of the Shepherds, the Sacrifice of Noah, the Expulsion from the Temple, into which he could introduce animals, painting them with such vigour and such forcible colour that Titian himself is said to have had a copy hanging in his studio. He loved to paint his daughters engaged in household tasks, and perhaps placed his figures with rather too obvious a reference to light and shade, and to the sun striking full on sunburnt cheeks and buxom shoulders. A friend, not a rival, of Veronese and Tintoretto, Gianbattista Volpado, records that when he was one day discussing contemporary painters with the latter, Tintoretto exclaimed, "Ah, Jacopo, if you had my drawing and I had your colour I would defy the devil himself to enable Titian, Raphael, and the rest to make any show beside us."

Bassano was invited to take up his residence at the Court of the Emperor Rudolph, but he refused to leave his mountain city, where he died in 1592. His funeral was attended by a crowd of the poorest inhabitants, for whom his charity had been boundless.

The "Journey of Jacob," to which we have already alluded, is among his most beautiful works. The brilliant array of figures is subordinated to the charm of the landscape. The evening dusk draws all objects into its embrace. The long, low, deep-blue distance stands out against a gleam of sunset sky. The tree-trunks and light play of leafy branches, which break up the composition, are from da Ponte's own country round Bassano. The pony upon which the boy scrambles, the cows, the dog among the quiet sheep, are given with all the loving truth of the born animal-painter. It is no wonder that Teniers borrowed ideas from him, and has more than once imitated his whole design.

The "Baptism of St. Lucilla" (in the Museum at Bassano) is one of his most Titianesque creations. The personages in it are grouped upon a flight of steps, in front of a long Renaissance palace with cypresses against a sky of evening-red barred with purple clouds. The drawing and modelling of the figures are almost faultless, and the colour is dazzling. The bending figure of S. Lucilla, with the light falling on her silvery satin dress, as she kneels before the young bishop, St. Valentine, is one of the most graceful things in art, and Titian himself need not have disowned the little angels, bearing palm branches and frolicking in the stream of radiance overhead.

Bassano has a "Concert," which is interesting as a family piece. It was painted in the year in which his son Leandro's marriage took place, and is probably a bridal painting to celebrate the event. The "Magistrates in Adoration" (Vicenza) again gives a brilliant effect of light, and its stately ceremonial is founded on Tintoretto's numerous pictures of kneeling doges and procurators in fur-trimmed velvet robes.

Jacopo da Ponte. BAPTISM OF S. LUCILLA. *Bassano.*
(Photo, Alinari.)

Madonnas and saints are usually built into close-packed pyramids, but in the "Repose in Egypt," now in the Ambrosiana, Milan, his arrangement comes very close to Palma and Lotto. The beautiful Mother and Child, the attendants, above all the St. Joseph, resting, head on hand, at the Virgin's feet and gazing in rapt adoration on the Child, are examples of the true Venetian manner, while the exquisite landscape behind them, and the vigorously drawn tree under which they recline, show Bassano true to his passion for nature.

Hampton Court is rich in his pictures. "The Adoration of the Shepherds," in which the pillars rise behind the sacred group, is an exercise in the manner of Titian's Frari altarpiece. His portraits are fine and sympathetic, but hardly any of them are signed or can be dated. His own is in the Uffizi, and there is a splendid "Old Man" at Buda-Pesth. Ariosto and Tasso, Sebastian Venier, and many other distinguished men were among his sitters; most of them are in half-length with three-quarter heads. The National Gallery possesses a singularly attractive one of a young man with a sensitive, acute countenance, robed in dignified, picturesque black, relieved by an embroidered linen collar. He stands by the sort of square window, opening on a distant landscape, of which Tintoretto and Lotto so often made use, in front of which a golden vase, holding a branch of olive, catches the rays of light.

Bassano has no great power of design, and his knowledge of the nude seems to have been small, but his brushwork is facile, and his colour leaps out with a vivid beauty which obliterates other shortcomings.

PRINCIPAL WORKS

Augsburg.	Madonna and Saints.
Bassano.	Susanna and Elders (E.); Christ and Adulteress (E.); The Three Holy Children (E.); Madonna, Saints, and Donor (E.); Flight into Egypt (E.); Paradise; Baptism of S. Lucilla; Adoration of Shepherds; St. Martin and the Beggar; St. Roch recommending Donor to Virgin; St. John the Evangelist adored by a Warrior; Descent of Holy Spirit; Madonna in Glory, with Saints (L.).
	Duomo: S. Lucia in Glory; Martyrdom of S. Stephen (L.); Nativity.
	S. Giovanni: Madonna and Saints.
Bergamo.	Carrara: Portrait.
	Lochis: Portraits.
Cittadella.	Duomo: Christ at Emmaus.
Dresden.	Israelites in Desert; Moses striking Rock; Conversion of S. Paul.
Hampton Court.	Portraits; Jacob's Journey; Boaz and Ruth; Shepherds (E.); Christ in House of Pharisee; Assumption of Virgin; Men fighting Bears; Tribute Money.
London.	Portrait of Man; Christ and the Money-Changers; Good Samaritan.
Milan.	Ambrosiana: Adoration of Shepherds (E.); Annunciation to Shepherds (L.).
Munich.	Portraits; S. Jerome; Deposition.
Padua.	S. Maria in Vanzo: Entombment.
Paris.	Christ bearing Cross; Vintage (L.).
Rome.	Villa Borghese: Last Supper; The Trinity.
Venice.	Academy: Christ in Garden; A Venetian Noble; S. Elenterino blessing the Faithful.
	Ducal Palace, Ante-Collegio: Jacob's Journey.
	S. Giacomo dell' Orio: Madonna and Saints.
Vicenza.	Madonna and Saints; Madonna; St. Mark and Senators.

Vienna.	The Good Samaritan; Thomas led to the Stake; Adoration of Magi; Rich Man and Lazarus; The Lord shows Abraham the Promised Land; The Sower; A Hunt; Way to Golgotha; Noah entering the Ark; Christ and the Money-Changers; After the Flood; Saints; Adoration of Magi; Portraits; Christ bearing Cross.

Academy: Deposition; Portrait.

PART III

CHAPTER XXVIII
THE INTERIM

Many of the churches and palaces of Venice and the adjoining mainland, and almost every public and private gallery throughout Europe, contain pictures purporting to be painted by Titian, Tintoretto, Veronese, and others of that famous company. Hardly a great English house but boasts of a round dozen at least of such specimens, acquired in the days when rich Englishmen made the "grand tour" and substantiated a reputation for taste and culture by collecting works of art. These pictures resemble the genuine article in a specious yet half-hearted way. Their owners themselves are not very tenacious as to their authenticity, and the visit of an expert, or the ordeal of a public exhibition tears their pretensions to tatters. In the Academia itself the Bonifazio and Tintoretto rooms are crowded with imitations. The Ducal Palace has ceilings and panels on which an effort to reproduce the kind of compositions initiated by the great artists, which make an effort tocapture their gamut of colour and to master their scheme of chiaroscuro, copying them, in short, in everything except in their inimitable touch and fire and spirit. It would have been impossible for any men, however industrious and prolific, to have carried out all the work which passes under their names, to say nothing of that which has perished; but our surprise and curiosity diminish when we come to inquire systematically into the methods of that host of copyists which, even before the masters' death, had begun to ply its lucrative trade.

We must bear in mind that every great man was surrounded by busy and attentive satellites, helping him to finish and, indeed, often painting a large part of important commissions, witnesses of the high prices received, and alive to all the gossip as to the relative popularity of the painters and the requests and orders which reached them from all quarters. The painters' own sons were in many instances those who first traded upon their fathers' fame. From Ridolfi, Zanetti, or Boschini we learn of the many paintings executed by Carlotto Caliari and the vast numbers painted by Domenico Robusti in the style of their respective fathers. Domenico seems to have particularly affected the subject of "St. George and the Dragon," and the picture at Dresden, which passes under Tintoretto's name, is perhaps by his hand. Of Bassano's four sons, Francesco "imitated his father perfectly," conserving his warmth of tint, his relief and breadth. Zanetti enumerates a surprising number of Francesco's works, seven of them being painted for the Ducal Palace. Leandro followed more particularly his father's first manner, was a good portrait-painter, and possessed lightness and fancy. Girolamo copied and recopied the old Bassano till he even deceived connoisseurs, "how much more," says Zanetti, writing in 1771, "those of the present day, who behold them harmonised and accredited by time." No school in Venice was so beloved, or lent itself so well to the efforts of the imitators, as that of Paolo Veronese. Even at an early date it was impossible not to confound the master with the disciples; the weaker of the originals were held to be of imitators, the best imitations were assigned to the master himself. "Oh how easy it is," exclaims Zanetti again, "to make mistakes about Veronese's pictures, but I can point out sundry infallible characteristics to those who wish for light upon this doubtful path; the fineness and lightness of the brushwork, the sublime intelligence and grace, shown particularly in the form of the heads, which is never found in any of his imitators."

Few Venetians, however, followed the style of only one man; the output was probably determined and varied by the demand. Too many attractive manners existed to dazzle them, and when once they began to imitate, they were tempted on all hands. It must also be remembered that every master left behind him stacks of cartoons, sketches and suggestions, and half-finished pictures, which were eagerly seized upon, bought or stolen, and utilised to produce masterpieces masquerading under his name.

As the seventeenth century advanced the character of art and manners underwent a change. Men sought the beautiful in the novel and bizarre, and the complex was preferred to the simple. Venetian art, in all its branches, had passed from the stately and restrained to the pompous and artificial. Yet the barocco style was used by Venice in a way of its own; whimsical, contorted, and overloaded with ornament as it is, it yet compels admiration by its vigorous life and movement. The art of the sei-cento in Venice was extravagant, but it was alive. It escaped the most deadly of all faults, a cold and academic mannerism—and this at a time when the rest of Italy was given over to the inflated followers of Michelangelo and the calculated elaborations of the eclectics.

Many of the things we most love in Venice, such as the Salute, the Clock-Tower, the Dogana, the Bridge of Sighs, the Rezzonico and Pesaro Palaces, are additions of the seventeenth century. The barocco intemperance in sculpture was carried on by disciples of Bernini; and as the immediate influence of the great masters declined, painting acquired the same sort of character. The carelessness and rapidity of Tintoretto, which, in his case, proceeded from the lightning speed of his imagination and the unerring sureness of his brush, became a mechanical trick in the hands of superficial students. True art had migrated elsewhere—to the homes of Velasquez, Rubens, and Rembrandt. As art grew more pompous it became less emotional. Painters like Palma Giovine spoilt their ready, lively fancy by the vice of hurry. The nickname of "Fa Presto" was deserved by others besides Luca Giordano, and Venice was overrun by a swarm of painters whose prime standard of excellence was the ability to make haste. Grandeur of conception was forgotten; a grave, ample manner was no longer understood; superficial sentiment and bombastic size carried the day. Yet a few painters, though their forms had become redundant and exaggerated, retained something of what had been the Venetian glory—the deep and moist colour of old. It still glowed with traces of its old lustre on the canvases of Giovanni Contarini, or Tiberio Tinelli, or Pietro Liberi; and though there was a perfect fury of production, without order and without law, there can still be perceived the survival of that sense of the decorative which kept the thread of art. We discover it in the ceiling of the Church of San Pantaleone, where Gianbattista Fumiani paints the glorification of the martyred patron, and which, fantastic and extravagant as it is, with its stupendous, architectural setting, and its acutely, almost absurdly foreshortened throng, is not without a certain grandiose geniality, ample and picturesque, like the buildings of that date. In Alessandro Varotari (il Padovanino), whose "Nozze di Cana" in the Academia is a finely spaced scene, in which a charming use is made of cypresses, we seem to recognise the last ray of the Titianesque. The painting of the seventeenth century passed on towards the eighteenth, and, from ceilings and panels, rosy nymphs and Venuses smile at us, attitudinising and contorted upon their cloudy backgrounds. Lackadaisical Magdalens drop sentimental tears, and the Angel of the Annunciation capers above the head of an affected Virgin, while violent colours, intensified chiaroscuro, and black greasy impasto betray the neighbourhood of the *tenebrosi*. When, towards the end of the seventeenth century, Gregorio Lazzarini set himself to shake off these influences, he went to the opposite extreme. Although a beautiful designer, he becomes cold and flat in colour, with a coldness and insipidity, indeed, that take us by surprise, appearing in a country where the taste for luminous and brilliant tints was so strongly rooted. The student of Venetian painting, who wishes to fill up the hiatus which lies between the Golden Age and the revival of the eighteenth century, cannot do better than compare Fumiani's vault in San Pantaleone with Lazzarini's sober and earnest fresco, "The Charity of San Lorenzo Giustiniani," in San Pietro in Castello, and with Pietro Liberi's "Battle of the Dardanelles" in the Ducal Palace. In all three we have examples of the varied and accomplished yet soulless art of this period. Not many of the scenes painted for the palaces of patricians in the seventeenth century have survived. They are to be found here and there by the curious who wander into old churches and palaces with a second-hand copy of Boschini in their hands; but in the reaction from the florid which took place in the Empire period, many of them gave place to whitewash and stucco. In the Ducal Palace, side by side with the masterpieces of the Renaissance, are to be found the overcrowded canvases of Vicentino, Giovanni Contarini, Pietro Liberi, Celesti, and others like them. Some of the poor and meretricious mosaics in St. Mark's are from designs by Palma Giovine and Fumiani. Carlo Ridolfi, who was a painter himself, as well as the painter's chronicler, has an "Adoration of the Magi" in S. Giovanni Elemosinario, poor enough in invention and execution. Two pictures by obscure artists disfigure a corner of the Scuola di San Rocco. The Museo Civico has a large canvas by Vicentino, a "Coronation of a Dogaressa," which once adorned Palazzo Grimani. We hear of a school opened by Antonio Balestra, who was the master of Rosalba Carriera and Pietro Longhi, and the names of others have come down to us in numbers too numerous to be quoted. Towards the end of the seventeenth century more light and novelty sparkles in the painting of the Bellunese, Battista Ricci, and assures us that he was no mere copyist; and, as the eighteenth century opens, we become aware of the strong and daring brush of Gianbattista Piazetta. Piazetta studied the works of the Carracci for some time in Bologna, and especially those of Guercino, whose style, with its bold contrasts of light and shade, has served above all as his model. He paints very darkly, and his figures often blend with and disappear into the profound tones of his backgrounds. Charles Blanc calls him "a Venetian Caravaggio"; and he has something of the strength and even the brutality of the Bolognese. A fine decorative and imaginative example of his work is the "Madonna appearing to S. Philip Neri" in the Church of S. Fava. The erect form of the Madonna is relieved in striking chiaroscuro against the mantle, upheld by *putti*. Radiant clouds light up the background and illumine the form of the old saint, a refined and spirited figure, gazing at the vision in an ecstasy of devotion. Piazetta is a bold realist, and many of his small pictures are strong and forcible. Sebastiano Ricci, Battista's son, is described as "a fine intelligence," and attracts our notice as having forged special links with England. Hampton Court possesses a long array of his paintings. In the chapel of Chelsea Hospital the plaster semi-dome is painted by him, in oils, with very good effect. He is said to have worked in Thornhill's studio, and his influence may be suspected in the Blenheim frescoes, and even in touches in Hogarth's work.

By the eighteenth century Venice had parted with her old nobility of soul, and enjoyment had become the only aim of life. Yet Venice, among the States of Italy, alone retained her freedom. The Doge reigned supreme as in the past. Beneath the ceiling of Veronese the dreaded Three still sat in secret council. Venice was still the city of subtle poisons and dangerous mysteries, but the days were gone when she had held the balance in European affairs, and she had become, in a superlative degree, the city of pleasure. Nowhere was life more varied and entertaining, more full of grace and enchantment.

A long period of peace had rocked the Venetian people into calm security. There was, indeed, a little spasmodic fighting in Corfù, Dalmatia, and Algiers, but no real share was retained in the struggles of Europe. The whole policy of the city's life was one of self-indulgence. Holiday-makers filled her streets; the whole population lived "in piazza," laughing, gossiping, seeing and being seen. The very churches had become a rendezvous for fashionable intrigues; the convents boasted their *salons*, where nuns in low dresses, with pearls in their hair, received the advances of nobles and gallant abbés. People came to Venice to waste time; trivialities, the last scandal, sensational stories, were the only subjects worth discussing. In an age of parodies and practical jokes, the more absurd any one could be, the more silly or witty stories he could tell, the more assured was his success in the joyous, frivolous circle, full of fun and laughter. The Carnival lasted for six months of the year, and was the occasion for masques and licence of every description. In the hot weather, the gay descendants of the Contarini, the Loredan, the Pisani, and other grand old houses, migrated to villas along the Brenta, where by day and night the same reckless, irresponsible life went gaily on. The power of such courtesans as Titian and Paris Bordone had painted was waning. Their place was adequately supplied by the easy dames of society, no longer secluded, proud and tranquil, but "stirred by the wild blood of youth and stooping to the frolic." "They are but faces and smiles, teasing and trumpery," says one of their critics, yet they are declared to be wideawake, natural and charming, making the most of their smattering of letters. Love was the great game; every woman had lovers, every married woman openly flaunted her *cicisbeo* or *cavaliere servente*.

The older portion of the middle class was still moderate and temperate, contented to live in the old fashion, eschewing all interest in politics, with which it was dangerous for the ordinary individual to meddle; but the new leaven was creeping through every level of society. The sons and daughters of the *bourgeoisie* tried to rise in the social scale by aping the pleasant vices of the aristocracy. They deserted the shop and the counting-house to play cards and strut upon the piazza. They mimicked the fine gentleman and the gentildonna, and made fashionable love and carried on intrigues. The spirit of the whole people had lost its elevation; there were no more proud patricians, full of noble ambitions and devoted zeal of public service; it was hardly possible to get a sufficient number of persons to carry on public business. It is a contemptible indictment enough; yet among all this degenerate life, we come upon something more real as we turn to the artists. They were very much alive. In music, in literature, and in painting, new and graceful forms of art were emerging. Painting was not the grand art of other days; it might be small and trivial, but there grew up a real little Renaissance of the eighteenth century, full of originality and fire, and showing a reaction from the pompous and banale style of the imitators.

The influence of the "lady" was becoming increasingly felt by society. Confidential little boudoirs, small and cosy apartments were the mode, and needed decorating as well as vast salas. The dainty luxury of gilt furniture, designed by Andrea Brustolon and upholstered in delicate silks, was matched by small, attractive works of art. Venice had lost her Eastern trade, and as the East faded out of her scheme of life, the West, to which she now turned, was bringing her a different form of art. The great reception rooms were still suited by the grandiose compositions of Ricci, Piazetta, and Pittoni, but another genre of charming creations smiled from the brocaded alcoves and more intimate suites of rooms.

It is impossible to name more than a fraction of these artists of the eighteenth century. There is Amigoni, admirable as a portrait-painter; Pittoni, one of the ablest figure-painters of the day; Luca Carlevaris, the forerunner of Canale; Pellegrini, whose decorations in this country are mentioned by Horace Walpole and of which the most important are preserved in the cupola and spandrils of the Grand Hall at Castle Howard. Their work is still to be found in many a Venetian church or North Italian gallery. Some of it is almost fine, though too often vitiated by the affected, exaggerated spirit of their day. When originality asserts itself more decidedly, Rosalba Carriera stands out as an artist who acquired great popularity. In 1700, when she was a young woman of twenty-four, she was already a great favourite with the public. She began life as a lace-maker, but when trade was bad, Jean Stève, a Frenchman, taught her to paint miniatures. She imparted a wonderfully delicate feeling to her art, and, passing on to pastel, she brought to this branch of portraiture a brilliancy and freshness which it had not known before. Rosalba has perhaps preserved for us better than any one else, those women of Venice who floated so lightly on the dancing waves of that sparkling stream. There they are: La Cornaro; La Maria Labia, who was surrounded by French lovers, "very courteous and very beautiful"; La Zenobio and La Pisani; La Foscari, with her black plumes; La Mocenigo, "the lady with the pearls." She has pinned them all to the canvas; lovely, frail, light-hearted butterflies, with velvet neck-ribbons round their snowy throats and coquettish patches on their delicate skin and bouquets of flowers in their high-dressed hair and sheeny bodices. They look at us with arch eyes and smile with melting mouths, more frivolous than depraved; sweet, ephemeral, irresponsible in every relation of life. Older men and women there are, too, when those artificial years have produced a succession of rather dull, sodden personages, kindly, inoffensive, but stupid, and still trifling heavily with the world.

Of Rosalba we have another picture to compare with those of her sitters. She and the other artists of her circle lived the merry, busy life of the worker, and found in their art the antidote to the evil living and the dissipation of the gay world which provided sitters and patrons. Rosalba's *milieu* is a type of others of its class. She lives with her mother and sisters, an honest, cheerful, industrious existence. They are fond of old friends and old books, and indulge in music and simple pleasures. Her sisters help Rosalba by preparing the groundwork of her paintings. She pays visits, and writes rhymes, and plays on the harpsichord. She receives great men without much ceremony, and the Elector Palatine, the Duke of Mecklenburg, Frederick, King of Norway, and Maximilian, King of Bavaria, come to her to order miniatures of their reigning beauties. Then she goes off to Paris where she has plenty of commissions, and the frequently occurring names of English patrons in her fragmentary diaries, tell how much her work was admired by English travellers. She did more than anybody else to promote the fashion for pastels, and her delightful art may be seen at its best in the pastel room of the Dresden Gallery.

Henrietta, Countess of Pomfret, has left us a charming description of a party of English travellers, which included Horace Walpole, arriving in Venice in 1741, strolling about in mask and *bauta*, and visiting the famous pastellist in her studio. It is in such guise that Rosalba has painted Walpole, and has left one of the most interesting examples of her art.

SOME EXAMPLES

Francesco da Ponte.

Venice.   Ducal Palace: Sala del Maggior Consiglio. Four pictures on ceiling (second from the four corners of the sala). On left as you face the Paradiso: 1. Pope Alexander III. giving the Stocco, or Sword, to the Doge as he enters a Galley to command the Army against Ferrara; 2. Victory against the Milanese; 3. Victory against Imperial Troops at Cadore; 4. Victory under Carmagnola, over Visconti. These four are all very rich in colour.

Chiesetta: Circumcision; Way to Calvary.

Sala dell' Scrutino: Padua taken by Night from the Carraresi.

Leandro da Ponte.

Venice.   Sala del Maggior Consiglio: The Patriarch giving a Blessed Candle to the Doge.

Sala of Council of Ten: Meeting of Alexander III. and Doge Ziani. A fine decorative picture, running the whole of one side of the sala.

Sala of Archeological Museum: Virgin in Glory, with the Avogadori Family.

Palma Giovine.

Dresden.	Presentation of the Virgin.
Florence.	Uffizi: S. Margaret.
Munich.	Deposition; Nativity; Ecce Homo; Flagellation.
Venice.	Academy: Scenes from the Apocalypse; S. Francis.
	Ducal Palace: The Last Judgment.
Vienna.	Cain and Abel; Daughter of Herodias; Pietà; Immaculate Conception.

Il Padovanino.

Florence.	Uffizi: Lucretia.	
London.	Cornelia and her Children.	
Paris.	Venus and Cupid.	
Rome.	Villa Borghese: Toilet of Minerva.	
Venice.	Academy: The Marriage of Cana; Madonna in Glory; Vanity, Orpheus, and Eurydice; Rape of Proserpine; Virgin in Glory.	
Verona.	Man and Woman playing Chess; Triumph of Bacchus.	
Vienna.	Woman taken in Adultery; Holy Family.	

Pietro Liberi.

Venice.	Ducal Palace: Battle of the Dardanelles.

Andrea Vicentino.

Venice.	Museo Civico: The Marriage of a Dogaressa.

G. A. Fumiani.

Venice.	San Pantaleone: Ceiling.
	Church of the Carità: Christ disputing with the Doctors.

A. Balestra.

Verona.	S. Tomaso: Annunciation.

G. Lazzarini.

Venice.	S. Pietro in Castello.
	The Charity of S. Lorenzo Giustiniani.

Sebastiano Ricci.

Venice.	S. Rocco: The Glorification of the Cross.
	Gesuati: Pope Pius V. and Saints.
London.	Royal Hospital, Chelsea: Half-dome.

G. B. Pittoni.

Vicenza.	The Bath of Diana.

G. B. Piazetta.

Venice.	Chiesa della Fava: Madonna and S. Philip Neri.
	Academy: Crucifixion; The Fortune-Teller.

Rosalba Carriera.

Venice.	Academy: pastels.
Dresden.	Pastels.

CHAPTER XXIX

TIEPOLO

We have already noted that to establish the significance of any period in art, it is necessary that the tendencies should unite and combine in some culminating spirits who rise triumphant over their contemporaries and soar above the age in which they live. Such a genius stands out above the eighteenth century crowd, and is not only of his century, but of every time. For two hundred years Tiepolo has been stigmatised as extravagant, mannered, as just equal to painting cupids, nymphs, and parroquets. In the last century he experienced the effect of the profound discredit into which the whole of eighteenth-century art had fallen. In France, David had obliterated Watteau; and the reputation of Pompeo Battoni, a sort of Italian David, effaced Tiepolo and his contemporaries. When the delegates of the French Republic inspected Italian churches and palaces, and decided what works of art should be sent to the Louvre, they singled out the Bolognese, the Guercinos and Guidos, the Carracci, even Pompeo Battoni and other such forgotten masters, a Gatti, a Nevelone, a Badalocchio; but to the lasting regret of their descendants, they disdained to annex a single one of the great paintings of the Venetian, Gianbattista Tiepolo.

Eastlake only vouchsafes him one line as "an artist of fantastic imagination." Most of the nineteenth-century critics do not even mention him. Burckhardt dismisses him with a grudging line of praise, Blanc is equally disparaging, and for Taine he is a mere mannerist, yet his influence has been felt far beyond his lifetime; only now is he coming into his own, and it is recognised that the *plein-air* artist, the luminarist, the impressionist, owe no small share of their knowledge to his inspiration.

The name of Tiepolo brings before us a whole string of illustrious personages—doges and senators, magnificent procurators and great captains—but we have nothing to prove that the artist belonged to a decayed branch of the famous patrician house. Born in Castello, the people's quarter of Venice, he studied in early youth with that good draughtsman, Lazzarini. At twenty-three he married the sister of Francesco Guardi; Guardi, who comes between Longhi and Canale and who is a better painter than either. Tiepolo appeared at a fortunate moment. The demand for a facile, joyous genius was at its height. The life of the aristocracy on the lagoons was every year growing more gay, more abandoned to capricious inclination, to light loves and absurd amusements. And the art which reflected this life was called upon to give gaiety rather than thought, costume rather than character. Yet if the Venetian art had lost all connection with the grave magnificence of the past, it had kept aloof from the academic coldness which was in fashion beyond the lagoons, so that though theatrical, it was with a certain natural absurdity. The age had become romantic; the Arcadian convention was in full force, Nature herself was pressed into the service of idle, sentimental men and women. The country was pictured as a place of delight, where the sun always shone and the peasants passed their time singing madrigals and indulging in rural pleasures. The public, however, had begun to look for beauty; the traditions which had formed round the decorative schools were giving way to the appreciation of original work. Tiepolo, sincere and spontaneous even when he is sacrificing truth to caprice, struck the taste of the Venetians, and without emancipating himself from the tendencies of the time, contrives to introduce a fresh accent. All round him was a weak and self-indulgent world, but within himself he possessed a fund of buoyant and inexhaustible energy. He evokes a throng of personages on the ceilings of the churches and palaces confided to his fancy. His creations range from mythology to religion, from the sublime to the grotesque. All Olympia appears upon his ample and luminous spaces. It is not to the cold, austere Lazzarini, or to the clashing chiaroscuro of Piazetta, or the imaginative spirit of Battista Ricci, though he was touched by each of them, that we must turn for Tiepolo's derivation. Long before his time, the kind of decoration of ceilings which we are apt to call Tiepolesque; the foreshortened architecture, the columns and cornices, the figures peopling the edifices, or reclining upon clouds, had been used by an increasing throng of painters. The style arose, indeed, in the quattrocento; Mantegna, the Umbrians, and even Michelangelo had used it, though in a far more sober way than later generations. Correggio and the Venetians had perfected the idea, which the artists of the seventeenth century seized upon and carried to the most intemperate excess. But Tiepolo rose above them all; he abandoned the heavy, exaggerated, contorted designs, which by this time defied all laws of equilibrium, and we must go back further than his immediate predecessors for his origins. His claim to stand with Tintoretto or Veronese may be contested, but he is nearest to these, and no doubt Veronese is the artist he studied with the greatest fervour. Without copying, he seems to have a natural affinity of spirit with Veronese and assimilates the ample arrangement of his groups, the grace of his architecture, and his decorative feeling for colour. Zanetti, who was one of Tiepolo's dearest friends, writes: "No painter of our time could so well recall the bright and happy creations of Veronese." The difference between them is more one of period than of temperament. Paolo Veronese represented the opulence of a rich, strong society, full of noble life, while Tiepolo's lot was cast among effeminate men and frivolous women, and full of the modern spirit himself, he adapts his genius to his time and devotes himself to satisfy the theatrical, sentimental vein of the Venice of the decadence. Full of enthusiasm for his work, he was ready to respond to any call. He went to and fro between Venice and the villas along the mainland and to the neighbouring towns. Then coveting wider fields, he travelled to Milan and Genoa, where his frescoes still gleam in the palaces of the Dugnani, the Archinto, and the Clerici. At Würzburg in Bavaria he achieved a magnificent series of decorations for the palace of the Prince-Archbishop. Then coming back to Italy, he painted altarpieces, portraits, pictures for his friends, and a fresh multitude of allegorical and mythological frescoes in palaces and villas. His charming villa at Zianigo is frescoed from top to bottom by himself and his sons, and has amusing examples of contemporary dress and manners.

When the Academy was instituted in 1755, Tiepolo was appointed its first director, but the sort of employment it provided was not suited to his impetuous spirit, and in 1762 he threw up the post and went off to Spain with his two sons. There he received a splendid welcome and was loaded with commissions, the only dissentient voice being that of Raphael Mengs, who, obsessed by the taste for the classic and the antique, was fiercely opposed to the Venetian's art. Tiepolo died suddenly in Madrid in 1770, pencil in hand. Though he was past seventy, the frescoes he has left there show that his hand was as firm and his eye as sure as ever.

His frescoes have, as we have said, that frankly theatrical flavour which corresponds exactly to the taste of the time. Such works as the "Transportation of the Holy House of Loretto" in the Church of the Scalzi in Venice, or the "Triumph of Faith" in that of the Pietà, the "Triumph of Hercules" in Palazzo Canossa in Verona, or the decorations in the magnificent villa of the Pisani at Strà, are extravagant and fantastic, yet have the impressive quality of genius. These last, which have for subject the glorification of the Pisani, are full of portraits. The patrician sons and daughters appear, surrounded by Abundance, War, and Wisdom. A woman holding a sceptre symbolises Europe. All round are grouped flags and dragons, "nations grappling in the airy blue," bands of Red Indians in their war-paint and happy couples making love. The idea of the history, the wealth, the supreme dignity of the House is paramount, and over all appears Fame, bearing the noble name into immortality. In Palazzo Clerici at Milan a rich and prodigal committee gave the painter a free hand, and on the ceiling of a vast hall the Sun in a chariot, with four horses harnessed abreast, rises to the meridian, flooding the world with light. Venus and Saturn attend him, and his advent is heralded by Mercury. A symbolical figure of the earth joys at his coming, and a concourse of naiads, nymphs, and dolphins wait upon his footsteps. In the school of the Carmine in Venice Tiepolo has left one of his grandest displays. The haughty Queen of Heaven, who is his ideal of the Virgin, bears the Child lightly on her arm, and, standing enthroned upon the rolling clouds, hardly deigns to acknowledge the homage of the prostrate saint, on whom an attendant angel is bestowing her scapulary. The most charming *amoretti* are disporting in all directions, flinging themselves from on high in delicious *abandon*, alternating with lovely groups of the cardinal virtues. At Villa Valmarana near Vicenza, after revelling among the gods, he comes to earth and delights in painting lovely ladies with almond eyes and carnation cheeks, attended by their cavaliers, seated in balconies, looking on at a play, or dancing minuets, and carnival scenes with masques and dominoes and *fêtes champêtres*, which give us a picture of the fashions and manners of the day. He brings in groups of Chinese in oriental dress, and then he condescends to paint country girls and their rustic swains, in the style of Phyllis and Corydon.

Sometimes he becomes graver and more solid. He abandons the airy fancies scattered in cloud-land. The story of Esther in Palazzo Dugnano affords an opportunity for introducing magnificent architecture, warriors in armour, and stately dames in satin and brocades. He touches his highest in the decorations of Palazzo Labia, where Antony and Cleopatra, seated at their banquet, surrounded by pomp and revelry, regard one another silently, with looks of sombre passion. Four exquisite panels have lately been acquired by the Brera Gallery, representing the loves of Rinaldo and Armida, and are a feast of gay, delicate colour, with fascinating backgrounds of Italian gardens. The throne-room of the palace at Madrid has the same order of compositions—Æneas conducted by Venus from Time to Immortality, and other deifications of Spanish royalty.

Tiepolo. ANTONY AND CLEOPATRA. *Palazzo Labia, Venice.*

Now and then Tiepolo is possessed by a tragic mood. In the Church of San Alvise he has left a "Way to Calvary," a "Flagellation," and a "Crowning of Thorns," which are intensely dramatic, and which show strong feeling. Particularly striking is the contrast between the refined and sensitive type of his Christ and the realistic and even brutal study of the two despairing malefactors—one a common ruffian, the other an aged offender of a higher class. His altarpiece at Este, representing S. Tecla staying the plague, is painted with a real insight into disaster and agony, and S. Tecla is a pathetic and beautiful figure. Sometimes in his easel-pictures he paints a Head of Christ, a S. Anthony, or a Crucifixion, but he always returns before long to the ample spaces and fantastic subjects which his soul loved.

Tiepolo is a singular contradiction. His art suggests a strong being, held captive by butterflies. Sometimes he is joyous and limpid, sometimes turbulent and strong, but he has always sincerity, force, and life. A great space serves to exhilarate him, and he asks nothing better than to cover it with angels and goddesses, white limbs among the clouds, sea-horses ridden by Tritons, patrician warriors in Roman armour, balustrades and columns and *amoretti*. He does not even need to pounce his design, but puts in all sorts of improvised modifications with a sure hand. The vastness of his frescoes, the daring poses of his countless figures, and the freedom of his line speak eloquently of the mastery to which his hand had attained. He revels, above all, in effects of light—"all the light of the sky, and all the light of the sea; all the light of Venice ... in which he swims as in a bath. He paints not ideas, scarcely even forms, but light. His ceilings are radiant, like the sky of birds; his poems seem to be written in the clouds. Light is fairer than all things, and Tiepolo knows all the tricks and triumphs of light."[6]

Nearly all his compositions have a serene and limpid horizon, with the figures approaching it painted in clear, silvery hues, airy and diaphanous, while the forms below are more muscular, the flesh tints are deeper, and the whole of the foreground is often enveloped in shadow. Veronese had lit up the shadows, which, under his contemporaries, were growing gloomy. Tiepolo carries his art further on the same lines. He makes his figures more graceful, his draperies more vaporous, and illumines his clouds with radiance. His faded blue and rose, his golden-greys, and pearly whites and pastel tints are not so much solid colours as caprices of light. We have remarked already that with Veronese the accessories of gleaming satins and rich brocades serve to obscure the persons. In many of Tiepolo's scenes the figures are lost in a flutter of drapery, subject and action melt away, and we are only conscious of soft harmonies of delicious colour, as ethereal as the hues of spring flowers in woodland ways and joyous meadows. With these delicious, audacious fancies, put on with a nervous hand, we forget the age of profound and ardent passion, we escape from that of pompous solemnity and studied grace, and we breathe an atmosphere of irresponsible and capricious pleasure. In this last word of her great masters Venice keeps what her temperament loved—sensuous colour and emotional chiaroscuro, used to accentuate an art adapted to a city of pleasure.

The excellence of the old masters' drawings is a perpetual revelation. Even second-class men are almost invariably fine draughtsmen, proving that drawing was looked upon as something over which it was necessary for even the meanest to have entire mastery. Tiepolo's drawings, preserved in Venice and in various museums, are as beautiful as can be wished; perfect in execution and vivid in feeling. In Venice are twenty or thirty sheets in red carbon, of flights of angels, and of draperies studied in every variety of fold.

Poor work of his school is often ascribed to his sons, but the superb "Stations of the Cross," in the Frari, which were etched by Domenico, and published as his own in his lifetime, are almost equal to the father's work. Tiepolo had many immediate followers and imitators. The colossal roof-painting of Fabio Canal in the Church of SS. Apostoli, Venice, may be pointed out as an example of one of these. But he is full of the tendencies of modern art. Mr. Berenson, writing of him, says he sometimes seems more the first than the last of a line, and notices how he influenced many French artists of recent times, though none seem quite to have caught the secret of his light intensity and his exquisite caprice.

PRINCIPAL WORKS

Aranjuez.	Royal Palace: Frescoes; Altarpiece.
	Orangery: Frescoes.
Bergamo.	Cappella Colleoni: Scenes from the Life of the Baptist.
Berlin.	Martyrdom of S. Agatha; S. Dominia and the Rosary.
London.	Sketches; Deposition.
Madrid.	Escurial; Ceilings.
Milan.	Palazzi Clerici, Archinto, and Dugnano: Frescoes.
	Brera: Loves of Rinaldo and Armida.
Paris.	Christ at Emmaus.
Strà.	Villa Pisani: Ceiling.
Venice.	Academy: S. Joseph, the Child, and Saints; S. Helena finding the Cross.
	Palazzo Ducale: Sala di Quattro Porte: Neptune and Venice.
	Palazzo Labia: Frescoes; Antony and Cleopatra.
	Palazzo Rezzonico: Two Ceilings.
	S. Alvise: Flagellation; Way to Golgotha.
	SS. Apostoli: Communion of S. Lucy.
	S. Fava: The Virgin and her Parents.
	Gesuati: Ceiling; Altarpiece.
	S. Maria della Pietà: Triumph of Faith.
	S. Paolo: Stations of the Cross.
	Scalzi: Transportation of the Holy House of Loretto.
	Scuola del Carmine: Ceiling.
Verona.	Palazzo Canossa: Triumph of Hercules.
Vicenza.	Museo Entrance Hall: Immaculate Conception.
	Villa Valmarana: Frescoes; Subjects from

Homer, Virgil, Ariosto, and Tasso; Masks and Oriental Scenes.

Würzburg.   Palace of the Archbishop: Ceilings; Fêtes Galantes; Assumption; Fall of Rebel Angels.

CHAPTER XXX
PIETRO LONGHI

We have here a master who is peculiarly the Venetian of the eighteenth century, a genre-painter whose charm it is not easy to surpass, yet one who did not at the outset find his true vocation. Longhi's first undertakings, specimens of which exist in certain palaces in Venice, were elaborate frescoes, showing the baneful influence of the Bolognese School, in which he studied for a time under Giuseppe Crispi. He attempts to place the deities of Olympus on his ceilings in emulation of Tiepolo, but his Juno is heavy and common, and the Titans at her feet appear as a swarm of sprawling, ill-drawn nudities. He shows no faculty for this kind of work, but he was thirty-two before he began to paint those small easel-pictures which in his own dainty style illustrate the "Vanity Fair" of his period, and in which the eighteenth century lives for us again.

His earliest training was in the goldsmith's art, and he has left many drawings of plate, exquisite in their sense of graceful curve and their unerring precision of line. It was a moment when such things acquired a flawless purity of outline, and Longhi recognised their beauty with all the sensitive perception of the artist and the practised workman. His studies of draperies, gestures, and hands are also extraordinarily careful, and he seems besides to have an intimate acquaintance with all the elegant dissipation and languid excesses of a dying order. We feel that he has himself been at home in the masquerade, has accompanied the lady to the fortune-teller, and, leaning over her graceful shoulder, has listened to the soothsayer's murmurs. He has attended balls and routs, danced minuets, and gossiped over tiny cups of China tea. He is the last chronicler of the Venetian feasts, and with him ends that long series that began with Giorgione's concert and which developed and passed through suppers at Cana and banquets at the houses of Levi and the Pharisee. We are no longer confronted with the sumptuosity of Bonifazio and Veronese; the immense tables covered with gold and silver plate, the long lines of guests robed in splendid brocades, the stream of servants bearing huge salvers, or the bands of musicians, nor are there any more alfresco concerts, with nymphs and bacchantes. Instead there are masques, the life of the Ridotto or gaming-house, routs and intrigues in dainty boudoirs, and surreptitious love-making in that city of eternal carnival where the *bauta* was almost a national costume. Longhi holds that post which in French art is filled by Watteau, Fragonard, and Lancret, the painters of *fêtes galantes*, and though he cannot be placed on an equal footing with those masters, he is representative and significant enough. On his canvases are preserved for us the mysteries of the toilet, over which ladies and young men of fashion dawdled through the morning, the drinking of chocolate in *négligé*, the momentous instants spent in choosing headgear and fixing patches, the towers of hair built by the modish coiffeur—children trooping in, in hoops and uniforms, to kiss their mother's hand, the fine gentleman choosing a waistcoat and ogling the pretty embroideress, the pert young maidservant slipping a billet-doux into a beauty's hand under her husband's nose, the old beau toying with a fan, or the discreet abbé taking snuff over the morning gazette. The grand ladies of Longhi's day pay visits in hoop and farthingale, the beaux make "a leg," and the lacqueys hand chocolate. The beautiful Venetians and their gallants swim through the gavotte or gamble in the Ridotto, or they hasten to assignations, disguised in wide *bauti* and carrying preposterous muffs. The Correr Museum contains a number of his paintings and also his book of original sketches. One of the most entertaining of his canvases represents a visit of patricians to a nuns' parlour. The nuns and their pupils lend an attentive ear to the whispers of the world. Their dresses are trimmed with *point de Venise*, and a little theatre is visible in the background. This and the "Sala del Ridotto" which hangs near, are marked by a free, bold handling, a richness of colouring, and more animation than is usual in his genre-pictures. He has not preserved the lovely, indeterminate colour or the impressionist touch which was the natural inheritance of

Watteau or Tiepolo. His backgrounds are dark and heavy, and he makes too free a use of body colour; but his attitude is one of close observation—he enjoys depicting the life around him, and we suspect that he sees in it the most perfect form of social intercourse imaginable. Longhi is sometimes called the Goldoni of painting, and he certainly more nearly resembles the genial, humorous playwright than he does Hogarth, to whom he has also been compared. Yet his execution and technique are a little like Hogarth's, and it is possible that he was influenced by the elder and stronger master, who entered on his triumphant career as a satirical painter of society about 1734. This was just the time when Longhi abandoned his unlucky decorative style, and it is quite possible that he may have met with engravings of the "Marriage à la mode," and was stimulated by them to the study of eighteenth-century manners, though his own temperament is far removed from Hogarth's moral force and grim satire. His serene, painstaking observation is never distracted by grossness and violence. The Venetians of his day may have been—undoubtedly were—effeminate, licentious, and decadent, but they were kind and gracious, of refined manners, well-bred, genial and intelligent, and so Longhi has transcribed them. In the time which followed, ceilings were covered by Boucher, pastels by Latour were in demand, the scholars of David painted classical scenes, and Pietro Longhi was forgotten. Antonio Francesco Correr bought five hundred of his drawings from his son, Alessandro, but his works were ignored and dispersed. The classic and romantic fashions passed, but it was only in 1850 that the brothers de Goncourt, writing on art, revived consideration for the painter of a bygone generation. Many of his works are in private collections, especially in England, but few are in public galleries. The National Gallery is fortunate in possessing several excellent examples.

Pietro Longhi.   VISIT TO THE FORTUNE-TELLER.   *London.*
(Photo, Hanfstängl.)

PRINCIPAL WORKS

Bergamo.	Lochis: At the Gaming Table; Taking Coffee.
	Baglioni: The Festival of the Padrona.
Dresden.	Portrait of a Lady.
Hampton Court.	Three genre-pictures.
London.	Visit to a Circus; Visit to a Fortune-Teller; Portrait.
	Mond Collection: Card party; Portrait.
Venice.	Academy: Six genre-paintings.
	Correr Museum: Eleven paintings of Venetian life; Portrait of Goldoni.
	Palazzo Grassi: Frescoes; Scenes of fashionable life.
	Quirini-Stampalia: Eight paintings; Portraits.

CHAPTER XXXI
CANALE

While Piazetta and Tiepolo were proving themselves the inheritors of the great school of decorators, Venice herself was finding her chroniclers, and a school of landscape arose, of which Canale was the foremost member. Giovanni Antonio Canale was born in Venice in 1697, the same year as Tiepolo. His father earned his living at the profession, lucrative enough just then, of scene-painting, and Antonio learned to handle his brush, working at his side. In 1719 he went off to seek his fortune in Rome, and though he was obliged to help out his resources by his early trade, he was most concerned in the study of architecture, ancient and modern. Rome spoke to him through the eye, by the picturesque masses of stonework, the warm harmonious tones of classic remains and the effects of light upon them. He painted almost entirely out-of-doors, and has left many examples drawn from the ruins. His success in Rome was not remarkable, and he was still a very young man when he retraced his steps. On regaining his native town, he realised for the first time the beauty of its canals and palaces, and he never again wavered in his allegiance.

Two rivals were already in the field, Luca Carlevaris, whose works were freely bought by the rich Venetians, and Marco Ricci, the figures in whose views of Venice were often touched in by his uncle, Sebastiano; but Canale's growing fame soon dethroned them, "i cacciati del nido," as he said, using Dante's expression. In a generation full of caprice, delighting in sensational developments, Canale was methodical to a fault, and worked steadily, calmly producing every detail of Venetian landscape with untiring application and almost monotonous tranquillity. He lived in the midst of a band of painters who adored travel. Sebastiano Ricci was always on the move; Tiepolo spent much of his time in other cities and countries, and passed the last years of his life in Spain; Pietro Rotari was attached to the Court of St. Petersburg; Belotto, Canale's nephew, settled in Bohemia; but Canale remained at home, and, except for two short visits paid to England, contented himself with trips to Padua and Verona.

Early in life Canale entered into relations with Joseph Smith, the British Consul in Venice, a connoisseur who had not only formed a fine collection of pictures, but had a gallery from which he was very ready to sell to travellers. He bought of the young Venetian at a very low price, and contrived, unfairly enough, to acquire the right to all his work for a certain period of time, with the object of sending it, at a good profit, to London. For a time Canale's luminous views were bought by the English under these auspices, but the artist, presently discovering that he was making a bad bargain, came over to England, where he met with an encouraging reception, especially at Windsor Castle and from the Duke of Richmond. Canale spent two years in England and painted on the Thames and at Cambridge, but he could not stand the English climate and fled from the damp and fogs to his own lagoons.

To describe his paintings is to describe Venice at every hour of the day and night— Venice with its long array of noble palaces, with its Grand Canal and its narrow, picturesque waterways. He reproduces the Venice we know, and we see how little it has changed. The gondolas cluster round the landing-stages of the Piazzetta, the crowds hurry in and out of the arcades of the Ducal Palace, or he paints the festivals that still retained their splendour: the Great Bucentaur leaving the Riva dei Schiavoni on the Feast of the Ascension, or San Geremia and the entrance to the Cannaregio decked in flags for a feast-day. From one end to another of the Grand Canal, that "most beautiful street in the world," as des Commines called it in 1495, we can trace every aspect of Canale's time, when the city had as yet lost nothing of its splendour or its animation. At the entrance stands S. Maria della Salute, that sanctuary dear to Venetian hearts, built as a votive offering after the visitation of the plague in 1631. Its flamboyant dome, with its volutes, its population of stone saints, its green bronze door catching the light, pleased Canale, as it pleased Sargent in our own day, and he painted it over and over again. The annual fête of the Confraternity of the Carità takes place at the Scuola di San Rocco, and Canale paints the old Renaissance building which shelters so much of Tintoretto's finest work, decorated with ropes of greenery and gay with flags,[7] while Tiepolo has put in the red-robed, periwigged councillors and the gazing populace. Near it in the National Gallery hangs a "Regatta" with its array of boats, its shouting gondoliers, and its shadows lying across the range of palaces, and telling the exact hour of the day that it was sketched in; or, again, the painter has taken peculiar pleasure in expressing quiet days, with calm green waters and wide empty piazzas, divided by sun and shadow, with a few citizens plodding about their business in the hot midday, or a quiet little abbé crossing the piazza on his way to Mass. Canale has made a special study of the light on wall and façade, and of the transparent waters of the canals and the azure skies in which float great snowy fleeces.

His second visit to England was paid in 1751. He was received with open arms by the great world, and invited to the houses of the nobility in town and country. The English were delighted with his taste and with the mastery with which he painted architectural scenes, and in spite of advancing years he produced a number of compositions, which commanded high prices. The Garden of Vauxhall, the Rotunda at Ranelagh, Whitehall, Northumberland House, Eton College, were some of the subjects which attracted him, and the treatment of which was signalised by his calm and perfect balance. He made use of the camera ottica, which is in principal identical with the camera oscura. Lanzi says he amended its defects and taught its proper use, but it must be confessed that in the careful perspective of some of his scenes, its traces seem to haunt us and to convey a certain cold regularity. Canale was a marvellous engraver. Mantegna, Bellini, and Titian had placed engraving on a very high level in the Venetian School, and though at a later date it became too elaborate, Tiepolo and his son brought it back to simplicity. Canale aided them, and his *eaux-fortes*, of which he has left about thirty, are filled with light and breadth of treatment, and he is particularly happy in his brilliant, transparent water.

The high prices Canale obtained for his pictures in his lifetime led to the usual imitations. He was surrounded by painters whose whole ambition was limited to copying him. Among these were Marieschi, Visentini, Colombini, besides others now forgotten. More than fifty of his finest works were bought by Smith for George III. and fill a room at Windsor. He was made a member of the Academy at Dresden, and Bruhl, the Prime Minister of the Elector, obtained from him twenty-one works which now adorn the gallery there. Canale died in Venice, where he had lived nearly all his life, and where his gondola-studio was a familiar object in the Piazzetta, at the Lido, or anchored in the long canals.

His nephew, Bernardo Belotto, is often also called Canaletto, and it seems that both uncle and nephew were equally known by the diminutive. Belotto, too, went to Rome early in his career, where he attached himself to Panini, a painter of classic ruins, peopled with warriors and shepherds. He was, by all accounts, full of vanity and self-importance, and on a visit to Germany managed to acquire the title of Count, which he adhered to with great complacency. He travelled all over Italy looking for patronage, and was very eager to find the road to success and fortune. About the same time as his uncle, he paid a visit to London and was patronised by Horace Walpole, but in the full tide of success he was summoned to Dresden, where the Elector, disappointed at not having secured the services of the uncle, was fain to console himself with those of the nephew. The extravagant and profligate Augustus II., whose one idea was to extract money by every possible means from his subjects, in order to adorn his palaces, was consistently devoted to Belotto, who was in his element as a Court painter. He paints all his uncle's subjects, and it is not always easy to distinguish between the two; but his paintings are dull and stiff as compared with those of Canale, though he is sometimes fine in colour, and many of his views are admirably drawn.

SOME WORKS OF CANALE
It is impossible to draw up any exhaustive list, so many being in private collections.

Dresden.	The Grand Canal; Campo S. Giacomo; Piazza S. Marco; Church and Piazza of SS. Giovanni and Paolo.
Florence.	The Piazzetta.
Hampton Court.	The Colosseum.
London.	Scuola di San Rocco; Interior of the Rotunda at Ranelagh; S. Pietro in Castello, Venice.
Paris.	Louvre: Church of S. Maria della Salute.
Venice.	Heading; Courtyard of a Palace.
Vienna.	Liechtenstein Gallery: Church and Piazza of S. Mark, Venice; Canal of the Giudecca, Venice; View on Grand Canal; The Piazzetta.

Windsor.	About fifty paintings.
Wallace Collection.	The Giudecca; Piazza San Marco; Church of San Simione; S. Maria della Salute; A Fête on the Grand Canal; Ducal Palace; Dogana from the Molo; Palazzo Corner; A Water-fête; The Rialto; S. Maria della Salute; A Canal in Venice.

CHAPTER XXXII
FRANCESCO GUARDI

An entry in Gradenigo's diary of 1764, preserved in the Museo Correr, speaks of "Francesco Guardi, painter of the quarter of SS. Apostoli, along the Fondamenta Nuove, a good pupil of the famous Canaletto, having by the aid of the camera ottica, most successfully painted two canvases (not small) by the order of a stranger (an Englishman), with views of the Piazza San Marco, towards the Church and the Clock Tower, and of the Bridge of the Rialto and buildings towards the Cannaregio, and have to-day examined them under the colonnades of the Procurazie and met with universal applause."

Francesco Guardi was a son of the Austrian Tyrol, and his mountain ancestry may account, as in the case of Titian, for the freshness and vigour of his art. Both his father, who settled in Venice, and his brother were painters. His son became one in due time, and the profession being followed by four members of the family accounts for the indifferent works often attributed to Guardi.

His indebtedness to Canale is universally acknowledged, and perhaps it is true that he never attains to the monumental quality, the traditional dignity which marks Canale out as a great master, but he differs from Canale in temperament, style, and technique. Canale is a much more exact and serious student of architectural detail; Guardi, with greater visible vigour, obliterates detail, and has no hesitation in drawing in buildings which do not really appear. In his oval painting of the Ducal Palace (Wallace Collection) he makes it much loftier and more spacious than it really is. In his "Piazzetta" he puts in a corner of the Loggia where it would not actually be seen. In the "Fair in Piazza S. Marco" the arch from under which the Fair appears is gigantic, and he foreshortens the wing of the royal palace. He curtails the length of the columns in the piazza and so avoids monotony of effect, and he often alters the height of the campaniles he uses, making them tall and slender or short and broad, as his picture requires. At one time he produced some colossal pictures, in several of which Mr. Simonson, who has written an admirable life of the painter, believes that the hand of Canale is perceptible in collaboration; but it was not his natural element, and he often became heavy in colour and handling. In 1782 he undertook a commission from Pietro Edwards, who was a noted connoisseur and inspector of State pictures, and had been appointed superintendent in 1778 of an official studio for the restoration of old masters.

Edwards had important dealings with Guardi, who was directed to paint four leading incidents in the rejoicings in honour of the visit of Pius IV. to Venice. The Venetians themselves had become indifferent patrons of art, but Venice attracted great numbers of foreign visitors, and before the second half of the eighteenth century the export of old masters had already become an established trade. There is no sign, however, that Joseph Smith, who retained his consulship till 1760, extended any patronage to Guardi, though he enriched George III.'s collection with works of the chief contemporary artists of Venice. It is probable that Guardi had been warned against him by Canale and profited by the latter's experience.

We can divide his work into three categories. 1. Views of Venice. 2. Public ceremonies. 3. Landscapes. Gradenigo mentions casually that he used the camera ottica, but though we may consider it probable, we cannot trace the use of it in his works. He is not only a painter of architecture, but pays great attention to light and atmosphere, and aims at subtle effects; a transparent haze floats over the lagoons, or the sun pierces though the morning mists. His four large pendants in the Wallace Collection show his happiest efforts; light glances off the water and is reflected on the shadowed walls. His views round the Salute bring vividly before us those delicious morning hours in Venice when the green tide has just raced up the Grand Canal, when a fresh wind is lifting and curling all the loose sails and fluttering pennons, and when the gondoliers are straining at the oars, as their light craft is caught and blown from side to side upon the rippling water. The sky occupies much of his space, he makes searching studies of it, and his favourite effect is a flash of light shooting across a piled-up mass of clouds. The line of the horizon is low, and he exhibits great mastery in painting the wide lagoons, but he also paints rough seas, and is one of the few masters of his day—perhaps the only one—who succeeds in representing a storm at sea.

Often as he paints the same subjects he never becomes mechanical or photographic. We may sometimes tire of the monotony of Canale's unerring perspective and accurate buildings, but Guardi always finds some new rendering, some fresh point of interest. Sometimes he gives us a summer day, when Venice stands out in light, her white palaces reflected in the sun-illumined water; sometimes he is arrested by old churches bathed in shadow and fusing into the rich, dark tones of twilight. His boats and figures are introduced with great spirit and *brio*, and are alive with that handling which a French critic has described as his *griffe endiablée*.

Francesco Guardi. S. MARIA DELLA SALUTE. *London.*
(*Photo, Mansell and Co.*)

His masterly and spirited painting of crowds enables him to reproduce for us all those public ceremonies which Venice retained as long as the Republic lasted: yearly pilgrimages of the Doge to Venetian churches, to the Salute to commemorate the cessation of the plague, to San Zaccaria on Easter Day, the solemn procession on Corpus Christi Day, receptions of ambassadors, and, most gorgeous of all, the Feast of the Wedding of the Adriatic. He has faithfully preserved the ancient ceremonial which accompanied State festivities. In the "Fête du Jeudi Gras" (Louvre) he illustrates the acrobatic feats which were performed before Doge Mocenigo. A huge Temple of Victory is erected on the Piazzetta, and gondoliers are seen climbing on each other's shoulders and dancing upon ropes. His motley crowds show that the whole population, patricians as well as people, took part in the feasts. He has also left many striking interiors: among others, that of the Sala del Gran Consiglio, where sometimes as many as a thousand persons were assembled, the "Reception of the Doge and Senate by Pius IV." (which formed one of the series ordered by Pietro Edwards), or the fine "Interior of a Theatre," exhibited at the Burlington Fine Arts in 1911, belonging to a series of which another is at Munich.

In his landscapes Guardi does not pay very faithful attention to nature. The landscape painters of the eighteenth century, as Mr. Simonson points out, were not animated by any very genuine impulse to study nature minutely. It was the picturesque element which appealed to them, and they were chiefly concerned to reproduce romantic features, grouped according to fancy. Guardi composes half fantastic scenes, introducing classic remains, triumphal arches, airy Palladian monuments. His *capricci* include compositions in which Roman ruins, overgrown with foliage, occupy the foreground of a painting of Venetian palaces, but in which the combination is carried out with so much sparkle and nervous life and such charm of style, that it is attractive and piquant rather than grotesque.

England is richest in Guardis, of any country, but France in one respect is better off, in possessing no less than eleven fine paintings of public ceremonials. Guardi may be considered the originator of small sketches, and perhaps the precursor of those glib little views which are handed about the Piazza at the present day. His drawings are fairly numerous, and are remarkably delicate and incisive in touch. A large collection which he left to his son is now in the Museo Correr. In his later years he was reduced to poverty and used to exhibit sketches in the Piazza, parting with them for a few ducats, and in this way flooding Venice with small landscapes. The exact spot occupied by his *bottega* is said to be at the corner of the Palazzo Reale, opposite the Clock Tower. The house in which he died still exists in the Campiello della Madonna, No. 5433, Parrocchia S. Canziano, and has a shrine dedicated to the Madonna attached to it. When quite an old man, Guardi paid a visit to the home of his ancestors, at Mastellano in the Austrian Tyrol, and made a drawing of Castello Corvello on the route. To this day his name is remembered with pride in his Tyrolean valley.

SOME WORKS OF GUARDI

Bergamo.	Lochis: Landscapes.
Berlin.	Grand Canal; Lagoon; Cemetery Island.
London.	Views in Venice.
Milan.	Museo Civico: Landscapes.
	Poldi-Pezzoli: Piazzetta; Dogana; Landscapes.
Oxford.	Taylorian Museum: Views in Venice.
Padua.	Views in Venice.
Paris.	Procession of the Doge to S. Zaccaria; Embarkment in Bucentaur; Festival at Salute; "Jeudi Gras" in Venice; Corpus Christi; Sala di Collegio; Coronation of Doge.
Turin.	Cottage; Staircase; Bridge over Canal.
Venice.	Museo Correr: The Ridotto; Parlour of Convent.
Verona.	Landscapes.
Wallace Collection.	The Rialto; San Giorgio Maggiore (two); S. Maria della Salute; Archway in Venice; Vaulted Arcades; The Dogana.

BIBLIOGRAPHY

It is an advantage to the student of Italian art to be able to read French, German, and Italian, for though translations appear of the most important works, there are many interesting articles and monographs of minor artists which are otherwise inaccessible.

Vasari, not always trustworthy, either in dates, facts, or opinions, yet delightfully human in his histories, is indispensable, and new editions and translations are constantly issued. Sansoni's edition (Florence), with Milanesi's notes, is the most authoritative; and for translations, those of Mrs. Foster (Messrs. Blashfield and Hopkins), and a new edition in the Temple classics (Dent, 8 vols., 2s. each vol.).

Ridolfi, the principal contemporary authority on Venetian artists, who published his *Maraviglie dell' arte* nine years after Domenico Tintoretto's death, is only to be read in Italian, though the anecdotes with which his work abounds are made use of by every writer.

Crowe and Cavalcaselle's *Painting in North Italy* (Murray) is a storehouse of painstaking, minute, and, on the whole, marvellously correct information and sound opinion. It supplies a foundation, fills gaps, and supplements individual biographies as no other book does. For the early painters, down to the time of the Bellini, *I Origini dei pittori veneziani*, by Professor Leonello Venturi, Venice, 1907, is a large book, written with mastery and insight, and well illustrated; *La Storia della pittura veneziana* is another careful work, which deals very minutely with the early school of mosaics.

In studying the Bellini, the late Mr. S. A. Strong has *The Brothers Bellini* (Bell's Great Masters), and the reader should not fail to read Mr. Roger Fry's *Bellini* (Artist's Library), a scholarly monograph, short but reliable, and full of suggestion and appreciation, though written in a cool, critical spirit. Dr. Hills has dealt ably with *Pisanello* (Duckworth).

Molmenti and Ludwig in their monumental work *Vittore Carpaccio*, translated by Mr. R. H. Cust (Murray, 1907), and Paul Kristeller in the equally important *Mantegna*, translated by Mr. S. A. Strong (Longmans, 1901), seem to have exhausted all that there is to be said for the moment concerning these two painters.

It is almost superfluous to mention Mr. Berenson's two well-known volumes, *The Venetian Painters of the Renaissance*, and the *North Italian Painters of the Renaissance* (Putnam). They are brilliant essays which supplement every other work, overflowing with suggestive and critical matter, supplying original thoughts, and summing up in a few pregnant words the main features and the tendencies of the succeeding stages.

In studying Giorgione, we cannot dispense with Pater's essay, included in *The Renaissance*. The author is not always well informed as to facts—he wrote in the early days of criticism—but he is rich in idea and feeling. Mr. Herbert Cook's *Life of Giorgione* (Bell's Great Masters) is full and interesting. Some authorities question his attributions as being too numerous, but whether we regard them as authentic works of the master or as belonging to his school, the illustrations he gives add materially to our knowledge of the Giorgionesque.

When we come to Titian we are well off. Crowe and Cavalcaselle's *Life of Titian*(Murray, out of print), in two large volumes, is well written and full of good material, from which subsequent writers have borrowed. An excellent Life, full of penetrating criticism, by Mr. C. Ricketts, was lately brought out by Methuen (Classics of Art), complete with illustrations, and including a minute analysis of Titian's technique. Sir Claude Phillips's Monograph on Titian will appeal to every thoughtful lover of the painter's genius, and Dr. Gronau has written a good and scholarly Life (Duckworth).

Mr. Berenson's *Lorenzo Lotto* must be read for its interest and learning, given with all the author's charm and lucidity. It includes an essay on Alvise Vivarini.

My own *Tintoretto* (Methuen, Classics of Art) gives a full account of the man and his work, and especially deals exhaustively with the scheme and details of the Scuola di San Rocco. Professor Thode has written a detailed and profusely illustrated Life of Tintoretto in the Knackfuss Series, and the Paradiso has been treated at length and illustrated in great detail in a very scholarly *édition de luxe* by Mr. F. O. Osmaston. It is the fashion to discard Ruskin, but though we may allow that his judgments are exaggerated, that he reads more into a picture than the artist intended, and that he is too fond of preaching sermons, there are few critics who have so many ideas to give us, or who are so informed with a deep love of art, and both *Modern Painters* and the *Stones of Venice* should be read.

M. Charles Yriarte has written a Life of Paolo Veronese, which is full of charm and knowledge. It is interesting to take a copy of Boschini's *Della pittura veneziana*, 1797, when visiting the galleries, the palaces, and the churches of Venice. His lists of the pictures, as they were known in his day, often open our eyes to doubtful attributions. Second-hand copies of Boschini are not difficult to pick up. When the later-century artists are reached, a good sketch of the Venice of their period is supplied by Philippe Monnier's delightful *Venice in the Eighteenth Century* (Chatto and Windus), which also has a good chapter on the lesser Venetian masters. The best Life of Tiepolo is in Italian, by Professor Pompeo Molmenti. The smaller masters have to be hunted for in many scattered essays; a knowledge of Goldoni adds point to Longhi's pictures. Canaletto and his nephew, Belotto, have been treated by M. Uzanne, *Les Deux Canaletto*; and Mr. Simonson has written an important and charming volume on Francesco Guardi (Methuen, 1904), with beautiful reproductions of his works. Among other books which give special information are Morelli's two volumes, *Italian Painters in Borghese and Doria Pamphili*, and *In Dresden and Munich Galleries*, translated by Miss Jocelyn ffoulkes (Murray); and Dr. J. P. Richter's magnificent catalogue of the Mond Collection—which, though published at fifteen guineas, can be seen in the great art libraries—has some valuable chapters on the Venetian masters.

www.ingramcontent.com/pod-product-compliance
Lightning Source LLC
Chambersburg PA
CBHW070906180526
45168CB00005B/1947